THE FIRST CENTURY OF
ENGLISH FEUDALISM
1066–1166

THE FIRST CENTURY OF
ENGLISH FEUDALISM
1066–1166

BEING

THE FORD LECTURES

DELIVERED IN THE UNIVERSITY OF OXFORD

IN HILARY TERM 1929

BY

SIR FRANK STENTON

FELLOW OF THE BRITISH ACADEMY

SECOND EDITION

GREENWOOD PRESS, PUBLISHERS
WESTPORT, CONNECTICUT

Library of Congress Cataloging in Publication Data

Stenton, Frank Merry, Sir, 1880-1967.
    The first century of English feudalism, 1066-1166.

    Reprint of the 2d ed., 1960, published by Clarendon
Press, Oxford, Eng., which was published as Ford lec-
tures, 1929.
    Includes index.
    1. Feudalism--England. I. Title. II. Series:
Oxford. University. Ford lectures, 1929.
DA185.S8 1979   942.02   78-26688
ISBN 0-313-20915-4

2ₙd ed. 1961 np 1979.

© Oxford University Press 1960.

First published 1952
Second edition (revised and reset) 1961

This reprint has been authorized by the Oxford University
Press.

Reprinted in 1979 by Greenwood Press, Inc.
51 Riverside Avenue, Westport, CT 06880

PREFACE TO THE SECOND EDITION

I N the lectures on which this book is based I attempted
to get behind the abstract conception of feudalism to
the actual relations between the king, his barons, and
their men in the aristocratic society imposed by war upon
the ancient Old English state. Apart from chronicles and
documents produced by the king's secretariate, the private
charters which begin to be numerous in Stephen's reign
offered materials for such a study which had not been
closely examined from this point of view. The proposal
for a second edition of the lectures has given me an opportunity to take account of documents overlooked in 1929
or published since that date which could be incorporated
into the book without changing its character. Many important texts, then in manuscript, are now in print. Eight
volumes of the Lincoln *Registrum Antiquissimum* have
appeared, and *Sir Christopher Hatton's Book of Seals* has
been published. Sir Charles Clay has edited seven volumes
of *Early Yorkshire Charters*, Professor Barraclough has
issued a volume of *Early Cheshire Charters* in facsimile,
Dr. Charles Johnson and Professor H. A. Cronne have
continued the *Regesta Regum Anglo-Normannorum* down
to 1135. Among works of reference, *The Complete Peerage*
has been brought to a conclusion by Mr. G. H. White.
Among studies bearing on particular aspects of the period,
I have been especially indebted to the late Mr. Lewis
Loyd's *The Origins of some Anglo-Norman Families*, which
has provided a new technique of investigation into the
subject indicated by its title, to the critically displayed
evidence for the Scandinavian element in early Norman
society in Dr. Adigard des Gautries's *Les Noms de Per-
sonnes Scandinaves en Normandie de 911 à 1066*, and to
Mr. Reginald Lennard's picture of the agrarian background of the Norman settlement in his *Rural England
1086–1135*. The unexpected discovery of a new text of
the *Gesta Stephani* has made it necessary to rewrite the

sections of the book dealing with King Stephen and the earl of Chester, where I have followed the reconstruction of events provided by Dr. A. L. Poole in the introduction to the edition of this chronicle by Mr. K. R. Potter. The work of the late Professor Sidney Painter, notably *Studies in the History of the English Feudal Barony* published in 1943, connects the meagre evidence for the early history of English feudalism with the abundant records of the thirteenth century.

I may add that the omnicompetence of the Anglo-Norman monarchy in ordinary times has been made more intelligible than ever before by the evidence for effective pre-Conquest centralization supplied by Dr. Florence Harmer's *Anglo-Saxon Writs*, and by the work now in progress on the managed currency issued during the last century of the Old English state.

FRANK M. STENTON

Whitley Park Farm, Reading
28 January 1961

PREFACE TO THE FIRST EDITION

M Y election as Ford's lecturer in 1927 suggested
to me the possibility of dealing with certain
features of Anglo-Norman society which though
familiar in outline are not often chosen as a centre of inquiry. Much study has been given in recent years to the
rural economy of this age and, on the other hand, to the
composition and functions of the king's court and household. Much work of the first importance has been done
upon the history of individual fiefs and families. But comparatively little has been written on the aristocratic society
of the Norman age considered as a whole, from the standpoint of the honour, and it seemed that a study of its
organization might illustrate some features of Anglo-
Norman history which cannot be seen so well from the
angle of the manor or the Curia Regis. It was clear from
the first that no study of this subject which might be
attempted at the present time could be in any sense complete, for the materials are widely scattered, and a large
proportion of them are still in manuscript. Nevertheless,
it seemed possible to emphasize some significant facts, to
indicate the lines along which further knowledge may
profitably be sought, and to suggest some conclusions to
which this work seems likely to lead. One of these conclusions should perhaps be mentioned here, for it explains
the title which has been given to this book. The more
clearly the Anglo-Norman aristocracy of barons and
knights is seen in the light of records written from its own
standpoint, the more widely it seems to differ from the
native aristocracy which preceded it, and the more misleading it seems to apply the adjective 'feudal' to any
aspect of English society before the Norman Conquest.

The illustrations of Anglo-Norman feudalism which
are quoted in the following chapters are derived, whenever possible, from materials relating to lay rather than
ecclesiastical fiefs. The evidence as to the organization of

feudalism on ecclesiastical baronies is of peculiar importance owing to the early date at which it begins. But the fiefs of bishops and abbots, large as some of them were, answered when all is told, for only a small proportion of the knight-service which the Norman kings could claim from their tenants in chief, and the feudalism which they represent has a certain artificiality which makes it unsafe to generalize from their history. The evidence as to the organization of secular baronies is scattered and fragmentary, but the conclusions to which it points stand at least for the ideas of the French military society of the eleventh century, un-complicated by pre-Conquest traditions or the ecclesiasti-cal character of the chief lord of the fee.

The plan of the lectures given in 1929 is followed closely in the present book, though some subjects are considered here in much more detail than was then possible, and, in particular, the section on feudalism in Stephen's reign with which the last lecture ended has been expanded into a separate chapter. In accordance with a suggestion made to me when the lectures were given, the documents introduced by way of illustration are quoted in a translated form. These translations should not be regarded as literal render-ings of the original Latin, which is often too formal for an intelligible word-for-word reproduction in English. On the other hand, this formality makes it sometimes difficult to arrive quickly at the real meaning of a document, and as a full Latin version is always given in the Appendix, it seemed permissible to keep the translations in the body of the book. The Appendix is confined to documents to which reference has already been made in the book, and may perhaps be useful as a small collection of texts illustrating the early organization of feudalism in England.

In the preparation of this book I am indebted to Pro-fessor Tait for one of the most interesting of early grants of land for knight-service, and to Mr. Lewis C. Loyd for references which show the real nature of the feudal *equita-tio* or *chevauchée*. Through the kindness of Canon Foster I have been able to refer, not only to the great collection of charters in Lincoln Cathedral, now appearing under his editorship, but also to the remarkable volume of copies and facsimiles of early charters known as Sir Christopher Hatton's Book of Seals. To my wife I am indebted for help without which this book could never have been written. The collection of charters on which it is founded was begun by her, I have consulted her on all the points where the study of Anglo-Norman feudalism impinges on that of early Angevin law and administration, she has compiled the index, and has taken a great, if not the greatest, part in the work of preparing the book for publication.

F. M. S.

Whitley Park Farm, Reading
8 November 1931

CONTENTS

INTRODUCTORY

THERE is a particular reason why any one lecturing on English feudalism in the spring of 1929 should introduce the name of John Horace Round into his first sentence. To every student of English feudal society, Mr. Round's death in the summer of 1928 was a notable event. It marked the close of forty years of passionate devotion to the interests of medieval scholarship, and the disappearance of a personality, little known in recent years, but always present to the minds of those working along the lines with which Round's name was associated. Few scholars in England have ever dominated a whole field of scholarship as Round, in the years of his full power, dominated all inquiry which centred upon the problems of early feudal society. The time has not yet come for any final estimate of his work, and the task will never be easy. Round never produced a long, continuous, piece of historical writing. His strength lay in analysis rather than synthesis, in the power of his attack upon individual problems, and the insight with which he perceived the inadequacy of accepted explanations. In reality his books are all collections of essays, and innumerable other essays, each making a definite addition to our knowledge of English feudalism, are scattered in periodicals such as the *Ancestor* and the *Archaeological Journal*, in the publications of local societies, and in contributions to the Victoria History of the Counties of England. And yet, detailed as Round's work might be, occupied as he continually was with the minor *personalia* of English feudalism, he never forgot that the facts which he ascertained were only of value as materials towards a better understanding of history. None of his work can be neglected in any estimate of his contribution to learning, for all of it is marked by the quality which gives distinction to the great essays published in *Geoffrey de Mandeville* or *Studies in Peerage and Family History*. But as yet it cannot be appreciated as a whole.

B

Nevertheless, it can be said at once that Round's work forms an essential part of the very remarkable movement which rather more than thirty years ago created the modern study of English feudal institutions. Compared with similar movements in other fields of scholarship, it was remarkably short. The fifteen years which ended with the death of Maitland in 1906 saw the appearance of the most essential part of Maitland's own work. Between 1892 and 1901 Liebermann published the studies upon the law-books of the Norman age which preceded his monumental edition of the *Gesetze*, and the text of that edition itself appeared in 1903. To the earlier part of this period belong most of the works which gave Round his unique place among English historians. *Geoffrey de Mandeville* appeared in 1892, *Feudal England*, incorporating essays already famous, appeared in 1895, the *Commune of London*, in 1899, synchronizing with the *Calendar of Documents preserved in France*, *Studies in Peerage and Family History*, in 1901. Of all Round's greater works, only the *King's Sergeants* falls outside this central period, and that was published nearly twenty years ago. It is, in fact, already difficult to reconstruct the condition of feudal studies before Round began to work upon them. There had been great genealogists before him. Stapleton and Eyton were not isolated figures in their respective generations. Individual historians, Freeman among them, had always realized the services which genealogy could render to history. But no one had yet expressed, as Round was to express, the truth that the fabric of feudal history is composed of genealogical detail, that innumerable events which are unintelligible as related by contemporary writers presuppose an elaborate nexus of family alliances and rivalries. The fact that William, King Stephen's younger son, was count of Boulogne and Mortain, lord of the honours of Warenne and Eye was a commonplace of genealogical knowledge, but it was Round who first showed how it explained Stephen's willingness to recognize Henry of Anjou as his heir.

There is always a certain danger that the respect which

is due to the memory of a great scholar may lead to some exaggeration of the completeness of his work. Round spent so many years in concentration upon feudal studies, his touch was so sure in his treatment of their detail, that it is hard to realize how fragmentary were the materials which lay before him, and how many problems he left unsolved. He rarely entered into the fundamental questions which underlie the history of English feudal organization. In other words he accepted the existence of a centralized feudal state in England without inquiring into its origins. He gave little of his attention to the internal organization of the individual honours of which that society was composed, and he was always inclined to regard the independent action of a twelfth-century baron as an encroachment upon royal authority. The very success of his early work may have contributed something to this attitude. He had shown that the whole elaborate system of knight-service in England could be traced to the conditions which the Conqueror had imposed on his leading followers, and he was perhaps too ready to assume that King William and his sons had controlled feudal justice and feudal administration as they certainly controlled the military organization which they had created for the defence of the realm. It is also worth remembering that much of Round's work was devoted to the great record in which the authority of the Norman monarchy is most clearly expressed. The shadow of the king falls across every page of Domesday Book. No one knew better than Round how limited was the scope of this record, and how clear in it are the signs of an exceptional effort made upon a great occasion. But the student of Domesday Book will always emphasize the power which called it into being, and of the materials which show the purely feudal aspect of Anglo-Norman society, comparatively few were accessible in print when Round began to write.

It is, moreover, impossible to read a list of Round's published writings without realizing that the whole course of his work was influenced by his interest in a particular part of England. In a sense, no doubt, all England, and more than England, was his province. He moved as freely along or beyond the Welsh border as in Middlesex or Kent. But the family from which he came had an ancient connexion with Essex, and most of the feudal houses whose fortunes he turned into material for English history were seated in this or adjacent shires. Through all the work of his most productive years there runs, for instance, a continuous interest in the house of Clare. He established its pedigree in the Norman age, showed for the first time its unique importance, and traced the fortunes of its members into Wales and Ireland. As late as 1899 there was still a possibility that he would write a detailed history of this family in the Norman period. The book would probably have been the greatest piece of feudal history ever written in this country, but its interest would have centred on the border of Essex and Suffolk. *Geoffrey de Mandeville*, perhaps the most influential of his works, is essentially a collection of local studies. They extended over the whole field of Anglo-Norman administration, but they all arose from incidents in the career of the first Norman earl of Essex. Upon a smaller scale, the essay on the counts of Boulogne, published in *Peerage and Family History*, forms perhaps the most perfect example of Round's highly individual method, and the centre of the honour of Boulogne lay in the same county. In this method lies, in fact, the secret of Round's peculiar strength. With the abstract ideas which lay behind English feudalism, with the nature of lordship or the significance of homage, he had little concern. Every problem which he approached was for him, as it had once been for the men with whose history he was dealing, a matter of local interest. From first to last he was a realist, and the feudalism which he studied was firmly rooted in the ground.

But feudalism was a form of social order, and its territorial organization was only one of many aspects which it presents when it is studied as a whole. The descent of fees, however accurately it may be ascertained, tells nothing as to the social status of their holders. It is only on rare occasions that a charter which records a tenant's enfeoffment will say anything about his personal relations with his lord, or about the place which he is to fill in the feudal group of which he has become a member. The nature and organization of feudal justice are still almost impenetrably obscure, and although there is much to suggest that many men owed to their lords military service beyond that which their lords owed to the king, little is known of its nature or of the conditions under which it could be exacted. In a sense the work of the last generation has really accentuated the vagueness of our knowledge of feudal society. In 1897 Maitland wrote that although the age which lay beyond Domesday was very dark, the way to it lay through the Norman period. At the present time, at almost every point, the outlines of Anglo-Saxon society seem more firmly drawn, and along more intelligible lines, than those of the succeeding feudal order. The rigorous distinctions of personal status which run throughout Old English society essentially simplify its structure. The materials in which it is described abound in minute detail, and their fewness invites a concentrated attack. Above all it was a society with centuries of continuous history behind it, and many of its features which are enigmatical at first sight can easily be explained in the light of its recorded development. At every point where comparison is possible it contrasts with the feudal order which replaced its higher ranks in the eleventh century, where the social distinctions which cut most deeply were matters of usage, not of law.

It is in its bearing upon the origins of what became the most highly centralized of feudal states that the detail of Anglo-Norman feudalism has its chief interest. The Angevin monarchy can only be fully understood in the light of preceding conditions. But the sureness with which Liebermann established the points of contact between Old English and Anglo-Norman law, the precision with which Round traced the descent of individual fees, the general clearness with which the rural background of English feudalism has been revealed by two generations of scholars, only emphasize the obscurity of Anglo-Norman feudal organization. Of the evidence which will one day make this organization clear, much is as yet unprinted, little has been collected and analysed. All that is attempted here is a mere outline, suggested by materials relating directly to the century after the Norman Conquest, and in particular by those private charters of the twelfth century in which the characteristics of Anglo-Norman feudalism find their most authentic expression. It cannot be pretended that these materials cover the whole wide field of feudal organization. Much was too familiar to be set in writing at all, much that was written was written obscurely. But it is well, now and again, to leave the standpoint of the king and his court, and to consider, from within, the community of knights and barons over which they presided, and to note, when they will let us, the way in which its members regarded the social organization of their own day.

I

THE FEUDALISM OF THE NORMAN SETTLEMENT

IN one respect the student of early English society enjoys unique good fortune. The essential character of this society was changed by the Norman Conquest, and within a generation of this event, when the new order which it introduced was well established, but before the older order had been forgotten, the clerks in the king's service carried through a detailed description of all England south of the Tees and the Westmorland Fells. The efficiency of their work, shown in the digest which since the twelfth century has been called Domesday Book, is no less admirable than the scale on which it was conceived. The precision with which modern scholars have marked their occasional inconsistencies of terminology, and errors of fact or figure, is itself a tribute to their general competence. It is easy to draw false inferences from the facts which they have recorded, to see distinctions where none were meant, to mistake the exceptional for the normal. But the facts are there, the conditions under which they were put on record give them a peculiar significance, and under the analysis of the last forty years they have yielded an impression of eleventh-century society which is still vague at many critical points, but is at least intelligible, and consistent with the evidence surviving from an earlier time.

It is not surprising that work on the transition from Saxon to Norman England should tend to take the form of commentary on this famous text. The opinion which we may form of social conditions in King Edward's time must turn in the last resort upon our interpretation of Domesday Book. The Confessor's reign was far from prolific of materials which can be used for the reconstruction of contemporary society, and only a meagre thread of

evidence connects the Conqueror's survey with the code
of Cnut, and through it, with the general body of earlier
English law. The Old English writs issued by the Confessor, important as they are for political history and in the
development of diplomatic forms, tell little about social
conditions. The formal land-books of this reign are few,
and unlike the charters of Æthelred II, show no tendency
to diverge from the bare record of a grant into details of
personal history which might be useful if the tenure were
ever contested.[1] It is hard to remember that a period of
scarcely less obscurity lies between King William's death
and the accession of Henry II. Rural England in 1086 was
still essentially the England of King Edward's day. It is
only in the light of contemporary evidence, far from
abundant and still in great part unexplored, that we shall
ever understand the social changes of the next century,
the consolidation of feudal lordship, the definition of
classes, the blurring of ancient traditions. The private
charters which are among the essential materials for this
study do not become numerous before the reign of
Stephen, and it is only a small proportion of them which
throw much light on details of social organization. It
may well be, indeed, that we shall never understand the
society of Norman England as under Liebermann's
guidance it has become possible to understand the society
revealed by Old English law. The clash and intermingling
of races had destroyed the ancient simplicity of social
relationships, and the evolution of a new order was slow.
Domesday Book stands at the beginning of this evolution,
but it stands in isolation, and evidence of a different
character is needed to connect the society described in
1086 with the society revealed in the abundant records of
the thirteenth century.

In particular, far more evidence than we now possess is
needed for an understanding of Anglo-Norman feudalism.
Domesday Book, which tells so much about individual
barons and their fiefs, tells little, and that indirectly, about

[1] e.g. *Codex Diplomaticus*, 684, 689, 692, 703, 1289. On such passages
see F. M. Stenton, *The Latin Charters of the Anglo-Saxon Period*, 81–83.

feudal organization. Its compilers took for granted the existence of the new military society which had arisen in England since the Conquest. They used the word *miles* often enough, but they ignored the nature of the knight's relationship to his lord, as they ignored all else that was irrelevant to their work. It follows that to an extent which is not always realized our conception of the feudal society of King William's day rests on a series of uncertain inferences. The feudalism of the early Angevin period is illustrated by abundant records. It is natural to interpret eleventh-century society in the light of this evidence, to argue, for example, from the knights' fees of John's reign to the endowments, and through them to the status, of the first Norman *milites*. On the other hand there are facts which suggest that the early part of the twelfth century was a period of rapid change in the higher ranks of feudal society. Families rose and fell; the difficulty of tracing the descent of estates through this period is a commonplace of modern genealogy. It is easy to assume that the structure of society remained constant through all these vicissitudes of individual fortune. Yet the escheat or forfeiture of any great barony, every promotion of a favoured minister, contributed something to the centralization of feudalism which distinguished the Angevin monarchy. That the work of centralization began early is certain. William the Conqueror had made full use of his unique position. But we can draw few detailed conclusions from the highly organized feudalism of the age of Glanville as to the conditions prevailing among the survivors of that hazardous military adventure, the invasion of 1066.

There is little evidence to show their attitude as individuals towards the English people of whom they had become the masters, or towards the king who had set them in power. Behind the tenurial settlement recorded in Domesday Book lie twenty years, illustrated in the main by a discontinuous tale of events revealing little of the grounds of action, by narratives of pleas turning on Old English precedents, and by writs and charters put out by a royal secretariat pursuing formality as a professional virtue. In this impersonal atmosphere there is adventitious interest in the charter of 1077 in which Geoffrey de Wirce, a Breton lord of the first post-Conquest generation, records his foundation of Monks Kirby Priory.[1] He states that he desires to make a gift from the possessions 'which he has earned by service from William the illustrious king of the English', for the peace, well-being, and soul's health of his lord the King, and for the well-being of himself and his ancestors, and of Alveva his wife and her predecessors.[2] He has therefore granted to the monastery of St. Nicholas of Angers the village of Copston, and the derelict church of Kirby, which he has rebuilt and caused to be dedicated in honour of St. Mary and St. Denis, with the fittings of the church and a priest named Frano. He also grants all the property which another priest, named Osgot, is now holding, and shall be holding at his death or departure. There follow gifts of tithe in a number of midland villages, a gift of 20 arable acres in Monks Kirby itself, and a grant of the alms which his men shall give by way of tithes, and the less permanent gifts which they shall make from their own possessions. If this charter had been undated, it would hardly be inferred from its subject-matter that it was written within twelve years of the battle of Hastings. To all appearance it reflects the life of a society which is well-knit and firmly established. But there is at least a hint of personal feeling beneath the formalities of feudal tenure in its grantor's reference to his lord King William, from whom he has earned his land by service.

It is never easy to divide a period of unbroken development into definite phases, and no moment of catastrophe separates the companions of the Conqueror from the

---

[1] *Monasticon Anglicanum*, vii. 996. Dugdale found the charter in 1640 in the library of Sir Thomas Cotton. It has now disappeared, and the only authority for the text is the copy printed in the first edition of the *Monasticon* (1655, i. 562).

[2] Alveva is an Old English name. It is probable that the greater part of Geoffrey's fief came to him as his wife's inheritance.

barons of the Charter. Even the long war of Stephen's time, followed by a growth of royal power which left no room for feudal independence, had little effect on the feudal economy itself. If, however, a single year were to be chosen as marking the beginning of a new period in the development of English feudalism, it would be hard to choose a better starting-point than the year 1166. The legal innovations of this year were so important that its interest in the history of English feudal society is sometimes overlooked. The changes in civil and criminal procedure made by the Assize of Clarendon were the foundations of a new legal system. But within a smaller sphere there was equal significance in the king's demand, made this year, that his tenants in chief should send in to him, with other information, a list of all those holding of them by military service, that all who had not yet done allegiance to him might do it within a definite time.[1] The demand introduced no new element into the relationship between the king, his barons, and their knights. But it was a notable assertion of the principle that the king has a claim to the allegiance of under-tenants overriding the claims of any immediate lord, and it produced a series of baronial letters revealing much of the detail and something of the history of the system through which the tenants in chief were providing for the military service due to the king.[2] With these letters, the *Cartae Baronum* of 1166, the continuous history of most fiefs really begins, for a succession of Pipe Rolls, fuller than those of previous years, connects the *Cartae* with the records of the thirteenth century, and gives coherence to the details of feudal society. The existence of this information is in itself an important historical fact, for it is the direct result of a new extension of royal power over the feudal world. The meagreness of record evidence for the eighty years between Domesday Book and the *Cartae* is not, indeed, a

---

[1] On the king's purpose in making this demand see below, 137–8.

[2] *Liber Niger Scaccarii*, ed. Hearne, i. 49–340; *Red Book of the Exchequer* (Rolls Series), i. 186–445. Although the readings of the *Liber Niger* are quoted in the latter edition, a text based on the *Liber Niger* is badly needed.

sign of weak government. Domesday Book itself shows the achievement of which the Norman administration was capable, and the isolated Pipe Roll of 1130 shows how much record material has been lost. But Domesday Book was the result of a wholly exceptional effort, and the centralization represented by the Pipe Roll of 1130 was premature.[1] The records which are characteristic of this period are the writs and charters of kings and barons, and these records, by their very nature, are discontinuous. A single baronial charter reveals at most a situation within a particular fief at a particular moment, and nothing is easier than to mistake its implications. The difficulty of forming general conclusions about Anglo-Norman feudalism is due far less to the scarcity of evidence than to its fragmentary nature and its frequent obscurity.

Many problems in the early history of English feudalism would doubtless disappear if we knew more about Norman society on the eve of the Conquest.[2] Its main features have been reconstructed in recent years. Unless discoveries of which there seems little prospect are still to be made, it is unlikely that future work on early Norman society will do more than supplement the outline which Professor Haskins[3] has drawn. But a far completer reconstruction than is now possible would still leave much that is obscure in the early history of English feudalism. There seems no doubt that the greater men and older churches of the duchy held of the duke by military tenure, and that the knights whose service they owed him were generally grouped in units of five or ten. The households of Norman magnates were already organized on the lines which were to become familiar in England. There is good evidence that the duke and his barons could take aids and reliefs from their military tenants, assume the guardianship of

[1] See below, 221-2.

[2] The identification of the Norman seats of the Anglo-Norman baronage has been carried to a new level of precision in L. C. Loyd's important book, *The Origins of some Anglo-Norman Families*, published by the Harleian Society in 1951.

[3] In the studies represented by the first chapter of his *Norman Institutions* (1918).

heirs who were under age, and give heiresses away in marriage. The Normans of 1066 were certainly familiar with the conception of the honour, its peers, and its court. It is, in fact, easy to find Norman parallels for most of the organization and for much of the terminology of feudalism in England. But the converse is not equally true. The military society revealed by English records of the twelfth century had clearly derived much from Norman precedent, but it was no mere reproduction of an earlier Norman system. The outline of its structure is the same, but its details are simpler. Many ancient features had disappeared under new conditions before the series of English records begins,[1] others remained as somewhat meaningless survivals from the older continental order. The origins of English feudalism may go back through Norman custom to Frankish practice, but it remains essentially a creation of the eleventh century.

Even in regard to the organization of military service, English feudalism was no mere repetition of a Norman model. In each country every important tenant in chief held his lands by the service of supplying his lord, on due summons, with a definite number of knights. But in Normandy the organization of this service was complicated in a way to which there is no parallel in England. To judge from the one record which refers in detail to eleventh-century conditions, the Bayeux Inquest of 1133,[2]

---

[1] Such, for example, as the distinction between service *totis armis* and *plainis armis* for which there seems no evidence in England: see below, 15–16.

[2] The Bayeux Inquest is discussed at some length by Haskins, op. cit. 15–20, and by Round in *Family Origins*, 201–16, and was used extensively by Guilhiermoz in his *Essai sur l'origine de la noblesse en France*. Round's study is important, partly because of his identifications of individuals mentioned in the Inquest, but still more because of his demonstration of the relationship between the published texts of the returns and the fragment headed 'Nomina militum tenentium de ecclesia Baiocensi' printed in the *Red Book of the Exchequer* (ii. 645–7). The text of the Inquest as printed without emendation by Léchaudé d'Anisy in 1835 (*Archives du Calvados*, ii. 425–51; for other editions see Haskins, op. cit. 15) is corrupt in itself, and as Round has shown, represents an original lacking various entries preserved in the *Red Book of the Exchequer*. But

it seems that Norman custom recognized three occasions on which the duke might require knight service from his tenants. If he summoned his army to his banner for the defence of the land, every man holding a knight's fee must obey. But the duke might also require knights for less serious war within the borders of Normandy, or for fulfilling his own service to the king of France, and for these purposes he only required a part of the total service which his tenants owed him. From the fief of the bishop of Bayeux he demanded only one knight out of five for service *in marchis Normannie*, and one knight out of ten for service due to the king of France, on each of the two latter occasions requiring forty days service from the knights who actually appeared. It is possible that forty days was the usual term of feudal military service in England. But the other arrangements indicated here are very unlike anything in English feudal custom, which gave the king the right of calling out the whole feudal army on every occasion which seemed necessary to him and his barons.

The difference between English and Norman feudalism was not only a matter of organization. In England, throughout the reigns of the Conqueror and his sons, private warfare was regarded as an offence against the king. In Normandy it was discountenanced by every efficient duke, but ancient habits were too strong for its suppression. Even the Conqueror had recognized that his barons must sometimes be allowed to fight out their quarrels. Admitting that private warfare was inevitable, he set himself to limit its range, forbidding the holding of prisoners for ransom, robbery from defeated enemies, the burning of houses and mills, and general plunder.[1] But the context in which

with all its imperfections the Inquest is by far the most important evidence which we possess as to Norman feudal organization under the Conqueror and his sons. It is the only record which describes at length the organization of a great Norman fee at a time when eleventh-century conditions were still within living memory, and it is the inevitable starting point of any inquiry into the details of the feudal system with which the Norman invaders of England were familiar.

[1] See the *Consuetudines et Justicie* of William the Conqueror, ed. Haskins, op. cit. Appendix D.

these limitations were drawn shows that disputes which we should expect to be settled in the duke's court might well give rise to private war. A rule that no one in pursuit of a claim to land may burn any house or mill, or ravage or take plunder,[1] allows the settlement of such claims by war between the parties so long as they observe the restrictions which the duke has set. Service to a lord whose enemies had brought war upon him could be mentioned as a matter of course in a formal Norman document written late in the Conqueror's reign. An agreement between William Paganel and the abbot of Mont St. Michel begins with a stipulation that one of William's tenants shall do forty days' service in castle-guard, 'if William shall have war in respect of the land which the king of the English has given him with his wife'.[2] Words like these are inconceivable in an English document written under the Conqueror or either of his sons, and they illustrate the fundamental difference which separated the newly established English feudalism from that of contemporary Normandy. Resemblance between two societies can only be superficial when one expects a man to fight in his lord's quarrel and the other makes the beginning of private war a cause of forfeiture.

It is equally significant that many words and phrases used with precision in eleventh-century Normandy became rare or acquired a more generalized sense soon after their transplantation to England. The history of the phrase *feudum loricae*—*fief del haubert*—is a curious illustration of the difference between Norman and Anglo-Norman feudal terminology. In ancient Normandy, as indeed generally in France and Germany, a fundamental distinction was drawn between the knight who served with what was regarded as a full provision for war and the knight of a more limited equipment.[3] It was essentially the possession of a hauberk of mail which brought a knight

---

[1] *Consuetudines et Justicie*, chap. 6.
[2] Printed by Haskins, op. cit. 21, 22, and by Stapleton, *Archaeologia*, xxvii. 27.
[3] Guilhiermoz, *Essai sur l'origine de la noblesse en France*, 172 et seqq.

into the higher class, and the man who did service thus
provided came naturally to be called a *miles loricatus*, and
a fee which owed this service, a *feudum loricae*. The distinction was long maintained in Normandy, but in England every knight enfeoffed for the king's service was
expected to come to war with a full equipment,[1] and
feudum loricae rapidly became a mere synonym for *feudum
militis*. The currency of such phrases a generation after
the Conquest is proved by the reference to the knights
qui per loricas terras suas deserviunt in the coronation
charter of Henry I,[2] and by a later charter of the same king
ordering Eudo his dapifer to be put in seisin of all the
appurtenances of certain manors *exceptis illis militibus
qui cum loricis serviunt*.[3]   Even under Henry II the
tradition of the *feudum loricae* survived in England.
William de Turville, in that reign, granted to William the
fisherman three yardlands, two acres, an essart, and a
fishery at Taplow in Buckinghamshire *pro tercia parte
feodi loricae*.[4] Later examples than this can no doubt be
found,[5] but in view of the extreme rarity of such phrases
in early charters of enfeoffment it is clear that they formed
no part of the common phraseology of the twelfth century.
In regard to the knight's equipment, as in regard to many
other matters of feudal organization, the Norman kings in
England had been free to simplify the earlier practice of
their duchy.

More interesting, because more closely connected with
the structure of society, is the difference between the

[1] It is possible that the small fees created on the honour of Mortain and
some other honours were not originally regarded as *fiefs del haubert* in the
strict sense. But there seems no direct evidence of this.

[2] Stubbs, *Select Charters*, 9th ed., 119.

[3] *Colchester Cartulary* (Roxburghe Club), i. 25.

[4] Public Record Office, Rentals and Surveys $\frac{20}{8}$; Appendix, No. 3. It
is clear that in this context the phrase has no special reference to actual
military service, nor to any particular kind of knight's fee. It clearly means
nothing more than the *pro servicio terciae partis unius militis* of a normal
charter of enfeoffment for the fractional part of a knight's service.

[5] Such as the statement in the Hundred Rolls that the abbot of Tavis-
tock held fifteen and a half knights' fees 'in fe de Haubergh', quoted by
Maitland, *History of English Law*, 2nd ed., i. 256.

Norman and the English use of the word *vavassor*. The origin of the word is obscure, but in the eleventh century it was current in every part of feudal Europe in the general sense of vassal. In the greater part of France the word seems to have carried a certain sense of distinction. The vavassor of early feudal documents is inferior to the baron, but normally he is a knight, and he is raised above the landless men of the military class by the possession of a fief which may well be of considerable extent.[1] The Norman use of the word was different. In the Bayeux Inquest of 1133, the first document to show the position of the Norman vavassor in any detail, he appears as a free tenant burdened with military duties which, in part at least, are determined by the size of his holding.[2] When the duke summoned an army for the defence of the land, every vavassor who held more than fifty acres was bound to serve with a horse and *plana arma*, namely hauberk, shield, and sword. On one of the bishop's fees it is stated that there are many vavassors 'who ought to guard the castle and give an aid of twelve pounds towards its keeping'. The normal holding of the vavassor was obviously less than a normal knight's fee, and *vavassoriae* were often grouped to provide the whole or some simple fraction of a knight's service. Of the services other than military which lay upon the vavassor, the Inquest says little, beyond a statement that when the bishop was obliged to go to Rome on the business of his Church, his vavassors must give him an aid according to the amount of their several holdings, but other Norman documents show him paying relief and rent and doing carrying-service, and make it clear that his lord had the wardship and marriage of his heirs.[3] A similar though less definite impression of his position is given by later Norman feudaries, notably the *Infeudationes Militum* of 1172, which shows a knight bound to

---

[1] See Guilhiermoz, op. cit. 150–4, 167–9.

[2] For the Bayeux Inquest see above, 13 n.

[3] See, for example, the references to *vavassores* in the charters abstracted by Round in his *Calendar of Documents preserved in France*, and the passages relating to vavassors quoted by Haskins, op. cit.

send three vavassors if he cannot do his castle-guard at Lions la Forêt,[1] and a group of vavassors in the Bessin bound to make up a knight's service for the abbot of Mont St. Michel unless they have already been called up by the arrière-ban.[2] The word in all these passages is clearly being used as a technical term, and the class to which it was applied was very numerous. In 1088 a Norman lord, not of the first rank, could say that a man like himself who was leaving a hundred vavassors to his sons might fairly keep one for himself when he retired from the world.[3] The military value of the class was far from negligible, and the social position of the vavassor was superior to that of a mere peasant. But the Bayeux Inquest, the ancient text which most clearly emphasizes his military duties, is precise in its distinction between the *vavassoria* and the knight's fee, between the *vavassor* and the *miles*.[4]

[1] *Red Book of the Exchequer*, ii. 637.

[2] Ibid. 626; Haskins, op. cit. 9: 'Abbas de Monte Sancti Michaelis, servicium vi militum in Abrincensi et Costanciensi, et i militem in Baio-cassino quem faciunt vavassores nisi fuerint in exercitum.' The last words are clearly intended to provide for the case which would arise if these vavassors had been called up by a general levy before they had been summoned by the abbot's officers. They are a useful indication of the vavassor's general position.

[3] Haskins, op. cit. 19.

[4] The distinctive position of the Norman vavassor was pointed out by Guilhiermoz (op. cit. 183–8), and illustrated by a large collection of references. But there is much to suggest that in the eleventh century the distinction was more pronounced than would be gathered from this work. While emphasizing the fact that *vavassor* was commonly used in contrast to *miles* in Normandy, Guilhiermoz considered that here, as elsewhere in France, it was also used in contrast to *baro*, thus covering the 'simple knight'. This, if correct, would materially reduce the significance of the distinction drawn in early texts between the *vavassor* and the *miles*. The chief reason given by Guilhiermoz for believing that in the eleventh century the vavassors of Normandy included knights is the use of the word in this extended sense in English texts like the *Leis Willelme* and the *Leges Henrici Primi*. But these texts are poor evidence to set against the restricted sense borne by the word *vavassor* in Domesday Book (below, 19–20), agreeing, as it does, with the information as to eleventh-century conditions given by the Bayeux Inquest, and by early Norman charters. In England, for reasons suggested in the text, *vavassor* had come to be used, by the beginning of the twelfth century, in the extended sense common in France at

It was in this restricted sense that the word *vavassor* was brought to England. In Domesday Book, as in the Norman documents which have just been quoted, it denotes men of very modest estate. The heading *Terra Vavassorum* in the Suffolk Domesday covers the holdings of a considerable number of very small free men.[1] In Buckinghamshire two *vavassores* appear as rendering thirty-two shillings and six pence to their lord,[2] and under the Isle of Wight there is a reference to a vavassor with two cows.[3] At first sight there seems little sense in the application of the term to the English free men of Suffolk. But in reality there must have been something more than a vague resemblance between those free men and the *vavassores* with less than fifty acres whose existence is implied by the Bayeux Inquest. There cannot have been much difference of social or economic condition between Godwine, the 'vavassor' who held twelve acres as a free man at 'Turulvestune' in Suffolk, and his contemporary, the vavassor in the Côtentin with ten acres, whom the East Anglian magnate Roger Bigot gave to the church of St. Martin at Séez.[4] Even within the military sphere, there are English parallels to the service of the Norman vavassors. In the early surveys in the *Liber Niger* of Peterborough many sokemen are described as serving with the knights of the abbey[5] in a way which recalls the military burdens laid on *vavassores* and their tenements in

this time, and English influence must have made for the extended use of the term in Normandy itself. There is undoubted evidence of the generalized use of the term by later Norman writers. Wace, for example, normally contrasts vavassor with baron. But the only conclusive evidence as to the original meaning of the term is that of early charters and custumals reflecting early conditions, and although these materials are less numerous than could be wished, they are on the whole remarkably consistent in pointing to a restricted use of *vavassor* in Normandy at the time of the conquest of England.

[1] D.B. ii. 446, 447.   [2] D.B. i. 146 b.   [3] D.B. i. 53.
[4] Round, *Calendar of Documents preserved in France*, No. 659; D.B. ii. 446.
[5] e.g. *Chronicon Petroburgense* (Camden Society), 172: 'In Estona ix sochemanni qui habent i hidam et iii virgas in Lerecestrescira et serviunt cum militibus quantum illis jure contingit.'

the Bayeux Inquest, compiled eight years later. In view of this parallel it may be wondered whether the peculiar use of *vavassor* in the earliest Norman feudaries—a use to which there seems nothing strictly comparable elsewhere in France—may not result from the presence in Normandy of many free landholders, derived, like the sokemen of the English Danelaw, from a Scandinavian settlement in the past. In any case there is no need to accuse the Domesday clerks of misusing words in their identification of the small English free men of Suffolk with the *vavassores* of contemporary Normandy.

But the use of *vavassor* in this restricted sense is confined in England to the generation immediately following the Conquest. The sokemen of the Midlands and East continued to be known by their Old English name, and no foreign description was ever permanently attached to the free men of East Anglia to whom the word *vavassor* was actually applied in Domesday Book. Barons and knights from many French provinces had settled in England in this generation, and it is not strange that the Norman conception of the vavassor should soon disappear in favour of the looser usage common throughout the rest of France. Already by the early part of the twelfth century the word was being used to cover men whose position was very different from that of the vavassor of the Bayeux Inquest. Many charters of this period imply that two great classes, barons and vavassors, comprised the whole of feudal, or at the least military, society. Henry I and Henry II each address writs to the barons and vavassors who owe castle-guard at Rockingham,[1] and Henry I speaks of the barons and vavassors who hold land by military service of the church of Ely.[2] In such a context the word *vavassor* obviously covers knights and military tenants of every class below the indeterminate but high rank of baron. This vagueness was not confined to the

[1] Add. MS. 28024, f. 53 b; Appendix, No. 44. For the castle-guard due from different honours at Rockingham see below, 213.

[2] Bentham, *History and Antiquities of the Church of Ely*, Appendix, No. xix.

king's chancery. At the middle of the twelfth century a
Lincolnshire knight could address a charter to all the
barons and vavassors of Lincolnshire.[1] Under Henry I,
when Hugh de Flamville was claiming land on the boundary between two Yorkshire villages, it was provided that
he should establish his claim 'by taking an oath with
eleven others, so that of those swearing with Hugh, half
ought to be vavassors as he is, and the other half ought to
be drengs'. Hugh's place in the Flamville pedigree has
not yet been fixed. He may have been the head of the
house. But the provision shows that *vavassor* had become
a word of very general application in Yorkshire before the
death of Henry I.[2]

Evidence to the same effect comes from the earl of
Chester's fee in Gloucestershire. Before the summer of
1141 Earl Rannulf sent his mandate to Richard de Veim
and his other vavassors of Bisley, commanding them to do
their service to Miles the king's constable as willingly as
they had ever done it.[3] The vavassors of this letter are
evidently the earl's feudal tenants on his fee of Bisley, and
there fortunately exists evidence to show that there were
knights among them. Some twenty years later Hugh earl
of Chester, Earl Rannulf's son, made an elaborate charter
restoring to Humphrey de Bohun, son-in-law of Miles the
Constable, the fee of Bisley 'to hold by the service of
three out of the five knights who are acknowledged to be
there', providing also that if more than five knights should
be found on the fee the earl should have half the service
due from the additional number.[4] The knights of this

---

[1] *Feodary of the Templars* (British Academy Records of Social and
Economic History), 248: 'Willelmus de Eschebia omnibus baronibus (et)
vavasoribus de Lincolnshyre et amicis et vicinis suis Francis et Anglis
salutem.' The charter which follows is a grant to the preceptory of Temple
Bruer.

[2] Farrer, *Early Yorkshire Charters*, i, No. 637. As it cannot be later than
1130, this document is earlier than the Bayeux Inquest. Its early date
emphasizes the contrast between the vague English use of *vavassor* and the
precision with which the term was still employed in Normandy.

[3] Duchy of Lancaster, Ancient Correspondence, 1; Appendix, No. 1.

[4] Cott. Chart. x. 7; Appendix, No. 2. These documents are discussed

charter had obviously been established on the fee for a considerable period, and there can be no doubt that they or their predecessors are covered by the *vavassores* of Earl Rannulf's letter. Even the earls of Chester, great lords in Normandy as they were, had abandoned in regard to their English fees the Norman distinction between the *miles* and the *vavassor*. This indefinite use of the word *vavassor* can, indeed, be traced throughout the materials for the early history of English feudalism. Whoever the author of the *Leges Henrici Primi* may have been, he knew the practice of King Henry's court from within, and to him, as indeed to Bracton, more than a century later, the class of *vavassores* included men who stood high in the feudal scale—*Habent autem vavassores qui liberas terras tenent placita que ad witam vel weram pertinent super suos homines et in suo et super aliorum homines si in forisfaciendo retenti vel gravari fuerint.*[1] These *vavassores* were obviously men of high position, with tenants of their own for whose good behaviour they were responsible—*viri magnae dignitatis*, as Bracton calls their successors.[2] The king himself used the same word in the same extended sense when he provided that if a plea arose between the *vavassores* of any baron of his own 'honour' that is, the whole realm of England, it should be heard in their lord's court.[3] A still more definite indication of the English vavassor's social position is given by that compendium of Anglo-Norman custom which passes under the name of *Leis Willelme*. Its compiler was attempting to equate the heriots which had been due from the various ranks of the Old English nobility with the reliefs paid by the different classes of

by Farrer, *Honors and Knights Fees*, ii. 51. The large number of knights established on this fee is remarkable, for in 1086 there were less than ten hides belonging to the earl of Chester's fief at Bisley, and there is no reason to think that any land was subsequently added to the estate. The existence of small military tenancies like those at Bisley must have contributed towards the twelfth-century generalization of the term *vavassor* in England.

[1] *Leges Henrici Primi*, ed. Liebermann, c. 27. Clause 26. 3, speaks of the *curia vavasoris.*

[2] *De Legibus et Consuetudinibus Angliae*, ed. Woodbine, ii. 32.

[3] Writ touching the shire and hundred courts, ed. Liebermann, c. 3. 1.

contemporary feudal society. He identifies the Old English earl with the Norman count, the Old English king's thegn with the baron, and the 'average thegn' of Cnut's laws with the vavassor. A vavassor, he says, 'shall be quit of relief by his father's horse, his helmet, shield, hauberk, his lance and sword, and if he is so ill-provided that he has neither horse nor arms he shall be quit by payment of a hundred shillings'.[1] The passage is valuable as a clue to the origin of the knight's hundred shilling relief. But it also shows that the Norman settlers in England could not maintain the clear social distinctions with which they had once been familiar. They were a miscellaneous multitude, painfully adapting themselves to the conditions which had arisen through centuries in an ancient kingdom. They had themselves no great store of words from which to draw indefinite terms of social significance. *Baron* already gave the impression of rank, *miles* had a precise meaning which no military society could afford to abandon. *Vavassor* was a convenient term for conveying the general sense of vassalage, of dependency in tenure.

The *vavassores* of the twelfth century form, in fact, a link between two distinct orders of society. On the one hand, according to the *Leis Willelme*, they represent the ordinary thegns, the lesser country gentlemen, of pre-Conquest England. On the other hand, they are evidently the predecessors of the *milites* on whom the administration of royal justice had come to depend before the end of the twelfth century. Most of them were doubtless knights in the technical sense. The *Leis Willelme* assume that every vavassor ought to have a knight's equipment. But the word vavassor has in England no precise military implication. It is an indefinite term, vaguely denoting a man's social position. Before the end of the twelfth century the outlines of English society had hardened. Knighthood itself had acquired a new social significance. The *vavassores* of the Anglo-Norman time represent the preceding phase of transition. The term is vague because the structure of society was still indefinite.

[1] *Leis Willelme,* ed. Liebermann, c. 20. 2 *a*. Cf. II Cnut 71. 2.

This indefiniteness was not due to any single cause. For one thing, the French invaders of the eleventh century were far too few to establish at once a uniform organization, even of military service in its narrowest sense. They were compelled to adapt themselves to the various types of agrarian development which they found in England, and to the last the feudalism of the less manorialized north and east differed from that of Wessex and the Midlands.[1] Under such conditions the evolution of anything that can properly be called a feudal system was bound to be slow. It was still further delayed by the fact that there was no coherent body of feudal custom common to all the invaders. The Normans brought with them a tradition of centralization which, however often it might be broken by individuals, determined the general character of English feudalism. But the Normans formed only one of the elements from which English feudal society arose. In 1086 men bearing names derived from places outside the Norman border appear in every part of England. It is not always realized how greatly their presence must have complicated King William's essential task of bringing all his followers into the same general scheme of feudal relationships. The one principle which all his men would admit, the principle of dependent tenure, left an indefinite number of questions open for future settlement. Most of them at length were doubtless settled in conformity with previous Norman usage. The king's court was essentially a Norman body, and most of his leading followers were Normans. But the Norman kings were not a race of great legislators. They worked by the settlement of individual cases as they arose, and no court working under the conditions which prevailed in the eleventh century can have settled all the questions of feudal organization which must have arisen in a newly conquered country. There can be no question that inferior courts—courts held by magnates for their tenants—contributed

---

[1] This point was emphasized by Vinogradoff, *English Society in the Eleventh Century*, 55–60, though with some exaggeration of the territorial compactness of knights' fees in southern England.

much towards the body of feudal law which existed at the middle of the twelfth century.[1] And many of these courts were composed of men who can have known nothing, at first hand, of earlier Norman practice.

The lands to the east of Normandy had supplied many knights to the army of the Conquest, and lords from Flanders, Picardy, and the Boulonnais can easily be traced in Domesday Book. Their settlement had begun early. Before the autumn of 1069 the Conqueror had promised to do justice if anyone, 'French or Flemish or English' did wrong to Archbishop Ealdred of York.[2] But in the eleventh century Flanders like Normandy was a highly developed feudal state, and there can have been little in Norman custom which would seem strange to the average Flemish knight. The settlement which really complicated the first phase of English feudalism came from Brittany. There had been a large Breton contingent in the army of Hastings. The Bretons formed one of the three divisions in which it advanced against the English position,[3] and many Breton lords received land in England. At their head came the earl of Richmond, a cadet of the ducal house, with a fee of the first importance in Lincolnshire, East Anglia, and the neighbouring shires, apart from his northern castlery of Richmond itself. Other Breton lords came high in the second rank of English barons. In the south-west Judhael of Totnes held a fief which in the twelfth century bore a *servitium debitum* of more than seventy knights.[4] In Lincolnshire Oger the Breton, the

[1] For the work of honorial courts in the twelfth century see below, Chapter II.

[2] Farrer, *Early Yorkshire Charters*, No. 12; Davis, *Regesta*, No. 33, and Appendix ii, *bis*. It may be noted that the earldom of Chester would certainly have had a strong Flemish complexion if Gherbod *avocat* of St. Bertin, to whom it was first granted, had not thrown up his English command.   [3] W. Spatz, *Die Schlacht von Hastings*, 48.

[4] For Judhael of Totnes see Round, *Feudal England*, 327. His foundation charter of Totnes Priory is printed in the *Monasticon*, iv. 630, and, more in accordance with its true form, by Oliver, *Monasticon Dioecesis Exoniensis*, 241. The 'Carta Tenementi de Totanesse', as the return of 1166 from this fee is called, is printed in the *Red Book of the Exchequer*, i. 257–8.

lord of Bourne, Eudo son of Spirewic, the lord of Tattershall, and Alfred of Lincoln, the first holder of what became the Bayeux barony,[1] have an important place in feudal history. In the Midlands Hascuit Musard held a scattered fief with a residence at Miserden in Gloucestershire, which still preserves his name,[2] and Maino 'Brito' was lord of a compact estate of which the head was at Wolverton in Buckinghamshire. In Essex Tihel de Helion of Helion's Bumpstead has made familiar the name of a remote Breton parish, Helléan near Ploermel.[3] There is, in fact, hardly a county in which this Breton element is not found, and in some counties its influence was deep and permanent. In Lincolnshire, for example, the Breton colony founded by Earl Alan of Richmond can still be traced, late in the twelfth century, by the personal names which give a highly individual character to records relating to the country round Boston, itself a town of Breton creation, and Louth. In these districts, as also in the North Riding of York, the Breton settlers of the eleventh and twelfth centuries preserved their ancient personal nomenclature with a conservatism resembling that of the Anglo-Scandinavian peasants among whom they lived.[4] It is safe to assume that a settlement which left such clear

[1] The Breton origin of Alfred of Lincoln was first pointed out by Round in *Feudal England*, 328. The origin of Eudo son of Spirewic is indicated by his father's name. In the ninth-century documents in the Cartulaire de Redon, the name Sperewi frequently occurs in a context composed exclusively of ancient Celtic names.

[2] See Round, *Victoria History of Warwickshire*, i. 280. The name Hascuit reappears in various forms among the tenants of the honour of Richmond in the twelfth century.

[3] Round, *Helion of Helion's Bumpstead* (Essex Archaeological Society's Transactions, viii. 187–91).

[4] The history of the Richmond fee in Lincolnshire has not yet been worked out, and few of the numerous documents which relate to it have been published. The Breton personal names in this district have therefore received little attention, and, indeed, cannot be studied in any detail as yet. But it is impossible to mistake the significance of names like Conan, Mengi, Constantine (with its short form Coste), Brian, Justin (with its short form Just), Alan, Tengi, Lauda, and no figure is more prominent in the earliest Lincolnshire Assize Rolls than the Simon Brito (or le Bret) who was an important tenant on the Richmond fee in the south-east of the county.

traces behind it was something more than the establishment of a few score knights and sergeants in military
tenancies. It must have had the character of a genuine
migration, though a migration upon a small scale.

Little can be said in definite terms of the society which
had been familiar to the Breton followers of the duke of
Normandy. Contemporary records are few, and those
which have survived are rarely as explicit as we could wish.
Nevertheless, enough material has been preserved to show
a fundamental difference between Breton and Norman
feudalism at this date. The whole history of Brittany
shows that the duke's authority was small when measured
by Norman standards. We are told, for example, that in
1126 Duke Conan son of Alan Fergant, a duke whose title
was uncontested, gave the custody of Redon Abbey to
Pope Honorius II, *cum milites suos a Rotonensis infestatione
monasterii cohibere non posset.*[1] In the letter which he
addressed to the pope the duke himself complains that
*accumulata Britannorum perfidia amodo custodire ut deceret
eam non possum.*[2] It is hard to imagine the weakest of
Norman dukes making a similar confession. But the
differences between Breton and Norman society lie deeper.
In the eleventh century Breton knighthood was essentially
a personal distinction, a mark of social status rather than a
qualification for military service. Feudalism itself was an
exotic institution in Brittany, imposed upon a society
which in 1066 was still Celtic in character and in much of
its organization. The evidence which comes from this time
shows a most curious blending of Celtic and feudal ideas.
When a monastic recorder styles a man *Miles quidam
nomine Daniel filius Eudoni (sic) matthiern,*[3] the French
knight and the Celtic chief are brought into close association. The same type of evidence shows that though
knighthood was a familiar dignity, a knight must often

---

[1] *Cartulaire de l'Abbaye de Redon* (Documents Inédits), 449.
[2] Ibid. 298.
[3] Ibid. 311. This document is assigned by the editor of the Redon
cartulary to the year 1066, and is apparently one of the latest records in
which the ancient Celtic word *mactiern* occurs.

have owed the estate which maintained him, not to a grant from any lord, but to his inheritance of a share in the ancestral lands of his family. But the paraphrase of a passage from the cartulary of Redon will illustrate this aspect of Breton knighthood better than any general discussion.

'A certain knight of noble race named Morvan shaken with the fear of death, inspired by the Holy Spirit, leaving the vanity of this world to seek the Lord, came to the monastery and sought the advice of Abbot Almod and Jarnogon the monk whom he had known from childhood, who with the brethren willingly offered him the habit of a monk. Thereupon he came armed to the holy altar, and there laid down the arms of knighthood, putting off the old man, putting on the new, and gave to the monastery a horse worth ten pounds, with his own *alod* of Trefhedic, that is, the eighth part of that place which fell to him among his kin, free from rent to any man under heaven, subject only to the church and monks.'[1]

There is no reason to suppose that Morvan and his kin were unusually conservative in their generation. In any case the passage shows what was possible in Brittany at the moment when the duke of Normandy was crossing to England, and illustrates the diversity of the customs which formed the continental background of English feudalism. It is more than probable that the Breton knights in England quickly adapted themselves to the habits of thought which prevailed among their French and Norman associates. But for a time they must have felt alien among the invaders of an alien land.[2]

[1] *Cartulaire de l'Abbaye de Redon*, 312. The charter is dated 1066.

[2] It is important to remember that the entry into England of Bretons and men from other French provinces outside Normandy was not confined to the Conqueror's day. William II, for example, established two brothers from Maine, Winebald and Hamelin de Ballon, in the marcher lordships of Caerleon on Usk and Abergavenny, and gave lands in England itself to each of them (Round, *Peerage and Family History*, 181–215). It was to Henry I that Alan fitz Flaald of Dol, ancestor of the Fitz Alan earls of Arundel and the Stewart kings of Scotland, owed his English lands (ibid. 115–46), and Brian son of Alan Fergant, count of Brittany, the famous Brian fitz Count of Stephen's reign, was brought up at King Henry's court and received the honour of Wallingford from him. The reign of

It is impossible to trace in detail the assimilation of the various elements introduced from time to time to form the feudal society of Norman England. The assimilation is often taken for granted by historians, for it is implied by the formal language of the Anglo-Norman chancery itself. To this body the king's subjects were of two races alone, French, without distinction between province and province, and English. The language of private charters tells the same story. It seems extraordinary when Ilbert de Carenci, at or shortly after the end of the twelfth century, addresses a charter relating to Cambridgeshire to all his men *Francis et Anglis et Flandrensibus*.[1] Ultimately, assimilation was doubtless inevitable, but the rapidity with which it came about is one of the most remarkable, if least considered, facts in Anglo-Norman history. If William's followers had received their lands in compact territorial blocks, nothing could have prevented the formation of a series of racial groups, each preserving the integrity of its own distinctive custom. The scattering of estates, which isolated individual Flemings, Bretons, Picards from others of their race, emphasized the elements common to all French society. Above all the fundamental distinction between Frenchmen and Englishmen overrode all the matters of detail in which the custom of one French province differed from that of another. The Conqueror could ignore all these lesser distinctions in the legislation which he issued for his new kingdom, but it was the force of circumstances rather than royal policy which brought the invading races together.

For indeed, the feudal law which prevailed in England at the accession of Henry II was no mere complex of discrepant customs. The various rules whose observance can be inferred from the practice of this and an earlier time

Henry I saw the establishment of many new families in England, but, as Round showed in the essay last quoted, the most important of them came from the Côtentin, of which Henry had been lord before his succession to the English throne.

[1] Augmentation Office Miscellaneous Books, 40, No. 5. For Ilbert de Carenci see Farrer, *Feudal Cambridgeshire*, 3, 176.

obviously form part of a common system. The difficulty which is often felt in approaching the feudalism of the reigns of Henry I or Stephen is not due to any survival of ancient provincial customs, but partly to the obscurity of the materials, and partly to the fact that however strongly they may emphasize the royal supremacy over all men they are preoccupied with the fundamental relationship of man and lord. To a modern reader a word like *ligius* or its derivative *ligantia* suggests the duty of a subject to his sovereign, a royal claim to obedience which overrides all feudal relationships.[1] To the author of the *Leges Henrici Primi*, as, indeed, to Glanville two generations later,[2] the relationship expressed by the statement that one man is the *ligius* of another is only one of the forms assumed by the general feudal bond. Although one man may well hold of many lords, the *Leges* assert that he owes especial obedience to one of them, and imply that this is the lord of whom he holds his usual residence.[3] He must never sit in judgement on this particular lord, even in a case in which the king is interested,[4] and conversely, if he himself is taken or impleaded by any of his other lords, he to whom he is *ligius* must be his pledge.[5] If he is killed it is this lord who will receive his *manbot*, and if the host is summoned, it is this lord whose contingent he must join.[6] The word is, in fact, a technical term denoting the closest feudal relationship conceived by the men of the Norman age. It was long before *ligius* and *ligantia* lost their original force. Early in the reign of Henry II, Geoffrey

[1] In Maitland's discussion of ligeance in the *History of English Law*, i. 298–300, it is treated in connexion with the very different conceptions of homage and fealty, and its feudal interest is obscured.

[2] Glanville, *Tractatus*, ix. 1.

[3] Clauses 43. 6, 55. 2, and 82. 5 all assert that a man should be the 'residens' of the lord to whom he is *ligius*.

[4] C. 32. 2: 'Nemo dominum suum iudicet uel iudicium proferat super eum cuius ligius sit, si etiam de principis causa sit.'

[5] C. 43. 6 a: 'Si multis homagium fecerit et ab aliquo eorum captus et implacitatus sit, ille cuius residens et ligius est erga quoslibet alios iure potest eum plegiare, nec debet ei denegari qui manbotam inde haberet.'

[6] This is evidently the meaning of the statement in c. 82. 5 that a man 'ought to be in war' with the lord of whom he is *ligius*.

Ridel, himself the son of a royal justice, granted land to John de Stutville, a fellow baron, with the provision, 'I have made this gift and grant to the aforesaid John on the day when he did homage and liegance to me at Northampton, but if it shall happen that any fee or inheritance comes to him for which he ought to make liegance, let him do it, saving my service belonging to me'.[1] Liegance was obviously a matter of immediate practical importance when these words were written.[2] The Curia Regis of

[1] F. M. Stenton, *Danelaw Charters*, No. 457. The writer of this charter is evidently providing for the possibility that John de Stutville may become possessed of a more important fee than that which he holds of Geoffrey Ridel. If this happens, Geoffrey will not insist that John remains his *homo ligius*.

[2] Now and then, though rarely, an early charter will describe a man who is neither of knightly condition nor of French extraction as the *homo ligius* of his lord. The clearest illustration of the position of such men comes from a memorandum written by the Chapter of Lincoln Cathedral at the middle of the twelfth century (*Registrum Antiquissimum of Lincoln Cathedral*, ii. 192): 'Notum sit presentibus et futuris Radulphum de Cadamo fratrem nostrum . . . utilitati prebende sue providendo in futuro concessisse et dedisse . . . Edrichio homini suo ligeo et heredibus eius xii acras terre ex orientali parte et x acras terre arabiles ex parte occidentali . . . in prebenda sua de Hasgreby solutas et quietas et liberas de villenagio et ab omni servicio tenendas in feudo et hereditate de eo et successoribus eius canonicis prebende predicte reddendo annuatim x solidos. . . . Et sciendum est quod si prefatus Radulphus vel successores eius canonici quesierint auxilium de hominibus de Hasgreby, idem Edrichius vel heredes eius nichil . . . propter terram prenominatam faciant preter x solidos prenominatos. . . . Preterea in omnibus que ad rectam iusticiam (*sic*) pertinebunt erit ipse Edrichius sicut homo ligius prebende de Asgreby, et idem Edrichius et heredes eius sicut liberi tenentes predicte ecclesie sancte Marie Lincolniensis et huic Radulfo prefato canonico . . . erunt obedientes et obnoxii.' There is no reason to think that Edric of Asgarby differed materially either in status or tenure from innumerable other free men around him. The statement that he is the *ligius* of the canon of whom he holds his land emphasizes the fact that he is bound particularly to his service against all other lords of whom he or his heirs may come to hold. In the Norman age it was as true of the free peasant, the sokeman, as of the knight that one man might hold of divers lords. In stating that Edric shall be as the liege man of the prebend 'in all things which belong to right justice', the memorandum is presumably insisting that he shall be attentive to the interests of the prebend and its canons whenever a case affecting them appears in the courts of shire, riding, or wapentake.

the Norman kings had made less impression than is always realized on the intractable core of feudal senti-
ment represented by the relationship of the *ligius* to his
lord.

Its success had lain in other directions. In its relations
with the feudal world its great achievement had been to
establish the effective supremacy of the crown by the
settlement of innumerable questions brought before it by
individuals. In dealing with the king's own tenants its
authority was in accordance with the strictest feudal
principles. Every tenant in chief was the liege man of the
king, for the king was the lord of whom he held his *caput
honoris*, and the baronial element was an essential, though
fluctuating, part of the Curia Regis. In the history of the
English constitution the court of the Anglo-Norman
kings usually appears as a small group of royal servants,
preoccupied with judicial, financial, and administrative
business. It is men of this type who usually attest the
writs of William II and Henry I. But at any moment this
body could be reinforced by the greatest magnates of the
land, and there can be no doubt that to the baronial class
the social side of the Curia Regis was at least as important
as the routine activity of its expert members. The king's
barons of every race were on common ground in his court.
Their presence gave opportunity for the informal discussion which must have preceded the establishment of
any general rules of feudal law. Many of them must have
been familiar with the king and his leading ministers from
earliest youth, for the king's rights of wardship brought
the heirs of many noble families for education into the
king's *curia*.[1] The distinction drawn instinctively by his-

[1] This aspect of the Curia Regis, to which little attention is generally
paid, is well illustrated by the curious epitaph of William son of Walter
de Aincurt, preserved in Lincoln Cathedral, and printed in facsimile by
Dugdale in his *Baronage of England* and by Hearne in his edition of *Sprott's
Chronicle*: 'Hic iacet Wi[llelmus] filius Walteri Aiencuriensis consanguinei
Remigii episcopi Lincoliensis qui hanc ecclesiam fecit. Prefatus Willelmus
regia styrpe progenitus dum in curia regis Willelmi filii magni regis Willelmi
qui Angliam conquisivit aleretur iii [ka]l' Novemb' obiit.' The description
of William de Aincurt as born of royal stock, a fact otherwise unknown,

torians between the *curia regis* in which the king had social intercourse with his barons, and the Curia Regis from which the later departments of state are derived, is drawn for the convenience of the modern student. The king's court of the eleventh and twelfth centuries was undoubtedly the judicial centre of the kingdom, the place from which writs were issued and where ultimate judgement was given, but this was not its only aspect to the magnates of the time. To the barons of the Conquest and their immediate successors it was the place where they were entertained by the king in the company of their fellows, discussed their affairs with him, and gave him their advice if he asked for it. And although a body of magnates, meeting in what was rather a social assembly than a court of law, might be slow in deciding questions in which men of their own class were interested, the weight of their decision was irresistible.

The records which have come down from the Anglo-Norman Curia Regis are for the most part brief and formal notifications of royal acts or commands. They hardly ever refer to any general principle or rule, and as most of them come from the archives of religious houses, they throw less light than could be wished on the dealings of the king with his barons. On innumerable occasions in the Norman period the king must have been compelled to consult with his barons about the disposal of escheated fiefs, the marriage of heiresses, or the settlement of conflicting claims to large estates. The lines along which he acted must have governed the whole of English feudal practice, but few documents of the time so much as show him in the company of his barons, and his treatment of individual cases has generally to be inferred from later evidence. Moreover, the few documents which illustrate the king's behaviour as the supreme feudal overlord are generally expressed in conventional and unemphatic language which obscures their real significance. In 1107 Robert count of Meulan obtained from Henry I a charter authorizing

suggests that an unrecorded family relationship may not infrequently have connected individual barons with the Conqueror.

the count's plan for the ultimate division of his great inheritance in England and Normandy between his twin sons Waleran and Robert.[1] The king is represented as granting the English lands to Robert, the younger twin, except for the large estate of Sturminster, which the count has given to Waleran, with the king's consent. If Robert shall die or prove incapable of ruling land, the English inheritance shall pass to Waleran, and if Waleran shall die or prove incapable of possessing land, the Norman inheritance shall pass to Robert.[2] If both the boys shall die, leaving the count without a male heir, the whole inheritance in England and Normandy shall pass to his daughter at his death, so that she shall be married therefrom by the king's advice. Provision is made for the security of the grants which the count has made or shall make to churches or to his men with the king's assent. Finally, the king appoints that if either the English or the Norman lands shall be lost, the remainder of the inheritance shall be shared between the brothers. The charter is only known from late and imperfect copies. But no other document expresses so clearly the firmness with which the king could control the devolution of even the greatest fiefs in England and Normandy.[3]

The king's overriding authority in the feudal sphere appears again in a later writ by which Henry I disposes of the inheritance of his justice, Geoffrey Ridel, drowned in the wreck of the White Ship in 1120. For its early date it is an elaborate record, but it is elliptical in its phrasing, and in reading it there should be borne in mind that Geoffrey Ridel had married Geva, daughter of Hugh I earl of Chester, and that Ralf and Richard Basset were father and son.[4]

---

[1] *Regesta Regum Anglo-Normannorum*, ii, No. 843.

[2] The fact that the verbs *regere* and *possidere* could be used indifferently in a context like this is a curious illustration of contemporary thought about the nature of feudal lordship.

[3] The essential part of the arrangement took effect in 1118, when Robert count of Meulan died; his Norman lands, with Sturminster, passing to Waleran, and his English lands, with his earldom of Leicester, passing to Robert.

[4] The following table indicates the relationship of the principal persons

'Henry king of the English greets the bishop of Lincoln and earl David and the earl of Leicester and earl Rannulf of Chester and all the barons and lords of whom Geoffrey Ridel held lands, and all the sheriffs within whose jurisdiction he held them. Know that I have given to Richard Basset the daughter of Geoffrey Ridel to wife, and the custody of Geoffrey Ridel's land until Robert Ridel can be a knight and marry the granddaughter of Ralf Basset, namely the daughter of one of his daughters. Thereupon, the aforesaid Richard shall have twenty *libratae* of land of my fee in demesne, in marriage with his wife, and four enfeoffed knights, and if Robert shall die without heir by his wife, I grant to Richard Basset and the heir whom he shall have by the daughter of the aforesaid Geoffrey the whole land of Geoffrey Ridel, of whomsoever he held it. And if the daughters of Geoffrey Ridel shall not be married during the life of Robert their brother or while under the wardship of Richard Basset, he shall provide for them according to my advice and discretion. And this gift and compact have been made at the request and with the advice of Rannulf earl of Chester and William his brother and Nigel de Albini and [Robert Ridel's] other kin and Geva his mother and Geoffrey the earl's chancellor and Simon dean of Lincoln and William son of Rannulf and Thomas de St. John and Geoffrey de Clinton and Pain fitz John and William de Albini and Umfrey de Bohun and Robert Musard and Robert Basset and Osmund Basset and Turstin Basset and William constable of earl Rannulf of Chester and Ralf fitz Norman and Hugh Maubanc, at Woodstock.'[1]

In this charter the king is dealing, in a feudal environ-

interested in this arrangement, but does not attempt a complete representation of the families with which it deals.

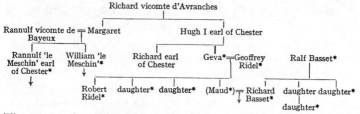

The persons who are named in the document or whose existence is implied by its language are indicated by an asterisk.

[1] Sloane Roll, xxxi. 4, m. 5; Appendix, No. 4. The charter falls between the death of Earl Richard of Chester, 25 Nov. 1120, and the succession of 'Earl David' to the Scottish kingdom in April 1124.

ment, with the sort of business which must continually have come before his greater barons in their relations with their own tenants. The provisions which he made for the descent of Geoffrey Ridel's land and the support of his children illustrate more than one detail of feudal custom, notably, the significance of knighthood as a sign that a military tenant has come of age, the practice by which the king would occasionally increase a baron's honour by the grant of knights already enfeoffed on the royal demesne,[1] and the care with which members of the higher baronage regarded the interests of those connected with them by family relationship. But for general history the details of this arrangement are less interesting than the composition of the body which the king took into counsel on the matter. It included representatives of each of the two great classes in the contemporary baronage. Geoffrey Ridel had been one of King Henry's new men. He owed much to the king's favour, and as the present document shows he had acquired land from many different lords. But he had married into the greatest of all baronial families, and the earl of Chester and three of his barons[2] stand here for the feudalism of the Conqueror's day. Humphrey de Bohun, Geoffrey de Clinton, William de Albini, Thomas de St. John, Nigel de Albini, and Pain fitz John represent in different ways the new baronage which had risen into importance since the accession of William II. It would be a mistake to regard this body as showing the normal composition of the king's court. The earl of Chester's barons are not likely often to have visited the king in the South. But it certainly illustrates the various elements which could combine at any time to form that court, and its meeting shows the care with which the king moved in matters interesting his greater barons. Even within the

[1] On grants of enfeoffed knights in general see below, 60, n. 1.

[2] Of these men, William the Constable was baron of Halton, Ralf fitz Norman was brother of Hugh fitz Norman, the first baron of Mold, Hugh Maubanc was baron of Nantwich. For these baronies see Tait, *Introduction to the Domesday Survey of Cheshire* (Chetham Society, vol. lxxv), and for Ralf fitz Norman, who may have been a *dapifer* to the first earl of Chester, see Tait, *Chartulary of Chester Abbey* (Chetham Society, vol. lxxix), 33.

purely feudal sphere, the Anglo-Norman monarchy was no autocracy.

It was only with the consent of a body, similar to this in composition, though far more numerous, that the king could legislate on matters of feudal interest. It is not strange that traces of such legislation are hard to find. Even when the king had brought his large and miscellaneous court into agreement on a general feudal issue, there was no immediate necessity for its decision to be set down in a formal record. In matters affecting the procedure of the communal courts, the treatment of royal pleas, or the punishment of grave offences, it was necessary that the king's officers in the shires should be told at once about any important innovations. Writs conveying information of this kind have survived from the chanceries of William I and Henry I.[1] But within the sphere of what may be called feudal law, the men who had approved a definition or an innovation were themselves immediately responsible for carrying it into effect. No decision affecting, for example, the rules of succession to lands held by military tenure could have been reached in the king's court without the consent of the baronage as a whole, nor could it have been carried out unless individual barons had been prepared to apply it to concrete cases in the courts of their respective honours. Even the Angevin kings, interested as they were in the detail of law, were slow to legislate on matters within the province of the honorial court. On more than one question of importance to feudal society, Magna Carta seems to have been the first general expression of the king's will. It may be added that a particular case might at any time produce a judgement from the king which cut across the best-established rules

[1] Such as the writ of William I forbidding bishops and archdeacons from holding pleas *de legibus episcopalibus* in hundred courts or bringing matters affecting the health of souls before the judgement of laymen (Stubbs, *Select Charters*, 9th ed., 99), the writ of Henry I about the holding of the shire and hundred courts and the pleas which might be taken there (ibid. 122), and the less-known writ of the same king describing the measures to be taken to secure the purity of the currency, and the punishment of those who made false money (Liebermann, *Gesetze*, i. 523).

of feudal law. In 1208 a jury reported that King Henry I had given the barony of Marshwood to a younger, in preference to the eldest son of a previous holder, 'because he was a better knight'.[1]

Up to the present few references to general rules of law have been noticed in the private charters of the Anglo-Norman time. The charters which are most characteristic of this age follow the model which the royal writ has made familiar. As a class they are the work of men who wished to place a transaction on record in the fewest possible words, and they ignore everything beyond the business immediately in hand. Even the more elaborate records of gift which religious houses generally obtained from their benefactors, valuable as they often are for matters of genealogy, rarely diverge into matters of law. Under these conditions a curious document of Stephen's reign preserved in the cartulary of Binham Priory becomes interesting through an incidental reference to a certain *statutum decretum* about the partition of fees among heiresses, of which there seems to be no other trace. The relevant words are few, but the charter as a whole shows the kind of writing possible to a clerk who felt himself at liberty to indulge in free composition, and few of his contemporaries have left a similar example of their powers. It is the first of a series of charters recording the way in which Binham Priory became possessed of its estate at Barney in Norfolk.[2]

'Roger de Valognes greets all his friends and men, French and English. It is generally known to many that Walter de Valognes, my kinsman, before he became a monk, gave Barney with the land of Thursford and with all things that are there and belong thereto, within wood and without, for his soul's health and mine, and for the soul's health of all our kin, living and dead, to the church of blessed Mary of Binham, to remain for ever to the use of the monks

[1] *Pipe Roll 10 John* (ed. D. M. Stenton), 113. The passage is only found in the Chancellor's Roll.

[2] Cott. Claud. D. xiii, f. 49; Appendix, No. 5. Roger de Valognes, who issued this charter, was son of Peter de Valognes, tenant in chief in 1086, and father of the Robert de Valognes who accounted for nearly thirty-five knights' fees in the *Carta* which he sent in to the king in 1166 (*Red Book of the Exchequer*, i. 360–2).

who serve and shall serve God there, with the assent and in the presence of Rohaise his wife, before the abbot of St. Alban's and before clerks and knights. We know also that Agnes his daughter, with the same Walter her father, has placed the aforesaid land upon the altar with a knife before all who were standing around, Agnes, namely, who was Walter's heir in respect of this land of Barney according to the appointed law that where there is no son the daughters divide their father's land by the spindles, nor can the elder take from the younger her half of the inheritance without violence and injury. Now I myself, Roger de Valognes, moved by the love of God and the blessed and glorious virgin Mary mother of our lord Jesus Christ, have granted that this gift should be made, and do now confirm it thus made, at the request and prayer of the aforesaid Walter, for the service of the third part of one knight only, for the soul of my father who first gave Barney to the church of Binham, and commanded Walter that this should be done, and for the soul of my mother and for the soul's health of myself, my wife Agnes, and my sons who are of one mind with me in this and grant the same themselves, and for the common salvation of all our kin alive and dead. Moreover I have done this at the advice and with the approval of many wise men, moved especially by the exhortation, the request, and the counsel of the lord Theobald archbishop of Canterbury and primate of all England, who showed me by most reasonable and unanswerable arguments that a noble gentleman who has the fee of six knights should give not only the third part of a knight's land to God and holy church for the soul's health of himself and his kin,[1] but the whole of a knight's land or more than that, adding also that if this man's heir should try to take away the alms which is interposed as a bridge between his father and Paradise, by which his father may be able to pass over, the heir, so far as he may, is disinheriting his father from the kingdom of heaven, and therefore should not obtain the inheritance which remains, since he who has killed his father has proved himself no son. All this the archbishop by careful argument has impressed upon us, and therefore

[1] These words deserve to be compared with the phrase quoted by Haskins (*Norman Institutions*, 19) from a Norman charter of 1088, 'rectum esse dicebat ut qui suis filiis centum vavassores dimittebat sibi atque monachis cum quibus victurus atque moriturus erat unum saltim ex illis proprie et solute retineret.' See above, 18. The difference between the hundred vavassors of this passage and the fee of six knights of the present charter is some measure of the difference between the respective position of the knight of English feudalism and the Norman vavassor. For the English extension of the latter term to cover knights see above, 20–23.

let Walter's aforesaid gift of Barney remain firm for ever with all its appurtenances to the church of blessed Mary of Binham, as freely, well, and honourably as Walter best held it in my father's time or in mine. As to him, therefore, who shall desire to take away this alms from the church of Binham, let him have his lot with Dathan and Abiron and Judas the traitor in the depth of Hell. As for him, however, who shall confirm it to the church, support, and maintain it, may his soul be in the lot of the elect and enjoy eternal life. Amen.'

There is much of general interest in this extraordinary charter, especially perhaps in the words attributed to Archbishop Theobald which imply, very clearly, that a fee of six knights was at least an adequate provision for a man who could be described as *vir nobilis et liberalis*. For once we obtain a reference to the social as distinct from the legal position of one among the many lords of large mesne tenancies whose names occur in the records of the twelfth century.[1] But the importance of the charter lies in its reference to the *statutum decretum* which governed the partition of fees among co-heiresses. That the law of the late twelfth century prescribed such partition has long been known. It would seem from this charter that already in Stephen's reign there existed a general rule to this effect, definite enough to be described in a phrase which in itself suggests a legislative act. For the phrase *statutum decretum* is at least remarkable.[2] It would not naturally have occurred to a clerk who merely wished to say that a division of a fee was in accordance with accepted custom. *Mos patriae, consuetudo regni* were

[1] Walter de Valognes with his six knights' fees is a good example of the honorial barons whose position is described below in Chapter III.

[2] By itself *statutum* means nothing more definite than 'that which is appointed'. Robert earl of Leicester, for example, put on record that if one of his heirs fails in doing or observing the homage due to the bishop of Lincoln for a manor which he holds of the bishop, 'episcopus cohercebit eum per illam terram secundum iudicium curie sue iuxta statutum regni' (*Registrum Antiquissimum of Lincoln Cathedral*, ii. 5). No legislation can ever have been put forth on so fundamental a matter of feudal organization. But the earl's *statutum regni* does not give the definite impression of an enactment which is conveyed by the *statutum decretum* of the Binham charter.

familiar phrases; *statutum decretum* does not belong to the ordinary language of the charter-writer. Its use in the present context suggests, at least, that the compiler of this charter knew of some recent general decision of the king's court which ruled that where there was no son to inherit a man's fee it should be divided among his daughters *per colos*. In any case, these curious words prove that one of the questions most closely affecting the leading members of feudal society had been settled already in the dark age which preceded the accession of Henry II.

II

THE HONOUR AND THE LORD'S HOUSEHOLD

I F it is hard to trace the influence of the king's court upon the development of feudal custom into law, it is because few judicial records have descended from the *Curia* of the Norman kings. Historians have never doubted the importance of its work, the leading members of its personnel are well known, and the width of its jurisdiction is proved by contemporary evidence. In passing from the king's court to the courts of even his greatest tenants, we are confronted at once by the obscurest institution in Anglo-Norman history. The existence of feudal courts to which all the peers of a great fee were subject is proved by the familiar passage in the *Leges Henrici Primi* which states that every lord may summon his man to stand to right in his court, and that if the man lives in the remotest manor of his lord's honour, he must come to the plea if his lord summons him.[1] Of the composition of that court, its procedure, and the kind of business which came before it, the *Leges* tell us very little. The private charters of the twelfth century, which reveal many aspects of feudal society, are disappointingly vague in their references to the assemblies in which a lord did justice between his men. They commonly take the form of an address by a lord to his men, and they often state that he is acting upon his men's advice. But only a small proportion even of the charters which show something of a lord's dealings with his men refer in explicit language to his court.

Their language is, however, precise enough to make one important distinction reasonably plain. A clerk who

---

[1] Stubbs, *Select Charters* (9th ed.), 126 (*Leges*, 55. 1, 1a). The whole tenor of the *Leges* on this subject shows that the right of a lord to hold a court for his feudal tenants was not confined to tenants in chief of the king.

is thinking of the court of his lord's honour, the judicial assembly of his tenants, generally describes it as his lord's *Curia* without further qualification. The courts of the various manors of which an honour was composed usually appear in twelfth-century charters as the 'hallimot' of this or that place. The form of the word is itself an important historical fact. It stands for an Old English *heall gemot*,[1] 'hall moot', and its currency in the first half of the twelfth century is good evidence that what can only be described as a manorial court had been a well-established English institution before the Conquest.[2] Twelfth-century charters tell little of the work of these bodies and hardly anything of their composition, but show, at least, that now and then they could give an independent opinion on matters affecting their lords' interests. At about the middle of that century, for example, Geoffrey de Ivoi restores certain land to the nuns of Godstow after

[1] The origin of the word has been obscured by the fact that it often appears in the form *halimotum*, under which, for example, it was indexed by Liebermann (*Gesetze*, ii. 1, 109), though he quotes variant readings which give *hallimotum* and was fully aware of its derivation. By itself the form *halimotum* suggests that the first element of the word was the OE. *halig*, 'holy', and this has sometimes led to confusion. In the introduction to his *Select Pleas in Manorial Courts* (p. lxxvi) Maitland quotes a communication from Skeat suggesting the 'holy moot' derivation, which he did not feel free to reject though expressing the wish 'that on the whole it would be convenient if philology would suffer us to believe that we have to do with a "hall-moot" '. But most of the examples of the word in early sources preserve the *ll*, though some of them omit the initial *h*, and the usual form *hallimot* is the natural development of an OE. *heall gemot*, the medial *i* representing, as in many other words, the OE. particle *ge*.

[2] In view of the general drift towards the substitution of French for English terms after the Conquest, the preservation of the Old English term for the hall moot is remarkable testimony to the strength of the Old English traditions underlying this institution. The survival of the word shows that the well-known statement in the Cheshire Domesday (D.B. i. 265 b) that the manor of Acton 'has its pleas in its lord's hall' was not the note of an exception. On this phrase see Maitland, *Domesday Book and Beyond*, 91, and Tait, *Introduction to the Cheshire Domesday* (Chetham Society, vol. lxxv, N.s.), 48. Maitland, who regarded the phrase as the statement of a novelty, though he connected it with the term 'halimote or hall-moot', does not seem to have felt the significance of the Old English origin of the latter expression.

their right to it had been proved by the testimony of his hallimot, and he ends his charter of restitution by recording the attestation of the hallimot itself, 'through whose knowledge the recognition of the nuns' right has been fully made and confirmed, never to be revoked'.[1] But evidence so clear as this is hard to find, and the hallimots of the twelfth century rarely emerge from their obscurity except occasionally to attest the charters of their lords. There is little real danger of confusion between these local courts, mainly concerned with the affairs of peasants, and the assemblies of enfeoffed tenants round which the history of every honour turned.

Now and then an exceptional charter shows a lord attended by his men in a court which is evidently the judicial centre of his fee. In 1153 William de Braiose solemnly confirmed the gifts of one of his men to Sele Priory in the court of his castle of Bramber.[2] Between 1168 and 1170 Robert Blanchemains, earl of Leicester, then newly come into his great inheritance, received from four of his tenants in his court of Leicester the surrender of an estate in Northamptonshire which he proceeded to grant to the monks of Biddlesden.[3] The transfer of the honour of Huntingdon to Earl Simon of Northampton after the capture of the king of Scots in 1174 is reflected in a charter of this year made at Fotheringay, the head of the honour, 'in the first court of Earl Simon'.[4] Other charters, some of which will be quoted below in another context, bear the attestation of a court in session, or refer more or less incidentally to a judgement which a court has given, but it is only on the rarest of occasions that a charter will enter into a detailed record of transactions which have taken place in such an assembly. Moreover, the records which have come from the honorial courts of the thirteenth and later centuries may easily give a misleading impression of feudal justice in the days of its full

---

[1] Exch. K.R. Misc. Books, 20, f. cxlii. The use of *recognicio* in this local connexion and at this date is remarkable.

[2] Salter, *Early Oxford Charters*, No. 9.

[3] Harl. Chart. 84. H. 20.   [4] Harl. MS. 1063, f. 13.

vigour. The honorial court whose records are most often quoted is that held at Broughton in Huntingdonshire for the tenants of Ramsey Abbey.[1] It was a formal and dilatory body, largely occupied with excuses for non-attendance. But the fourteenth-century court rolls of the honour of Clare, a small portion of which has recently been printed,[2] show a highly efficient institution, administered by men who have clearly learned much from the practice of the king's court. It is obviously unsafe to argue back from the slow and ineffective procedure of the court of Broughton to the general character of feudal justice in the Norman age.

There can, in fact, be no question that courts which can only be described as feudal profoundly influenced the development of English society in the twelfth century. In every rank of life it was the lord's duty to see that justice was done between his men. Wide as was the field covered by the king's court under the Conqueror and his sons, it could not lightly override the relationship between lord and man created by the tie of homage. It was only through tentative advances that it gained the power of intervening between a tenant and his lord. The barons who demanded in 1215 that the writ *Praecipe* should not be issued in a manner through which any free man should lose his court were maintaining what had been a fundamental principle of feudal society. The organization which knit this society together must have been in great part the work of feudal courts. The baronial courts of the Norman age did justice between their peers,[3] advised their lords in the crises which continually arose in the history of every great fee, and thereby evolved in course of time a coherent scheme of rights and duties out of the tangle of personal relationships produced by the sudden introduction of feudal tenure

---

[1] The general nature of this court has long been familiar, owing to the inclusion by Maitland of extracts from its rolls in his *Select Pleas in Manorial Courts* (Selden Society).

[2] By Dr. W. O. Ault, *Court Rolls of the Abbey of Ramsey and of the Honour of Clare* (1928), 75–110.

[3] On this word see below, 60–61, and 91, n. 5.

into England. By the middle of the twelfth century the essential part of their work had been done. It remained for the justices who served Henry II and his successors to elaborate a feudal jurisprudence which would ignore the customs of individual fees. But the speed and assurance with which they moved owed more than is always realized to the feudal courts which their work was destined to supersede.

There is more than one reason for the rarity of texts which illustrate the course of early feudal justice. No doubt feudal assemblies, like all others of their time, relied much on their collective memory. Written evidence was only a supplement to the testimony of a court whose tradition was continuous however much its personnel might change. It was not to any charter but to the better and more ancient men of his honour that William de Roumara, afterwards earl of Lincoln, appealed when he wished to know the truth about the prebend of Asgerby, which his father had given to St. Mary of Lincoln.[1] But even so, the rarity of this evidence is remarkable. There must have been many occasions which emphatically called for the production of a written record. The partition of a fee was a complicated business, and there were endless possibilities of future dispute in the assignment of a widow's dower. If such transactions were rarely reduced to writing, one principal reason is that the clerks in the service of the average lord were men of little skill. They could draft the straightforward record of an enfeoffment or a grant of land in alms, but many of them were curiously helpless as soon as they left the elementary formulas which the king's chancery had made familiar. The record of a plea, in

---

[1] *Registrum Antiquissimum of Lincoln Cathedral*, i. 79: 'Ego Willelmus de Roumara uolens scire ueritatem de prebenda Asgerbie inquisiui eam a melioribus et antiquioribus hominibus meis de honore meo et aperte cognoui et didici ab eis quod Rogerus filius Geroldi pater meus et Lucia mater mea dederunt . . . sancte Marie Lincolnie . . . Asgerbiam . . . in prebendam et puram elemosinam.' Although more than one writ of Henry I confirming this gift still survives at Lincoln, there is no record of any charter of Roger son of Gerold. The circumstances of the gift must have been left to the memory of the men of Roger's honour.

which successive stages must be distinctly marked, and technical distinctions accurately drawn, lay altogether beyond the power of most of them. The clerks who served the Curia Regis itself soon found their limitations when they passed from matters of fact to those of law. Nothing could be more incompetent than the style of the *Leges Henrici Primi*, which certainly comes from this body,[1] and upwards of a century later, the clerks of the king's court were by no means uniformly successful in giving a coherent account of the business which had come before them. Even if the feudal law of the Anglo-Norman time could be studied in its application to individual cases, it is probable that much of its procedure would still be very dark.

The cases which we actually possess are very few, they are most inadequately recorded, and we know little of the law and custom, and often less of the facts, which lay behind them. Nevertheless, however dense its obscurity, any early record which expresses the result of deliberation in a feudal assembly deserves attention. The document which follows, preserved among the collections of the Lincolnshire antiquary Gervase Holles,[2] comes from the middle of the twelfth century, and probably from the closing years of Stephen's reign.[3] It describes in considerable detail, but with the omission of many material facts, the terms of an agreement made between two Lincolnshire barons, Roger of Benniworth and Peter of Goxhill, in the presence of their lord William of Roumara, earl of Lincoln, at Bolingbroke, the head of his honour.

[1] Liebermann, *Über das englische Rechtsbuch 'Leges Henrici'*, 44–47. See also below, 220.

[2] Lansd. MS. 207 E, p. 201; Appendix, No. 6.

[3] Earl William of Lincoln survived the accession of Henry II, for as *Willelmus comes de Roumara* he addressed a letter to the justiciar, sheriff, and king's ministers of Lincolnshire saying that he was prepared to testify to a transaction which had taken place in the court of King Henry *avi nostri regis* (Bodleian Library, Stixwould Charters, No. 3). But he plays no recorded part in the history of Henry II's early years, and none of his numerous charters are demonstrably later than 1154. He was certainly dead by 1161 (*Complete Peerage*, vii. 669, 670), and he probably died in 1155.

The lands which formed the subject of the agreement, lying at East Halton near Grimsby, Holton le Moor near Caistor, Wilsthorpe in Kesteven, and Shernborne in north-west Norfolk, formed part of the fee held of Ivo Taillebois in 1086 by Odo of Benniworth, Roger's grand-father.[1] It is not clear that Peter of Goxhill had any claim by inheritance to a share in this fee. When the agreement was made, neither he nor Roger were in seisin of any part of the estate at issue. Its language suggests that they were really allies against an unnamed third party, possibly some member of the Benniworth family, possibly Earl William, the overlord. In any case the agreement was intended to record the fact that Roger and Peter had mutually promised to share the expenses of recovering the estate, and to define the part which each was to receive when they had been successful.

'Be it known that this is the pact between Roger of Benniworth and Peter of Goxhill by which they have been brought into agree-ment at Bolingbroke in the presence of Earl William touching their claim to the land of Gervase of Halton, and touching the other inheritance of Odo of Benniworth, namely Wilsthorpe, Holton, and Shernborne. Namely that Gervase of Halton throughout his life shall hold half his land of Halton with all its appurtenances of Roger of Benniworth, and the other half of Peter of Goxhill. And this Peter of Goxhill holds and shall hold his half of Roger of Benniworth in fee and inheritance; he and his heirs of Roger and his heirs. And this Roger shall hold these aforesaid lands with all their appurtenances of Earl William and his heirs in chief, since Peter of Goxhill and Gervase of Halton have allowed that Roger is the rightful heir of these lands. Moreover, by this same pact which is here made touching the acquisition of the lands of Gervase, namely the land of Halton, Wilsthorpe, Holton, and Shernborne,

---

[1] These lands are entered in D.B. i. 350 b (Holton le Moor), 351 b (Wilsthorpe), and ii. 244 b (Shernborne). Odo's land at East Halton is entered at i. 350 b under the names of 'Chelvingehou' (Killingholme) and 'Lobingeham'; the latter place being now absorbed into Killingholme and East Halton. For the Lincolnshire identifications see Canon Foster's notes and index to the *Lincolnshire Domesday* (Lincoln Record Society, vol. xix). The fee of Odo of Benniworth, of which this is only a part, is a good example of the 'baronial' mesne tenancies which are discussed below, Chapter III.

this Roger and this Peter shall acquire them by their common power and their common money. And this Peter shall hold half of Roger in fee and inheritance, and of these and of the other lands in question Roger shall hold half in his demesne. And he who shall put more money towards acquiring these lands shall have the greater part of the land until his money is returned to him, to hold to him and his heirs, saving the tenures which this Roger and this Peter held in chief of Earl William on the day when they made this concord. And this Roger and this Peter have pledged their faith, one to another, in the presence of Earl William, to observe without guile the pact which is here made plain, these being witnesses. . . .

'After the aforesaid convention was made in Earl William's presence, on the day when Roger the Marshal put Roger of Benniworth in seisin of the service of Gervase of Halton, the agreement was renewed and re-acknowledged between Roger of Benniworth and Peter of Goxhill. In the first place, it was agreed between them that Gervase of Halton shall hold his whole fee, throughout his life, as he ever best and most freely held it. But after his death, it was agreed between the aforesaid Roger and Peter that the whole land of Halton shall be divided, so that Peter shall hold half of that land of Roger. Therefore, in the same place where this agreement was made, Peter did homage to Roger in respect of that half. And immediately after Roger was seized of the service of Gervase, and after Peter had done his homage to him, Roger, before all, gave Peter seisin of the aforesaid half, to hold of him and his heirs. Moreover, it was agreed between them that all their acquisitions of the fee of Odo of Benniworth should be divided, so that Peter and his heirs shall hold the half of their acquisitions of Roger and his heirs, saving the tenures which they hold, and held on that day, in chief of William de Roumara earl of Lincoln. This agreement Roger has bound himself and his heirs to observe on the security of his faith. And Peter also has bound himself and his heirs to observe it on the security of his faith. And after them, on the part of Roger of Benniworth, Matthew his brother has bound himself to the observance of this agreement on the security of his faith. And on the part of Peter of Goxhill, Garcier de Campania has bound himself to observe this agreement on the security of his faith. These being witnesses. . . .'

Alike in form and in matter, this document is interesting. Here, for once, we are brought into the authentic atmosphere of feudalism. The features which make the document difficult to a modern reader,[1] its elaborate repetitions, and its painful insistence on ceremonial *minutiae*, are in themselves significant, for they show the mental habit of a society which can only deal empirically with legal problems and must therefore move very slowly when it is confronted by an abnormal tenurial situation.[2] It is not surprising that in this feudal environment, phrases which were to become familiar among the technicalities of the common law are used in a vaguer sense. Even in Stephen's reign no clerk of legal training would have described a lord's claim to the service of a tenant like Gervase of Halton as tenure 'in demesne'. It would also be hard to find an exact parallel to a partition of this kind, in which the share of each party is proportionate to the amount of money spent in acquiring the land at issue. There is abundant evidence from the reign of Henry II that the need of money often destroyed the integrity of a fee. Many lords were giving portions of their estates as security for loans, and many loans were never repaid. Few cases can be quoted from any part of the twelfth century in which a whole fee is deliberately divided because its heir has not the money to acquire it for himself. No other case has yet been observed in which a peer of the honour to which the fee belonged intervened to make up the necessary sum,[3] and received a portion of the fee to be held thenceforward of the rightful heir. The situation revealed by this document may not have been uncommon in the reign of Stephen. The Assize of Northampton seems, in

[1] In part, though only in part, the difficulty of the document is due to the incompetence of the clerk who wrote it. More than one of Earl William's own charters is marked by a similar obscurity of style, and was probably written by the same man.

[2] By a very curious chance we happen to know that one essential part of this agreement was carried into effect. A charter of Gervase of Halton, of which the original has been preserved, is addressed to Roger of Benniworth and Peter of Goxhill. It is therefore plain that Gervase did actually hold half his land of Roger and half of Peter as the agreement prescribed (Stenton, *Danelaw Charters*, No. 474).

[3] These arrangements give a remarkable illustration of the influence of money on feudal relationships, an influence which is often underestimated.

fact, to be referring to just such cases in its insistence on the right of the heir to enjoy the seisin of his ancestor.[1] But they were unlikely to occur when the assize of mort d'ancestor had provided a cheap and simple method for their solution in the king's court.

But this remedy had not been devised at the date of this partition, nor could the king intervene in the internal affairs of a great honour. The supreme authority here is not the king, but William de Roumara, earl of Lincoln. The present agreement was made at Bolingbroke, the head of his fief, and witnessed by a group of his leading tenants; the heir to the land at issue was put in seisin by his marshal. The feudal order illustrated here was independent of the king's direction or control. The honour of Bolingbroke was a feudal state in miniature. Within it the peers of the fee were tenants in chief, and any arrangement on which they were agreed needed no sanction except that which their lord could give. A few years later the process had begun which was to open all but the greatest honours to the king's justices. In his old age Philip of Kyme, the first witness to this agreement,[2] might have read the treatise on the laws of England, attributed to Rannulf de Glanville, and both he and Peter of Goxhill were to serve King Henry II as sheriffs of Lincolnshire.[3] It is not strange that few materials have survived to illustrate the organization of the honour in the time when it was still autonomous.

Nevertheless, it is easy to antedate the extension of the king's justice over feudal society. Henry II never made any direct attack on the great baronial franchises, and his reign was well advanced before the activities of his court can have seriously affected their solidarity. A very remarkable record drawn up between 1162 and 1166 shows

[1] Stubbs, *Select Charters* (9th ed.), 179.

[2] Philip of Kyme appears occasionally at the court of Henry II, and in 1177 he was one of the 'barons of England' who witnessed the king's award in the dispute between the kings of Castile and Navarre.

[3] Peter of Goxhill acted from 1163 to 1165, and for another year by deputy. Philip of Kyme acted from 1167 to Easter 1170 (Eyton, *Itinerary of Henry II*, 338).

the court of William Earl Ferrers still a self-contained unit of feudal organization, witnessing a transaction which permanently reversed the normal order of succession between the two elder sons of one of the chief tenants on the Ferrers fee.[1]

'This is the composition of a final concord between Henry son of Fulcher and Sewall his brother; namely that the said Henry has made Sewall the heir of the baronies of Fulcher and Henry, Fulcher's brother, and thereof, namely of these two baronies, Henry the elder brother has set him in the place of lord and first-born. And for this gift and acquittance Sewall has given half a mark of silver to Henry in the court of the lord Earl William, and more-over Sewall has given to Henry and his heirs the homage of Swain of Mapleton and the service of Ivonbrook and the service of Ible, saving the right of Simon son of Jordan, and the service of Okeover, saving the right of the heirs of Ralf son of Orm, and the service of all the dower which Jordan, Sewall's brother, gave to his wife, namely half Youlgrave, and Gratton with its appurtenances, and Weston, and a mill in Derby, and a mark of silver from Brushfield, and Ireton, and Okeover, and the church of Edensor, and the

[1] Below, Appendix, No. 7, from a fourteenth-century copy in the Darley cartulary. The document has also been edited by R. R. Darlington, *The Cartulary of Darley Abbey* (1945), ii. 518–19, where it is collated with a version printed by Evelyn Shirley, *Stemmata Shirleiana* (2nd ed.), 347, from a transcript by Dugdale. It is a document of the first importance for the construction of the remarkable Shirley pedigree. The following table should make plain the relationship of the chief persons who are mentioned, but ignores other members of the family:

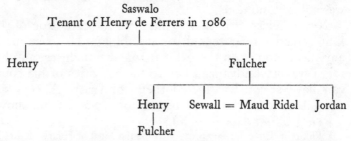

The date of the agreement can be fixed within narrow limits, for William Earl Ferrers does not seem to have obtained possession of his honour before Michaelmas 1161 (*Complete Peerage*, iv. 193) and Sewall appears in the earl's *Carta* of 1166 (*Red Book of the Exchequer*, i. 336) as holding all the fees which had once belonged to his father and uncle.

church of Shirley and whatever the father of Henry and Sewall had in the church of Youlgrave; and if the aforesaid lady shall change her life before her death, Henry and his heirs shall have all her aforesaid dower in their demesne.[1] And for this fine and gift Henry has given to Sewall five marks of silver, and by this composition and agreement, Henry and his heirs have confirmed (their inheritance) under oath, to Sewall and his heirs, if he shall have an heir by his wife, and if he shall not have an heir by his wife, the whole inheritance shall remain to Henry and his heirs. And for this gift and fine, Fulcher, Henry's son, has become the man of Sewall. And neither Sewall nor Henry may sell or give in pledge any part of their inheritance, save one to the other, and then, for a lower price than another would be willing to give. And the dower which Sewall had given to Maud Ridel his wife Henry and his heirs have confirmed to her, to hold as Earl William's charter confirms and attests the gift. And if one of them should not stand by this composition and observe it, and should refuse to make amends in obedience to the earl and his own friends, at the request of either, the earl shall take seisin of the fee of him who has departed from the agreement till the injury is made good. Of this deed and agreement, Earl William is both judge and witness, and these are witnesses; Robert the earl's brother and William Pantulf.'

Twenty years at most separate this document from the agreement between Roger of Benniworth and Peter of Goxhill, but its compiler was a draftsman of another class.

[1] Apart from Okeover in Staffordshire (which was possessed from the date of this document to the present century by the descendants of Ralf son of Orm, mentioned above) all the places dealt with here are in Derbyshire. Each of the brothers between whom this agreement was made founded a singularly tenacious family upon his estate. Sewall, the younger brother, was the ancestor of the Shirley family, of which the head was called to the House of Lords as Lord Ferrers in 1677 and created Earl Ferrers in 1711. Henry, the elder brother, whose descendants took their family name from Little Ireton in Derbyshire, was ancestor in the male line of Henry Ireton, son-in-law of Oliver Cromwell and Lord Deputy of Ireland. The descent of the baronies which were the subject of this agreement is, in fact, a very curious illustration of the continuity of English family history. It may be added that the name 'Saswalo' borne by the grandfather of the parties to this agreement, which here appears in the second generation as 'Sewall', and has sometimes been regarded as of English origin, represents the Romance 'Saxwalo', a rare, but adequately recorded name (Forssner, *Continental-Germanic Personal Names in England*, 223).

The example set by the king's clerks was evidently being felt outside the immediate sphere of his court. Nevertheless, here again, the clerk of a feudal magnate is using words in a sense which they would hardly have borne in the Curia Regis of his day. To him, writing from the standpoint of a great honour, the lands of its leading tenants were baronies.[1] But more significant than any verbal conservatism is the implication which runs all through this document that Earl William's authority will be sufficient to secure the observance of a most unusual family agreement, which cut straight across all the customs of inheritance accepted by feudal society, and gave to a younger son the tenurial position of the eldest born. It is for the lord who has sanctioned the agreement by his attestation to settle the disputes to which it may give rise— he is both *justicia* and *testis*, and he does not need to feel the king's authority behind him. Even in 1192, when this agreement was re-affirmed between Sewall son of Fulcher, and his nephew Fulcher son of Henry, the king's justices were not invoked. The document then drawn up took the form of a final concord in the court of William Earl Ferrers,[2] at Tutbury, the head of the Ferrers honour, and in the earl's presence.[3]

The body before which this partition was made is described in the record simply as the 'court' of Earl William. In many of the documents recording feudal business, transacted in a feudal assembly, there is not even this

---

[1] The use of this word gives a valuable indication of the conception of a barony which prevailed at the middle of the twelfth century. The *Carta* sent in by William Earl Ferrers in 1166 shows that the 'barony' of Henry, Sewall's uncle, had consisted of five knights' fees and that of Fulcher, Sewall's father, of four. The position of feudal barons of this type is discussed below, in Chapter III.

[2] The son of the earl who sanctioned the agreement which has just been translated.

[3] *Stemmata Shirleiana*, 347–8. The document begins: 'Anno ab incarnatione domini M°C nonagessimo secundo, anno scilicet in quo Willelmus comes de Ferrariis duxit Anneis in uxorem, sororem Ranulfi comitis Cestriae, facta est pax et finalis concordia in curia Willelmi filii Willelmi comitis de Ferrers apud Tutesberiam coram ipso comite, inter Sewallum filium Fulcheri et inter Fulcherum filium Henrici, nepotem suum.'

slight attempt to indicate its character. Before 1140, for example, William de Anisi, a tenant of Henry de Port, informed his own men that with his heir's consent he has given certain lands of his own acquisition at Sherfield English in Hampshire to Richard, a younger son. He states that on the advice of his friends and *pares* he has surrendered this land to Henry, his lord, who has given seisin of the land to Richard, and received Richard's homage for it, so that Richard shall hold the land thenceforward of Henry for the service of one knight, as it had formerly been held by William himself. He adds that Richard has paid on his behalf the sum of £11, being the arrearage of the service due from that fee to Henry, his lord. The charter is dated at Basing, the head of Henry de Port's barony, it is witnessed by more than thirty persons, many of whom can be identified as Henry's tenants, and it clearly represents a transaction which had taken place in Henry's court.[1] The charter is remarkable for the many points of early feudal practice which it illustrates; such as the distinction between the almost inalienable lands of a man's inheritance and the lands of his own acquisition with which he could deal more freely, the description of men on the same plane of tenure as each others *pares*, the giving of seisin and the taking of homage by a lord, above all, the transfer of a fee by its surrender to a lord, followed by its re-grant to a designated tenant—a procedure which curiously anticipates the surrender and admittance of the copyhold tenements of a later age. The charter shows a self-contained feudal community in action. Its ability to manage a complicated piece of internal business without the aid or control of the king's court is emphasized by the fact that William de Anisi, who set this feudal process in motion, was himself a member of the royal household. The seal which authenticates the charter describes him as *regis dispensator*, and later evidence shows that the description was correct.

It is not until the thirteenth century that a lord will

[1] Printed in facsimile with full notes in *Sir Christopher Hatton's Book of Seals*, No. 301.

commonly refer to the judicial assembly of his leading
tenants as the court of his 'honour'. This distinctive word
is used far less frequently in early documents than would
be inferred from the importance of the institution which
it represents, and its history shows again the indefiniteness of Anglo-Norman feudal terminology.[1] Even in the
thirteenth century, when its employment had become
specialized, it was not in any sense a technical term, but
certain features common to most honours emerge clearly
enough from the records of this age, and can be traced
sporadically in those of an earlier time. The honour, in the
usual sense of the word, was essentially the fief of a great
lord, charged with a definite amount of military service to
the king. The word was generally restricted to fiefs held
of the king in chief, but it could occasionally be applied
to an important mesne tenancy. Under Henry II Osmund
de Stutville, who held a considerable fee of the Warenne
honour dependent on his manor of Gressenhall in Norfolk,
speaks of his 'honour' of Gressenhall in a charter to Castle
Acre Priory.[2] The administrative centre of an honour was
usually its lord's chief residence, and upon this estate,
which could not properly be subinfeudated or assigned in
dower, the king could distrain for the performance of the

[1] The description of an honorial court as the court of Ralf de Toeni or of
Earl Simon brings out the important fact that the basis of these assemblies
was simply the personal relationship of tenants to their lords, but makes it
sometimes difficult to determine the exact nature of a particular *curia*. A
remarkable charter published by Dr. Salter (*Oxford Charters*, No. 1)
states that a certain priest has failed to prove his right to a 'parrochia' in
the court of Philip de Braiose held at Washington in Sussex. This is not
the sort of business which would naturally come before an honorial court,
and the early date of this charter (*c.* 1095–1115) makes it possible that the
curia which it mentions is the court of the Rape of Bramber, then in the
hands of Philip de Braiose. (For the jurisdictional aspect of the rape see
Stevenson in *Eng. Hist. Rev.* xxviii. 297–8.) But all the circumstances of
this transaction are unusual, and difficulties of this kind rarely arise in
regard to courts held for lords of high position.

[2] Harl. MS. 2110, f. 35: 'Confirmaui deo et ecclesie Sancte Marie de
Acra . . . quicquid homines mei de honore de Gressinghal' dederunt et concesserunt.' For Osmund de Stutville see Farrer, *Honors and Knights' Fees*,
iii. 396–7.

service due to him. The unity of the honour was expressed in its court,[1] and was so clearly recognized that if a lord acquired more than one honour, by marriage, inheritance, or royal grant the separate existence of each was usually maintained with care.[2] The amalgamation of honours would often have meant an intolerable confusion of feudal custom. A large proportion of the honours existing under Henry III can be traced back to the eleventh century, and although the reign of Henry I saw the creation of many new fiefs of this type, the division of England between these great lordships goes back, in essentials, to the settlement after the Norman Conquest. Rarely as the word is used in early records, there is no doubt that the form of estate to which later generations applied the word honour was the characteristic unit of feudal organization under the Norman kings.[3]

The word *honor*, in its familiar sense of a great fee, was certainly current in the eleventh century. It occurs with this meaning in Domesday Book itself, which speaks of seisin obtained by Nigel de Albini, the lord of Cainhoe, *postquam ad honorem venit*.[4] It was used with the same significance by the Norman lords themselves. Robert

[1] The late G. J. Turner argued convincingly that 'at the time of the Norman Conquest all ordinary pleas of land between subject and subject were initiated by plaint in the seignourial courts. .... Pleas of land in seignourial courts could be removed by the demandant into the county court by the ancient process of tolt' (*Brevia Placitata*, Selden Soc. 66, lxviii). This process probably lies behind the charter made by Walter de Aincurt and John his son between 1156 and 1165, stating that they have released to a kinsman and tenant the service of one knight which had been in dispute between them, and that he has released to them his claim to a certain manor (I. H. Jeayes, *Derbyshire Charters*, No. 1397). The charter was attested by the shire court of Nottingham and Derby, and the plea which it implies had presumably been settled there.

[2] Thus the 'Honour of Hinckley', which seems to represent the midland fief forfeited by Aubrey de Couci, earl of Northumbria under the Conqueror, was still distinguished in the thirteenth century from the other lands of Robert fitz Parnel, earl of Leicester, to whose ancestors it had belonged since, at latest, the reign of Henry I (see L. W. Vernon Harcourt, *His Grace the Steward*, 96, 97).

[3] For a writ of Henry II granting an honour in its entirety to the husband of an heiress see Appendix, No. 8.   [4] D.B. i. 214.

Malet when founding a priory at Eye, the head of his great fee, provided that the monks should enjoy all the liberties which his lord King William granted him when he gave him his honour.[1] From this usage it was only a short step to the practice of calling an honour after the name of the chief place within it, and this practice, already established in Normandy before the Conquest, was naturally continued by the Norman barons who obtained fiefs in England. But *honor* was a word of many meanings, and its feudal specialization was a slow process. Besides the passages in Domesday Book where it already bears something of its later feudal sense, there should be set the well-known statement in the customs of the borough of Malmesbury that on occasion the king used to take one man from the borough 'as for an honour of five hides'.[2] To the man who wrote these words, *honor* can have meant nothing more definite than 'estate', and could have been applied to any one of the numerous manors assessed at five hides in southern England. It would be hard to find an exact parallel to this usage in later records, but in the Northern Danelaw, where manors of wide extent were common, the word *honor* could still be applied to an abnormally large single estate in the early thirteenth century.[3] In two charters of this date in the White Book of Southwell, the manor of Southwell, which covered many villages, is described as an honour in the first and as a soke in the second.[4] There is no need to accuse the writer of these charters of a confusion between honour

---

[1] *Mon. Ang.* iii. 405: 'Quare volo . . . ut teneant libere et quiete . . . habeantque socham et sacham et toll et theam et infangenetheof in Eya, in Donewyco, sive in aliis locis . . . habeantque omnes alias libertates quas dominus meus Willelmus rex Angliae mihi concessit quando honorem mihi dedit.' The passage gives, incidentally, a good illustration of the rights of jurisdiction which accompanied the grant of a great honour by the king.

[2] D.B. i. 64 b.

[3] See F. M. Stenton, *Danelaw Charters*, cviii.

[4] Southwell Cathedral, White Book, ff. 403, 404. In the first of these charters a man grants to his son the land which he holds *in honore de Swelle* [*sic*]. In the second charter, written some twenty years later, the land is stated to lie *in soca de Suthwella*.

and soke. To a man who lived within a great franchise like the soke of Southwell and in a highly feudalized county like Nottinghamshire the distinction between soke and honour must have been so obvious that it would never even need to be drawn. The interest of this curious usage lies in the fact that it is a survival from an earlier terminology in which *honor* stood for any estate which gave a man dignity, a position of authority in the life of his time.[1]

It is, in fact, only an indefinite meaning of this kind which will cover all the passages in which the word *honor* was employed in records of the Norman age. At one end of the scale comes the honour of five hides envisaged by the clerk who wrote the Domesday description of Malmesbury. At the other comes the honour which was in the mind of King Henry I when he ordered 'Si placitum est . . . inter vavasores alicujus baronis mei honoris, tractetur placitum in curia domini eorum'.[2] Like a five-hide manor in Wiltshire, the kingdom of England was an honour in the sense that it gave dignity and responsibility to its lord.[3] That the king's barons should apply this word to their fiefs was inevitable. The congeries of fees which constituted a great honour had a social as well as a military

[1] Maitland's statement that 'honour seems to be generally reserved for the very largest complexes of land' (*History of English Law*, ed. 2, i. 260) is not borne out by records made accessible since he wrote, such as the early Inquisitiones post mortem, where *honor* seems to be used interchangeably with *baronia* and even *feudum*. In vol. iv of the *Calendars of Inquisitions post mortem*, the fief of which Belvoir castle was the head is described as an honour on p. 2 and a barony on p. 222, and in vol. ii it appears as a fee on p. 180. On the whole, these inquisitions give the impression that *baronia* was more of a technical term than *honor*. The latter word could still be applied to estates like the Danelaw manors referred to above, such as the 'honour of Thurvaston' in Derbyshire held of the 'honour of the earl of Ferrers' by Robert son of Nicholas in 1273 (ibid. ii. 22).

[2] Stubbs, *Select Charters* (9th ed.), 122.

[3] The idea of an *honor* as an estate which gives a man distinction comes out very clearly in the quotations given by Ducange to illustrate this word. They suggest, in fact, that the word was specialized much earlier in England than abroad. But this specialization did not mean that the ancient sense of the word had disappeared.

significance. The reputation of a feudal lord in the world of his day, his influence at the king's court, and his standing in his own country largely turned on the number and quality of the enfeoffed knights who were bound to him by homage.[1]

Now and then these enfeoffed knights appear in charters as the peers, the *pares*, of the fee to which they belonged. In a feudal charter to be dated between 1121 and 1148 Abbot Anselm of Bury states that one of his leading tenants is to hold a knight's fee 'well, peaceably, honourably, and freely, as do his peers, namely, the knights of the abbey'.[2] The further idea that the military tenants on an honour form in some sense a community comes out when they are described not merely as *pares* but as *compares*—as when John Basset of Oakley addresses a charter *Henrico regi Anglorum . . . et omnibus comparibus suis de Gwalingeford*,[3] and Walter de Bolbec grants a manor to the abbot of Ramsey *per servitium duorum militum in omnibus servitiis quae facient compares sui de eodem feuodo*.[4] Within the honour its peers or compeers clearly form a group of men, all of the same general social class, holding on the same tenurial plane, and by a similar form of service. But in itself *par* means no more than equal, and it is in this sense that it is generally used in the Anglo-Norman period. The feudal sense of the word certainly underlies the passage in the *Leis Willelme* which states that if a man wishes to prove that his lord has made an agreement with him about land, he must vouch *ses pers de la tenure meimes* as witnesses.[5] But this precision is unusual, and no definition more precise than 'men of the same standing' will cover all the *pares* of English feudal texts. In Domesday Book William

[1] The assiduity with which the barons of Stephen's reign sought grants of enfeoffed knights from the king or the empress should not be attributed merely to a wish to increase their own military power.

[2] D. C. Douglas, *Feudal Documents relating to the Abbey of Bury St. Edmunds*, cxlvi and charter No. 122.

[3] Harl. MS. 3618, f. 132. The king is addressed here because the honour of Wallingford was in his hand.

[4] *Cartularium Monasterii de Rameseia* (Rolls Series), i. 153–4.

[5] *Leis Willelme*, c. 23.

de Perci vouches his *pares* to bear witness that he was seized of certain land when William Malet was sheriff of York.[1] The *Leges Henrici Primi* warn a man who is about to hold a plea in his own court 'or in any place where business is transacted' to bring together his *pares* and neighbours to afforce the court[2]—a passage helping incidentally to explain the frequency with which feudal charters are addressed to a grantor's friends as well as to his men. The same text speaks of pleas held on the boundary between *pares*,[3] and points out that pleas are very different *si par parem accuset, vel major minorem, vel minor majorem*.[4] The important rule which the *Leges* lay down that each man should be judged by his *pares* of the same country[5] certainly does not mean that he should only be judged by fellow tenants upon the same honour. And even within the honorial sphere itself, the judgement of peers can have meant nothing more in practice than judgement by a man's feudal equals.[6]

Other terms relating to essential features of honorial organization were used with equal vagueness in Anglo-Norman records. In the twelfth and following centuries every normal honour held by a lay baron included one estate regarded as its head both by its lord and his men, and by the king and his officers. The *caput honoris* was originally the place where the lord of the honour most

[1] D.B. i. 374.
[2] *Leges,* c. 33. 1.
[3] c. 9. 4.
[4] c. 9. 6 a.
[5] c. 31. 7: 'Unusquisque per pares suos judicandus est, et eiusdem provincie.' For these and other twelfth-century references to the word see Liebermann, *Gesetze,* ii. 1, and ii. 2, under *Standesgenossen.*
[6] Charter references to *pares* are so rare that the following example may be given from a Yorkshire charter written before 1157: 'Dominis suis karissimis Eustachio filio Johannis et Willelmo de Vecchi filio suo et Gaufrido fratri suo necnon et nepotibus suis Roberto de Valonia et Gaufrido fratri suo et omnibus tenentibus et hominibus domini Eustachii et filiorum suorum Francis et Anglicis, clericis et laicis, tam presentibus quam futuris, et omnibus paribus suis, suus fidelis Warnerus filius Wihomari salutem et amicitias' (W. T. Lancaster, *Ripley and the Ingilby Family,* 30). As this extraordinary address takes in a larger circle of people the farther it goes on, the *pares* who come last are presumably men of the grantor's social condition in general. See also p. 91, n. 5.

commonly resided. Early feudal charters rarely bear a note
of issue, but occasionally show a lord transacting business
at a manor or castle which afterwards appears as the head
of the family honour. The retention of the *caput honoris*
in its lord's hand was essential to the working of the whole
feudal economy, and the phrase is one of the most
familiar terms of English feudalism. It is therefore interesting to see that at its first appearance in English records the
phrase, like so much else of the language of feudalism,
had not yet acquired its precise significance. In 1086
Geoffrey de Mandeville founded a priory at Hurley in
Berkshire as a cell of Westminster Abbey, and declared
in his foundation charter that Hurley should always be
under his special protection and should be the 'head' of
his honour.[1] In such a context the phrase *caput honoris*
cannot possibly bear its usual sense. A baron who says
that a monastery which he has just founded is to be the
head of his honour can only mean that he wishes it to be
regarded as the place of greatest distinction within his
fief. It is, moreover, remarkable that this strange expression does not stand alone. Almost at the same time,
William de Warenne, the second earl of Surrey, states
that he wishes to keep 'St. Pancras' as his patron and the
head of his honour, 'St. Pancras' standing here both for
the Warenne Priory of Lewes and its patron saint.[2] The

[1] Armitage Robinson, *Gilbert Crispin*, 133: 'Quod locus ille, locus
quoque regio munimine insignitus, in protectione mea et defensione
semper sit precipuus et mei capud honoris, ab omnium hominum inquietu-
dine liber et quietus.' It is not easy to identify the real head of the great
Mandeville honour, but in the thirteenth century it appears to have been
Pleshy in Essex. See *Book of Fees*, 855, where land in Berkshire of the
Mandeville fee is described as *de honore de Plesseto*. The actual caput of
the honour in the Norman period was presumably the castle, of which the
motte and bailey earthworks still survive at Pleshy.

[2] Quoted by Farrer, *Honors and Knights' Fees*, iii. 312, from the Cartulary of Lewes, Cott. Vesp. E. xv. In the Introduction which he wrote for
this volume Professor Tait called attention to the remarkable statement by
the plaintiff in a plea of 1213 that the advowson of Knebworth church
was the *caput* of his honour, without which he could not have seisin (ibid.,
pp. viii and 208). But this is the *ex parte* statement of a litigant anxious to
recover an advowson given away by his father, and attempting to bring it

same idea probably explains the alternative description of
the fief of Roger de Busli, generally called the honour
of Tickhill from Roger's castle, as the honour of Blythe,[1]
where he had founded a priory in the Conqueror's time.
It is, in fact, another illustration of the indefinite use in
the early Norman period of words which were to become
specialized in later generations. Like *honor* itself, *caput
honoris* was no technical term to the clerks of the eleventh
century.

No map indicating the actual centres of the different
twelfth-century honours has yet been drawn—possibly no
complete map could be compiled from the materials at our
disposal. In feudal records an honour generally appears as
a complex of fees held of a particular lord, rather than as
a territory with a single estate as its centre.[2] Nevertheless,
more than a hundred of these estates can be identified by a
comparison of twelfth- and thirteenth-century evidence,
and a few general statements can be made about them.
The most important is that it was by no means necessary
that the head of an honour should be a castle. It is true
that most of the greatest honours had a castle at their
administrative centres. Before the end of the eleventh
century, to name only a few examples, castles had been
built at Dudley, Belvoir, Okehampton, Tickhill, and
Dunster,[3] the heads of the Domesday honours of William
fitz Ansculf, Robert de Toeni, Baldwin de Meules, Roger
de Busli, and William de Mohun. In such cases the

under the rule that the *caput* of an honour must not be alienated. It stands
apart from the early application of the term to the priories of Hurley and
Lewes. The Knebworth plea is now printed *Curia Regis Rolls*, vii. 138.

[1] This description appears early. William de Lovetot, the founder of
Worksop Priory, in a charter addressed to Archbishop Thurstan of York,
grants to the priory all the churches of his demesne of the honour of Blythe
(*Mon. Ang.* vi. 118; facsimile of original charter in *Transactions of the
Thoroton Society*, vol. ix).

[2] Unless a lord took his name from the head of his honour—like Judhel
'of Totnes' under William I or Michael 'of Hanslope' under Henry I—it
may well happen that the name of a particular *caput honoris* is not recorded
before the thirteenth century.

[3] On these and other eleventh-century castles see Mrs. Armitage, *The
Early Norman Castles of England.*

honour sometimes appears as dependent on its castle in thirteenth-century records. An inquisition of 1298, for example, states that Robert de Tibetot had held Bentley in Yorkshire of 'the honour of the castle of Tickhill'.[1] But there is neither trace nor record of any castle at Blankney, Hook Norton, Freiston, or Beckley, the heads of the Aincurt, Oilli, Craon, and St. Valery honours, and the Giffard earls of Buckingham seem to have been content with a house and park at Long Crendon,[2] the head of their fee. Even when a lord is known to have possessed an important castle, he by no means always regarded it as the head of his honour. The influence of the Fitzwalter barons was largely due to their possession of Baynard's Castle outside London. Their tenants by military service owed money for castle-guard there,[3] but the head of their honour was Little Dunmow in Essex. Ralf de Toeni, the lord of Clifford Castle in Herefordshire, chose Flamstead in Hertfordshire as his principal seat, no doubt because it lay conveniently between his estates on the Welsh border and in East Anglia, but there seems to be no evidence of any castle at Flamstead. It was, in fact, entirely at a lord's discretion whether or not he should build a castle at his chief residence, and many lords were satisfied with a house which might have defences but was certainly not a castle as the centre of their estates.[4] The *caput honoris* is important in the social and administrative rather than the military history of feudalism.

Greatly as the honours of the twelfth century varied in

[1] *Calendar of Inquisitions post mortem*, iii. 369.
[2] In 1086 Walter Giffard had a *parcus bestiarum silvaticarum* at Long Crendon. D.B. i. 147.
[3] See Cott. Tit. C. viii, f. 52, where land at Wicklewood in Norfolk is charged 'ad scutagium domini regis quando aduenerit ad xx solidos, ii denarios . . . et ad wardam Ca⟨s⟩telli Baignardi quando aduenerit, i denarium' (early thirteenth century).
[4] It is difficult to prove a negative, and some early castles whose existence is proved by records have disappeared, apparently without trace. See below, 197–8. But we are certainly not entitled to assume the wholesale disappearance of castles planned on the scale which, to judge from existing remains, was usually adopted when a Norman lord fortified the head of his honour.

size and composition, certain features are common to most of them. One of these is a commonplace of English history. The lands of a great baron were either scattered over a wide area, or if, like the fees of many powerful magnates of the Danelaw, they all lay in one part of England, they were dispersed among the fees of other lords. There were many reasons for the adoption of this method of distribution by the Conqueror. The administrative convenience of giving to one man all the scattered lands of one English thegn, the wish to extend as widely as possible the influence of trusted adherents or kinsmen, and a natural unwillingness to parcel out his new kingdom into compact lordships must all have moved him in the same direction.[1] It also deserves note that most of the later honours created by Henry I were formed in the same way. The honour of Bourne, given to Baldwin fitz Gilbert of Clare, lay in Lincolnshire, Northamptonshire, and Hertfordshire,[2] and that of Kington, formed for Adam de Port, comprised lands in Dorset, Somerset, and Wiltshire, in addition to the Herefordshire lordship which was its head.[3] The honour of Ongar, acquired by Richard de Lucy in the middle of the twelfth century, consisted of members derived from four pre-existing honours. It included fees in Essex of the honours of Boulogne and Gloucester, fees in Cornwall of the honour of Mortain, and fees in Sussex of the honour of Pevensey.[4]

[1] No single principle will account for this dispersal. There are clear cases in which the scattered lands of a single thegn have been given to a single Frenchman. The important honour of Geoffrey Alselin, on which see below 200, was almost entirely composed of manors held in 1066 by Tochi son of Outi. But in a much greater number of cases a Frenchman has received the lands of a considerable number of Englishmen, and it is generally impossible even to guess why certain manors have been chosen to form the fief of a particular individual.

[2] On the honour of Bourne see *Feudal England*, 164–5, and F. M. Stenton, *Facsimiles of Early Charters from Northamptonshire Collections*, 18–20.

[3] See Round, 'The Families of St. John and of Port' (*Genealogist*, New Series, xvi. 1).

[4] See Round, 'The Honour of Ongar', *Essex Archaeological Society's Transactions*, vii. 142–52.

It is, moreover, significant that despite the opportunities afforded by the troubles of Stephen's reign, there is no evidence of any general movement among the baronage towards the local consolidation of honours. It would seem, in fact, that the dispersal of a baron's fees, whatever part royal policy had played in its origin, worked to the profit of the baronage as well as of the king. To the leading members of feudal society it was an advantage to possess an interest in many parts of England. The position of an isolated feudal magnate might be strong for rebellion, but was far from satisfactory in the more ordinary course of life. The dispersal of a baron's fees enlarged the range of his influence, and brought him into relations with the alliances formed between other men of his class. To barons whose chief interest lay on the Welsh border, the possession of fees in central or southern England gave valuable military and financial reserves.[1] It is not strange that the scattering of honours characteristic of English feudalism in the eleventh century persisted throughout the Middle Ages.

It is easy to underestimate the complexity of the organization required for the administration of a great honour in the twelfth century. Its superficial history generally amounts to little more than the record of successions to the individual fees of which it was composed. In reality its lord was confronted with a variety of administrative and judicial duties similar to those which fell upon the king himself as lord of the greatest of all honours, the kingdom of England. At present we can only speak in most general terms of the organization through which this work was done. We can, in fact, hardly pass beyond the safe generalization that the administration of an honour turned on the household officers of its lord, for the administrative side of feudalism can only be approached

---

[1] The Magna Carta of Cheshire shows that the earl's 'knights of England' were very useful for the guard of Chester Castle, particularly in releasing the barons of Cheshire and their men from this duty when no immediate attack on the county was expected (*Chartulary of Chester Abbey*, ed. Tait, i. 105).

through the study of individual baronial households, and the material for this study is so scattered, its chronology is so uncertain, that when this book was first written few workers had entered this field. Professor Tait had, indeed, drawn the outlines of the system through which the Norman earls of Chester governed their great regality.[1] But they stood apart from most of their contemporaries in power, though not in rank, and at present we do not know how much of the elaborate organization at their disposal was due to their exceptional position.[2] The wide distribution of their honour and the extent of their liberties meant the addition of sheriffs and justices to a staff of household officers such as every magnate had in his service. It would be inaccurate to describe their administrative system as a reproduction of that which served the king. The honour of Chester never developed a secretarial department which can properly be called a chancery,[3] and its financial arrangements belong to a more primitive type than the royal exchequer. But in most other respects there is a close parallel between the organization revealed by their charters and that which centred around the king's household. It is now becoming apparent that other feudal magnates of the twelfth century were administering their several honours in the same way.

As the functions of royal officers become more specialized even the greatest barons could hardly find justification for describing their own officers by names which had acquired a definite official meaning. The baronial sheriff and the baronial justice belong to an early phase of English feudalism. In the first half of the twelfth century, each of the Sussex rapes was under a different sheriff, responsible to its lord,[4] but these baronial officers do not

---

[1] Ibid., vol. i, pp. xliv–l.

[2] On this and on the numerous problems presented by the feudal organization of Cheshire itself see G. Barraclough, *Early Cheshire Charters* (1957), pp. ix–xi; the Earldom and County Palatine of Chester (1953).

[3] *Chester Chartulary*, ed. Tait, pp. xlvii, xlviii.

[4] Round, *Calendar of Documents preserved in France*, p. li. The existence of a sheriff is proved for the 'honours' of Arundel, Pevensey, Lewes, Hastings, and Bramber.

appear after the end of Stephen's reign. William count of
Aumale, the lord of Holderness, was still addressing
charters to his steward, his sheriff, and his barons, after the
accession of Henry II,[1] and Mr. Denholm-Young has
shown that until Holderness came into the king's hand in
1268 it was still administered for its lord by an officer
styled a sheriff.[2] The baronial justice is an obscurer person
than the baronial sheriff, but he can be found on honours
beside that of Chester in the first part of the twelfth
century. He appears, for example, on the vast fief held
under Henry I by Stephen count of Mortain, afterwards
king. Three writs issued by Stephen, as count, in favour
of Eye Priory have been preserved in an eighteenth-
century copy of the Eye cartulary. In one Stephen addresses his justices and barons, French and English, of all
England; in another he addresses Malger the chaplain,
G. Blund, and his justices of England; and the address of
the third, if its text can be trusted, ran *Omnibus justificatoribus et omnibus baronibus suis Francis et Anglis*.[3] Stephen
was the greatest of English territorial magnates when
these writs were issued, and needed an administrative
organization hardly less elaborate than that of the king
himself. It is more remarkable to find the baronial justice
upon the isolated fee of Sturminster which fell to Waleran
count of Meulan on the partition of his father's lands.

'G. count of Meulan greets all his justices and ministers of Sturminster, present and future. I direct and strictly command you to
give each year to the canons of St. Denis of Southampton twenty
shillings from my *prepositura* of Sturminster, namely ten shillings at
the feast of St. John the Baptist and ten shillings at Michaelmas.
This gift I command to be observed strictly for ever. Robert son
of Roger of Southampton has entreated me much to this end, for
he had given the aforesaid pennies to the aforesaid canons.'[4]

---

[1] Farrer, *Early Yorkshire Charters*, No. 1334.

[2] N. Denholm-Young, *Seignorial Administration in England*, 48.

[3] Appendix, Nos. 10, 11, 13. The 'G. Blund' of the second writ is
Gilbert Blund, lord of the barony of Ixworth. A writ in favour of Castle
Acre Priory is addressed by Stephen to his justice of Norfolk and Suffolk.
Mon. Ang. v. 63.

[4] Add. MS. 15314, f. 109; Appendix, No. 14. See above, 34.

Whoever these justices of Sturminster may have been, they were certainly not among the leading *familiares* of the count of Meulan. Like the earlier justices of Count Stephen, who could be ordered to put a priory in seisin of a village church, or the contemporary justices of the earl of Chester,[1] they were evidently the minor executive officers of a large organization. Their title shows that they had judicial duties, and it may be that they earned this title by presiding in the courts of manors or hundreds in their lord's hand. But they were certainly more than justices in the narrow sense of the word, a sense, indeed, which had not yet become established in England. They were clearly responsible for the collection of their lord's revenue, and for payments which he might authorize. There is, in fact, a curious resemblance between the position of these obscure baronial justices and that of the justices of the king's court in the twelfth century. Their work lay within a smaller sphere, though the justices of a man like Count Stephen, who had added the honours of Eye and Lancaster to the English lands of the counts of Mortain and Boulogne, exercised authority over a great part of England. But in their combination of executive, financial, and judicial duties they obviously held in the feudal organization the place filled by the royal justices in the administration of that part of England which lay outside the greater franchises. In substance, if not in form, there is a close resemblance between Count Waleran's writ to his justices and ministers of Sturminster and the writs of *Liberate* which the king's chancery had already begun to address to the barons of his exchequer.

The exigencies of baronial administration might even lead to the creation of a financial department to which the actual name exchequer could be applied. It is, indeed,

---

[1] On the justices of the earls of Chester see Tait, *Chartulary of Chester Abbey*, vol. i, pp. xliv, xlv. Professor Tait points out that while in the thirteenth century the justice was the chief officer of the palatinate, 'there is no evidence that he occupied so important a position in the twelfth century', and that the formulas of address employed, in particular, by Earl Rannulf II show that the earl had more than one justice in his service.

curious that references to such a body should be as rare as in fact they are, for every lord with large estates must have felt the need of some permanent financial organization, and the example of the king's exchequer was familiar to all. Some of the few apparent references are really ambiguous. The word *scaccarium* could denote a mere reckoning-board, and its appearance in a charter does not necessarily imply the existence of a financial bureau. It is probably unsafe to argue closely from the occurrence of the word in the charter by which William earl of Gloucester grants land in Bristol to his harper for a dish of beans, rendered yearly at the earl's exchequer at Bristol.[1] At present the best evidence of a baronial exchequer of the Norman age comes from two unrelated charters, each of which refers to the exchequer of Henry I's minister, Robert count of Meulan. In one, the count's son Robert earl of Leicester grants £8. 6s. od. to the abbey of St. Leger de Préaux *ad scacarium meum . . . per annum sicut pater meus ei dedit et concessit*.[2] The second charter refers to a payment of 20 shillings a year from the earl's exchequer, which his father had granted, and he will continue to the collegiate church of St. Mary de Castro in Leicester.[3] The promise was honoured by the earl's successors, for the sum can safely be identified with the payment of 20 shillings at Michaelmas to the canons of Leicester which appears in 1209 as a charge upon the revenues of Earl Simon de Montfort.[4]

These references carry the baronial exchequer back to a time before the count of Meulan's death in 1118. But it must always have been an exceptional institution, which, like the baronial sheriff and justice, represented the enlargement for a special purpose of the normal baronial household. It is unfortunate that few early charters give anything like a complete picture of the household of a great lord at a particular moment. Individual officers of a lord frequently attest his charters. Robert bishop of Lincoln, for

[1] Stowe MS. 925, f. 122; Appendix, No. 15.
[2] A. du Moustier, *Neustria Pia* (1663), 524. I owe this reference to the late Mr. L. C. Loyd.   [3] *Ancient Charters*, ed. J. H. Round, 60.
[4] Pipe Roll of 11 John, ed. D. M. Stenton, 25.

example, can be seen at his manor of Louth, soon after
the accession of Henry II, accompanied by his butler,
chamberlain, usher, and marshal.[1] But few charters are
attested by as many as four household officers in succession, and it is not easy to reconstruct the series of a lord's
ministers from scattered and often undated evidence.[2] The
longest list of the members of a great twelfth-century
household hitherto noted occurs at the end of an elaborate
charter issued by Archbishop Theobald of Canterbury for
the priory of Stoke by Clare, and shows the archbishop
accompanied by a butler, dispenser, chamberlain, seneschal,
master cook, usher, porter, and marshal.[3] The relative
precedence of these officers is interesting. The high place
given to the butler and the low place of the seneschal are
both remarkable. On the other hand, the position of the
marshal at the end of the list agrees with other evidence
in suggesting that the early marshalship was an office of
no great dignity. In Normandy before the Conquest the
marshal appears as a horse-breaker.[4] In the *Constitutio
Domus Regis* which was written some fifteen years before
Archbishop Theobald's charter, the marshal only receives
a livery of two shillings a day against the five shillings
given to the other principal servants of the court. But at
present we are hardly in a position to say what is normal
or abnormal in the position occupied by different household officers in a list coming from Stephen's reign.

Sixty years later a dispute between the abbot of Westminster and one of the tenants produced a detailed description of the household which accompanied the abbot when
he travelled into a distant part of the country.[5] The tenant

---

[1] F. M. Stenton, *Danelaw Charters*, No. 284.

[2] The difficulty is increased by the fact that the ministers of a great lord
often attest his charters without indicating their positions in his household.
It is known, for example, that Adam son of Warin was *dapifer* of the first
earl of Clare early in Stephen's reign, but he rarely attests the earl's charters
under his household title.

[3] Cott. MS. Appendix xxi, f. 65; Appendix, No. 16.

[4] *Chartularium Monasterii Sanctae Trinitatis* (ed. Deville), 439: 'Quidam vir nomine Hugo equorum domitor, quod vulgo dicitur marescal.'

[5] Feet of Fines, C.P. 171/13/239; Appendix, No. 17.

in question, Ivo of Deene, admitted before the king's justices that he was bound to receive the abbot and his household at Deene in Northamptonshire, once a year, and the dispute was settled by a final concord which gives a remarkable picture of the household of a great lord in the early part of the thirteenth century.

'When it shall please the abbot to be entertained at Deene, Ivo ought to be forewarned fifteen days previously by notice given him in writing from the abbot. And on the day when the abbot is coming, seven servants of the abbot shall precede him, to whom shall be given charge of seven departments of the house; namely, to the seneschal the charge of the hall, to the chamberlain the custody of the chamber, to the pantler the custody of the dispence and the bread, to the butler the custody of the butlery and the drink, to the usher the custody of the door, to the cook the custody of the kitchen, to the marshal the custody of the marshalsea. And Ivo and his men shall honourably receive the abbot and the men coming with him, and shall find necessaries sufficient for them from Ivo's own goods, in food and drink and other necessaries belonging to honourable entertainment, on the first day of the abbot's coming, and on the morrow, until he and his men have had their meal honourably, so that after the day's meal neither the abbot nor his men may demand or have drink more than once by way of custom, nor may they have anything else of Ivo's unless they shall be willing to buy it. But if the abbot shall wish to remain for the whole night at Ivo's house, he shall buy at a just price whatever he may have, and reckoning having been made, and a tally, between the abbot's servants and Ivo and his servants, whatever the abbot and his men have had of Ivo's shall be accounted for and allowed to Ivo in the rent which he ought to pay at the next term. Moreover, Ivo shall find two wax candles to burn before the abbot on the first night of his coming, of which each shall be of one pound of wax, and the abbot's chamberlain shall have whatever remains unburnt of the candles, and Ivo shall give twelve pence to each of the aforesaid seven servants of the abbot.'

This very curious description is interesting for more than one reason. Any document which reveals a medieval household in being is valuable because it shows a very formal and highly organized institution functioning in the atmosphere of daily life. There can be no doubt that the abbot of Westminster travelled from place to place with an entourage comparable to that which accompanied the king himself, and this account of the elaborate arrangements which followed the arrival of the abbot's ministers at Deene gives reality to the household organization described in the *Constitutio Domus Regis*. The officers who served the abbot are no mere ministers of ceremony, and if their several duties are precisely defined, it is not to prevent one minister from encroaching on another's prerogatives, but to secure a proper entertainment for their master. Moreover, the household revealed by this record gives the impression of a very conservative institution. The distinction between the responsibility of the seneschal for the *aula* and that of the chamberlain for the *camera* is clearly marked, and is evidently of practical importance. The pantler, though responsible for the issue of provisions in general, is particularly concerned with the supply of bread, the marshal comes at the end of the ministers whose duties are expressly defined, and the candle-ends are the chamberlain's perquisites. At these points and at many others the record agrees with what is known of earlier practice, and it can safely be regarded as enumerating the ministers who were essential to the household of a great Anglo-Norman lord as it moved over the country.

Little is at present known of the more intimate economy of such households. They have left no accounts behind them, and the charters which give the names and sometimes the offices of their members barely touch upon their routine of life. Nevertheless, the charters, for all their appearance of formality and legal precision, stand in innumerable cases for the results of discussion in the crowded environment of a lord's household, and the officers who attended their lord as he dealt with his tenants were the men who carried out his orders or his compromises. Among the few English narratives which convey something of the atmosphere of an early baronial household, an episode in the *Historia Fundationis* of Byland Abbey deserves quotation.[1] At Archbishop Thurstan's request

[1] *Mon. Ang.* v. 350.

the young Roger de Mowbray had given the tithe of the food of his household to the monks:

'and a lay brother named Lyngulf was deputed to follow the court[1] of the lord Roger and collect each day the produce granted to the monks, and he sent it by a faithful messenger to the abbot and monks at Hood. And when the lord Roger was staying in remoter parts, the lay brother sold whatever belonged to the monks and sent the money to the abbot. But owing to the multitude of guests, who were never lacking to so great a lord in large number, it often happened that his *dapifer* and the provisioner of his house were obliged to borrow that produce from the lay brother, to prevent a failure of supplies in their lord's house. And when the time came to make good the produce which had been borrowed, the provisioner was extremely annoyed. . . . But the lord's *dapifer* named George, a wise and prudent man, considered how this inconvenience could be avoided, and having found a way, when his lord secretly discussed his affairs with his council,[2] he showed his lord, among other matters, how he had often borrowed the tithe of food from the lay brother, sometimes more of it and sometimes less, and advised his lord to make a gift of land to the value of the tithe of the provision of his house.'

The date of this episode was 1140, and it is interesting as showing the dapifer occupied with household duties, responsible, with a *provisor hospicii* beneath him, for the provisioning of his lord's household, and giving advice to his lord in a 'council' which meets privately, and seems to be a permanent body. The reference to this council is noteworthy, for while it is known that some lords of the later Middle Ages possessed councils distinct from the courts of their honours,[3] there is little trace of such bodies at an early period. On the other hand, it has recently been shown that on the honour of the constables of Chester in the mid-twelfth century, a body known as the 'small council' was a recognized institution, so well established

---

[1] *Ut curiam domini Rogeri sequeretur.*

[2] *Cum dominus suus secrete tractavit de negotiis cum consilio suo.* Despite the form *consilio*, there is no danger here of the confusion between 'council' and 'counsel' which obscures more than one similar passage.

[3] See Professor A. E. Levett's article 'Baronial Councils' in *Mélanges Lot*, 421–41.

that it could witness charters collectively.[1] In view of this evidence it is clear that the council of the Byland story should not be dismissed as an anachronism.

The story is more obviously accurate in the central position which it gives to the lord's *dapifer*. However complex an honour may be, its administration nearly always turned on the officer who is indifferently described as *dapifer* or seneschal. When a lord wishes to begin a charter with a personal address to one of his ministers, it is generally his *dapifer* who receives it.[2] On most honours the office had become hereditary long before the end of the twelfth century, and there is some temptation to regard the baronial *dapifer* of the thirteenth century as little more than the chief among a group of *ministeriales*, whose functions were mainly ceremonial. However this may have been—and here the organization of one honour differed from that of another—there is no doubt of the importance of the *dapifer* at an earlier time. It is the earliest baronial charters which bring out most clearly the practical nature of his duties. The following writ, issued before 1136 by Richard fitz Gilbert of Clare, is a good illustration of his place in the administration of a great honour. One of the lord's tenants has been withholding tithes from a monastery under his special protection, and the lord writes:

'I command you that you reseize my monks of Stoke in the tithe of Gestingthorpe, as Gerard son of Renger gave them seisin at the command of my *dapifer*, and as they were seized on the day when they gave up the land which was Robert your brother's, and afterwards, if you or any one else claim anything against them, let them stand to right where it is just. And if you do not this, let Adam my *dapifer* do it quickly, that I hear no complaint for lack of right.'[3]

The royal style in which this writ is cast, or, to speak more accurately, the employment by a great lord of formulas

[1] The charters which mention this 'small council' are discussed in a note to Charter No. 515 in *Sir Christopher Hatton's Book of Seals*, 355.

[2] *Gillebertus comes Lincolnie dapifero suo et omnibus hominibus suis Francis et Anglicis salutem* is an average example of these formulas (Harl. Chart. 50. F. 31).

[3] Cott. MS. Appendix xxi, f. 114 b. Below, Appendix, No. 10.

which he like the king found convenient, emphasizes the fact that there was no necessary difference between the form of royal and private documents in the Norman period. It also emphasizes the parallel between royal and baronial organization in this age. Within the sphere of the honour the *dapifer* is clearly doing the work done in the country at large by those men who went out from the king's household to act as royal justices. Whatever duties he may have had in his lord's household he is also his lord's executive officer within the honour at large.

The administrative duties of the *dapifer* are shown no less plainly in a letter of very different style[1] issued in the name of the second earl of Clare, a younger son of the Richard fitz Gilbert whose mandate to a tenant has just been quoted. The circumstances under which it was written are not made clear, but its wording implies that the earl was proposing to set out into remote parts.

'Roger de Clare, earl of Hertford, greets all his barons[2] and faithful men. As you regard my soul's health and my honour, I charge and command you to assist my monks of Stoke, their men and their business, in my place while I am absent, as they shall request you, and as they may need your help, and I moreover command you who are debtors to the monks, either in tithes or in rents, to pay fully that which is theirs at their will without delay. And if any of you shall design to withhold or delay his rents or tithes, then I command Reginald my *dapifer* that he do full and sufficient justice to my aforesaid monks, as to me in regard to my own rents.'

A letter addressed generally to a whole group of 'barons and faithful men' is bound to be less peremptory in style than a writ addressed to a single person. The earl's father had not felt it necessary to refer to his soul's health or his honour when commanding an individual tenant to do right. But the administrative system underlying the two documents is the same. In each case a great lord assumes

---

[1] Cott. MS. Appendix xxi, f. 21 b; Appendix, No. 19.

[2] For the significance of this address to the earl's 'barons' see below, Chapter III.

that his own written command needs no royal or ecclesiastical support to make it effective, and in each case he leaves it to his *dapifer* to deal with the disobedient. The disorders of Stephen's reign, which separate the two documents, had neither strengthened nor weakened the feudal authority of the head of the house of Clare.

In course of time the *dapifer* as an administrative officer comes to acquire great importance as the president of courts held in his lord's name, and in particular of those manorial courts which are the successors of the ancient hallimots. On individual fees the development may have begun early, but there is little evidence of it for much more than a century after the Norman Conquest. The *Leges Henrici Primi* assumes that the reeve of a manor will preside in its hall moot.[1] The *dapifer* of a great lord was usually himself a man of rank, with a considerable fee of his own, who certainly cannot have undertaken the routine duty of holding periodical local courts. Philip of Kyme, *dapifer* of Simon earl of Northampton, held approximately thirty knights' fees of many different lords.[2] Feudal charters of the twelfth century suggest that a lord usually presided in the court of his own honour, and that though the *dapifer* was generally present at such assemblies, he came, not as an officer essential to the holding of the court, but as a member of the lord's household and a tenant upon his fee. It is significant that in the *Leges Henrici Primi*, the *dapifer* never appears as the president of a feudal court. He can represent his lord in the courts of shire and hundred, and, like other members of his lord's household, can receive summonses addressed to him.[3] But

---

[1] This appears clearly in the description given in the *Leges* of the conditions under which rights of jurisdiction are exercised (c. 20, 1 a) *sub prepositis maneriorum in iis adiacentibus halimotis; sub prelatis hundretorum et burgorum; sub uicecomitibus.*

[2] On the family of Kyme and its feudal position see Farrer, *Honors and Knights' Fees*, ii. 118–25.

[3] In regard to summonses, the *Leges* make careful provision for cases likely to arise: 'Si quis . . . dapiferum vel quemlibet ministrum ita rebus suis prefecerit . . . et homini suo committet ut quodammodo locum eius habeat et quod fecerit factum sit' (c. 42. 2). It is clear that the *dapifer* is

throughout this work, the presumption is that a lord will transact his legal business in person, and that although he will generally use his *dapifer* when he is compelled to find a deputy, the office does not of itself make a man his lord's representative. The *dapifer* was important in the feudal organization because of the administrative duties which were continually being laid upon him, and in the twelfth century it was still for the lord to determine what those duties should be.

It would therefore be incorrect to suggest that the *dapifer* was the only household officer who could be employed for miscellaneous administrative duties. Even when a man held an office essential to the daily routine of his lord's household, he could be used for extraneous work. A dispenser, for example, must generally have been in attendance on his lord. Round described the king's dispensers as the 'issue department' of the royal household,[1] and the phrase could certainly be applied to the officers who bore this title in baronial service. Henry de Lacy, for instance, commands his dispensers to render the tithe of his hunting in flesh and hides to the monks of Pontefract.[2] Yet the following writ shows the second Earl Warenne using a dispenser for a piece of administrative work entirely unconnected with the arrangements of the earl's household.

'William earl Warenne greets Osmund his dispenser. I direct and command you quickly to reseize the monks of St. Pancras in ten *solidatae* of land which Hugh de Grigneuseville gave to God and St. Pancras for his soul. And I confirm this gift to them for the souls of my father and mother—those ten *solidatae* of land, I mean, which are in Caston.'[3]

the minister most likely to be chosen as his lord's representative, but no less clear that a lord can choose whom he wishes for this purpose.

[1] *The King's Serjeants*, 62.

[2] *Chartulary of St. John of Pontefract* (Yorkshire Archaeological Society), i. 34.

[3] Cott. MS. Vesp. F. xv, f. 33; Appendix, No. 20. The last words, which give important information as an afterthought, are curiously reminiscent of the postscripts often added to writs of William II and Henry I.

Interesting as it is in form, this writ has a further value as one of the earliest illustrations which we possess of the external activities of the officers of a baronial household. Within the household itself, the duties of each minister were definite, and such as were covered by his title. But the regular course of household duty which brought each minister into constant association with his lord meant, inevitably, that a lord would use one or other of his *ministri* when a trustworthy man was needed for a piece of occasional work within his honour at large. The *dapifer* was the natural person to use on these occasions. His office was one of dignity, and he was generally a man of influence within the honour. But the services of all a lord's ministers were at his disposal for the administration of his fee, and it was for him to choose whom he would send on a particular errand.

It is natural, but it is certainly unfortunate, that the officer who stands particularly for the military side of the baronial household should be the obscurest figure of this company. It would be going too far to say that the baronial constable is ignored by the private charters of the twelfth century, but as yet they have thrown little light on his position or duties. It is only the very greatest of lords—men of the earl of Chester's standing—who at all frequently include their constable or constables among the officers to whom they address charters. An individual constable occasionally attests his lord's grants of land. He will sometimes emphasize his office when he is issuing a charter under his own name. In Stephen's reign, when the constable of Alexander, bishop of Lincoln gave two churches to increase his son's prebend in Lincoln Cathedral, he styled himself *Willelmus conestabularius Alexandri episcopi Lincolie* without further definition.[1] There is, indeed, no doubt as to the importance of the constable in early feudal organization. His original function was, apparently, to command the knights of his lord's household. But in early records of English feudalism, baronial constables are associated with garrison rather than household

[1] *Registrum Antiquissimum of Lincoln Cathedral*, ii. 253–4.

duties, and stand apart from the general body of their lord's ministers. It seems to have been usual for a magnate of the highest rank, the lord of many castles, to place a separate constable in charge of each, and titles like constable of Chester or of Richmond suggest that the greatest man among a group of constables had the command of his lord's chief castle.[1] Like most feudal offices, constableships became hereditary at an early date, and their military importance tended to decline in the second half of the twelfth century, except in border country. On rare occasions a charter of an earlier time shows a baronial constable in the position of castellan. Soon after the death of Robert earl of Gloucester, when his widow and son restored the manor of Sherborne, apart from its castle, to the bishopric of Salisbury, they provided that the constable of Sherborne, whoever he might thereafter be, should pledge his faith to observe the bishop's rights, so long as he made no claim to the castle or its appurtenances.[2] But the military duties of the constable, which gave his office peculiar importance in time of war, are not often reflected in the documents from which our knowledge of twelfth-century feudalism is derived.[3]

Now and again, on some particular occasion, a lord will address a special mandate to his constable. It is significant that most of the occasions which are recorded have reference to the troubles of Stephen's reign. Between 1138 and 1153 Gilbert earl of Hertford commanded Simon son of Lambert his constable, and his *familia* of Desning to maintain the abbey of Colchester in its possession of an

[1] For the early constables of Chester see Tait, *Domesday Survey of Cheshire* (Chetham Society), 48–50, and Farrer, *Honors and Knights' Fees*, ii. 64 et seqq. For the constables of Richmond see the section on the Constable's Fee in *Early Yorkshire Chartery*, ed. C. T. Clay, v. 81–164.

[2] *Salisbury Charters and Documents* (Rolls Series), 32, 33.

[3] The title *constabularius* is not infrequently borne by witnesses to twelfth- and thirteenth-century charters. But in many cases it is probable that the individual so described was not in any sense a household officer, but the leader of one of those *constabulariae* of ten knights, in which lords of this period seem to have arranged their contingents to the feudal host. See V. H. Galbraith, *Eng. Hist. Rev.* xliv. 370, 371.

estate given by the earl's ancestors[1]—a command which obviously relates to the disturbed condition of eastern England in this period. There is a similar echo of the war in a letter written by the second earl of Derby to his constable and steward telling them that he has given certain land to Burton Abbey in recompense for harm which he has done, that he will put the abbey in possession of the land within fifteen days after his return from St. James of Compostella, and that they are to secure the abbey in enjoyment of his firm peace against all who make demands upon it.[2] The constable is introduced here because his lord is about to leave the country, and no one but the commander of his knights can make his peace effective. In each of these cases in fact the constable appears in his original military capacity. If such appearances are rare, it is because in quiet times there was no need for them.

More than one crisis in English medieval history was produced in whole or in part by the misbehaviour of those royal officers of whom the sheriff was the chief. The misdeeds of baronial officers are rarely described by chroniclers, but they sometimes attracted the king's attention. The Inquest of Sheriffs in 1170 directed that inquiry should be made into all payments which the seneschals and ministers of lords of every rank had exacted since the king last crossed into Normandy,[3] and the surviving returns to this inquiry show that it was necessary. No king before Henry II could have carried through an inquest of this kind, and in regard to an earlier age, though we may suspect that the baronial officer often acted high-handedly, we have little evidence of his offences or of his lord's attempts to check them. It so happens that an act of oppression committed by the seneschal of the first earl of Clare in Stephen's reign led in the next generation to

---

[1] *Colchester Cartulary*, i. 171. The *familia* addressed here is presumably a military household of knights and sergeants established at Desning under the constable's command.

[2] *William Salt Archaeological Society's Collections*, vol. v, part i, p. 50.

[3] Stubbs, *Select Charters* (ed. 9), 176.

G

a suit before the king's justices, and produced a very remarkable letter from the third earl.[1]

'Richard de Clare, earl of Hertford greets his beloved men Ralf de Chaure, William son of Godfrey, William Lencroe, Gervase de Samford, Godfrey de Heham, and David de Samford. I have been told that you have been ordered on behalf of the king's justices to swear that you have seen Stephen de Dammartin seised of the land of Pitley as of fee and inheritance, and here I interpose, for I do not wish you to incur the wrath and malediction with which God visits perjury. For I tell you all that while this Stephen had the stewardship and mastery[2] of all the land of Earl Gilbert, he unjustly and wrongfully occupied the land of Pitley which belonged to William the reeve of Bardfield and his heirs, for he cruelly and unjustly caused one of William's sons to be killed, because he knew and perceived him to be the nearest to his father's inheritance in regard to the possession of that land. And because the truth of the matter is as I have received it from my older men, I command you as my faithful men to swear nothing as to the fee and inheritance of this Stephen, for neither was his, neither fee nor inheritance, but only, as has been said, a wrongful and violent occupation.'[3]

Nothing can now be recovered of the story which must lie behind this letter, but there is no reason to question the earl's representation of the facts. We may be certain that acts of this sort were not confined to the period which it is convenient, if inaccurate, to call the anarchy of

[1] Cott. MS. Appendix xxi, f. 27; Appendix, No. 21.

[2] 'Senescalciam et magisterium.'

[3] It does not seem possible to fix the date of this letter at all closely. The third earl of Hertford succeeded his father in 1173 and died in 1217. The events to which the letter refers must have taken place towards the close of Stephen's reign. Gilbert, the first earl of Hertford, died between 1151 and 1153 (*Complete Peerage*, vi. 499), and it can only have been towards the end of his life that Stephen de Dammartin had the 'senescalchia et magisterium' of his land. Previously Stephen appears as one of the less important members of the earl's circle; he comes eighth among the witnesses to one of the earl's earlier charters (Harl. Chart. 76. F. 35) and is there preceded by his brother Alan. As the earl was succeeded by a brother of full age, his lands cannot have been held in custody by Stephen after his death. It is possible that the incident recorded in the letter took place in 1146 when Earl Gilbert was an hostage in the king's hand on behalf of the earl of Chester. The Pitley of the letter is now represented by Pitley Farm in Great Bardfield, Essex.

Stephen's reign. The interest of the present case does not lie in its date, but in its illustration of the essential weakness of early feudal organization. The administration of a great honour, of the kingdom of England itself, depended on officers who must themselves be powerful if they were to uphold their lord's authority. It was inevitable that such men in such a position should now and again take the law into their own hands, without their lord's knowledge if not in his despite. In the reign of Stephen the king's own household officers were setting a bad example to the servants of his barons. William Martel, Stephen's *dapifer*, is named first among four men of whose robberies and exactions the monks of Abingdon complained to Pope Eugenius III in 1147.[1]

[1] *Chronicon Monasterii de Abingdon*, ii. 200. An important household officer of the empress, John the Marshal, is the fourth of these men. Of the remaining two, William de Beauchamp claimed a royal constableship and dispensership (below, 225) and only one of the four, Hugh de Bolbec, had no official connexion with the royal household.

III

THE HONORIAL BARONAGE

IT is impossible to write many paragraphs about the early phases of English feudalism without using the word baron.[1] The word was freely employed by all writers of the Anglo-Norman period, and formed part of the ordinary language of royal writs already in the Conqueror's day. The literary writers never define it, because to them it was simply a term of social currency, and though in the language of charters and law-books it carried a definite implication of rank and power, its legal specialization lay in the far future. It is, no doubt, possible to trace an early tendency towards the restriction of the term to the lords who held important fees of the king. The *barones* who are addressed by Henry I and Stephen in innumerable writs represent, as a class, the king's greater tenants in chief by military service, distinct on the one hand from his knights, sergeants, and ministers of lesser rank, and, on

---

[1] The archaic use of *baro* in the sense of man, and married man in particular, produced the *baron et feme* of Anglo-French law language. It was suggested by Maitland (*History of English Law*, ii. 406) that this usage 'is probably due to the fact that the king's court has for the more part been conversant with the affairs of gentle-folk. The wife of a magnate, perhaps the wife of a knight, would naturally speak of her husband as "mon baron".' But this limitation of the activities of the king's court cannot be maintained, and there is evidence that women of much lower rank used this word when speaking of their husbands. Late in the reign of Henry III, two women named Maud and Elena who belonged to Offerton in north Derbyshire, executed a deed 'cum consensu boronum nostrorum Eustachii et Roberti' (Jeayes, *Derbyshire Charters*, No. 1788, from a charter at Brookhill Hall, Mansfield). The reading *boronum*, though eccentric, is certain, and the Peak of Derbyshire is the sort of country in which an ancient usage could well persist long after it had become rare or obsolete in the centre and south of England. The Offerton case, in fact, makes it unlikely that the use of *baron* in the sense of husband had ever been confined to any particular section of society, and suggests that it is nothing more than a linguistic survival.

the other, from the undifferentiated multitude of his *fideles*. But it was long before the tendency produced any significant result, and to the end of the Norman period the king's barons remained a large and indeterminate body, defined by a rough equality of rank and a general similarity of territorial position, but by nothing that even approximated to any rule of law.

Even within the circle which surrounded the king, men of very different condition were regarded as barons in this period. The barons of the Exchequer included great household officers, of whom more than one would have ranked as barons under the severest definition that could be given to the term. Aubrey de Vere, to whom Henry I granted the master chamberlainship of all England in 1133 by charter,[1] represented in the second generation the aristocracy of the Norman settlement. Other members of this new ministerial *noblesse*, less important by hereditary position than Aubrey de Vere, held considerable fees at the close of their careers. In, or soon after, 1123 Ralf Basset, who seems to have held an informal primacy among King Henry's justices, gave to a clerical son the patronage of all the churches of his demesne. These churches represented manors distributed over eight counties.[2] William

---

[1] Printed in facsimile in *Sir Christopher Hatton's Book of Seals*, No. 39, from the drawing commissioned by Dugdale for this volume.

[2] This appears from a charter of Archbishop Theobald recording that Ralf Basset, 'regis Henrici justiciarius', had given to Ralf the clerk his son by the hand of the late Archbishop William the *dominatus* and *advocatio* of all the churches of his demesne (Saltman, *Theobald Archbishop of Canterbury*, 414). The churches were those of Hawridge and Marsworth in Buckinghamshire with the chapel of Tiscot in Hertfordshire, the church of Oakley with the chapel of Clopham in Bedfordshire, the churches of 'Treotuna' (near Bruern Abbey) and Mixbury in Oxfordshire, with the chapel of Willaston, and the churches of Peatling and Stoney Stanton in Leicestershire, Quiddenham in Norfolk, Turkdean and Rissington in Gloucestershire, and Letcombe Basset in Berkshire. More than half the manors represented here had belonged to the Domesday fief of Robert de Oilli, and Marsworth and Tiscot were held of Robert in 1086 by a Ralf Basset who may well be the future justiciar himself. But the estate indicated by these churches represents as a whole Ralf's acquisitions of a later time, and, even so, should not be regarded as equivalent to his entire fee.

Mauduit, the chamberlain, received from Henry I the honour of Hanslope in addition to the small Hampshire fee which came to him by inheritance.[1] But other men of the same class seem never to have obtained any considerable estate from the king. Few names occur more frequently in Henry's early charters than Hugh of Buckland, the sheriff of eight counties, but his representative in 1166 held no more than a knight's fee 'of the old fee of King Henry's time'.[2] Moreover, these agents of King Henry's administration included men whose origin, to say the least, is obscure. Ordericus Vitalis may have been exaggerating in the familiar passage in which he speaks of the men— Ralf Basset and Hugh of Buckland among them—whom the king 'raised, so to speak, from the dust, and exalted above counts and illustrious castellans',[3] but the passage would have been pointless if, in origin these men had been noble in any sense of nobility recognized by Orderic's contemporaries. If they ranked as barons at King Henry's court, it was because this was the natural word to apply to the men who enjoyed the king's confidence. They were barons because it pleased the king to treat them as such.

When the word baron is used without qualification in a modern book it is safe to assume that its author is thinking of a tenant in chief of the king. In a general survey of constitutional history it is convenient to use the term in this limited sense. But the usage receives no support from the private charters of the Norman period, in which earls, bishops, and many lords of lesser rank continually speak of their own tenants as *barones*. Even in the thirteenth century the Magna Carta of Cheshire,[4] perhaps the most remarkable of English feudal charters, is in form a grant of liberties by a great lord to his barons, at their request. Up to the present the honorial barons of Norman England

[1] Round, 'Mauduit of Hartley Mauduit', *Ancestor*, v. 207–10.

[2] See the *Carta* of Hugh of Buckland, *Red Book of the Exchequer*, i. 307.

[3] *Historia Ecclesiastica*, ed. le Prevost, iv. 164. Orderic is inaccurate in including Hugh of Buckland among the men who owed their rise to Henry I. He had been in the service of William II (Morris, 'The Office of Sheriff in the Early Norman Period', *Eng. Hist. Rev.* xxxiii. 152, 156).

[4] Ed. Tait, *Chartulary of Chester Abbey* (Chetham Society), i. 102–7.

have hardly received the attention which they deserve. At the very beginning of the eighteenth century their existence was noted by Archdeacon Hody, one of the ablest members of a very remarkable group of historians, in his *History of English Councils and Convocations*.[1] He noticed that the phrase 'Si quis baronum regis vel aliorum comitatui secundum legem interfuerit' in the *Leges Henrici Primi* suggested a distinction between the barons of the king and other barons,[2] and he brought together a number of passages in which magnates of the eleventh and twelfth centuries refer explicitly to their barons.[3] In recent times individual scholars have referred to this honorial baronage,[4] but it is commonly ignored in modern discussions of baronial origins. This is perhaps natural, for the honorial baron, though not distinctive, is characteristic of the Norman and earliest Angevin periods, and by the end of the twelfth century he rarely appears except on the greatest regalities in the land.

His existence there has always been recognized. There has never been any doubt that on 'palatine' earldoms such as Chester and Durham, and on such exceptional honours as those of Lancaster and Richmond, the greater feudal tenants were called barons. In all these cases the evidence for the description begins early. Under Henry I, Rannulf Flambard, as bishop of Durham, refers to all his barons and *fideles* of 'Haliarefolc', the future county of Durham.[5]

---

[1] London, 1701, 287–9.

[2] *Leges*, c. 7. 7. Other passages in the Anglo-Norman law-books point in the same direction, 'so dass *baro* allein auch Aftervassall muss bedeuten können' (Liebermann, Glossary, ii. 1, under *baro*).

[3] The most interesting of Hody's documents is a charter of Bishop William Giffard of Winchester addressed *Omnibus baronibus et ministris suis Francis et Anglis*, derived from Rudborne's *Historia Major Wintoniensis*, which Wharton had recently made accessible in *Anglia Sacra*.

[4] e.g. Professor Tait in *Medieval Manchester and the beginnings of Lancashire*.

[5] Original charter, D. and C. Durham, 2 I. Pont. 7: 'R. dei gratia Dunelmensis episcopus Turstino eadem gratia Eboracensi archiepiscopo et omnibus baronibus Francis et Anglis de Euerwicsire et capitulo sancti Cuthberti et omnibus baronibus et fidelibus suis de Haliarefolc et omnibus baronibus Francis et Anglis de Norhumberlanda.'

Few charters have come down from the early lords of
Lancaster, but between 1153 and 1160 Reginald de
Warenne, on behalf of William count of Boulogne, King
Stephen's son, addressed a writ in favour of Shrewsbury
Abbey to the justices, sheriffs, and all the ministers of the
honour of Lancaster, and to all the barons and good men
of the same honour.[1] The Norman earls of Chester usually,[2]
and the Breton earls of Richmond very frequently,[3] include their barons among the persons to whom they
address their less solemn charters. The Norman earldom
of Shrewsbury was short-lived, but in the foundation
charter of Shrewsbury Abbey Earl Roger allows to his
barons, burgesses, and knights the liberty of making gifts
to the abbey,[4] and his son, Earl Hugh, addresses a charter
in favour of the same house to all his barons, sheriffs, and
ministers, French and English, of Shropshire.[5] The early
references are valuable, historically, for they show that
the barons who appear at a later time in Shropshire,
Cheshire, Lancashire, and Durham did not owe their
style to the mere analogy between their position and that
of a tenant in chief of the crown, but that they were the
representatives of men regarded as barons already in the
Norman period. Their titles come, in fact, from the time
before the conception of baronage was specialized, and
have the interest which always belongs to an historical
survival.

The evidence which reveals the honorial baronage of
this earlier time comes in the main from the private

---

[1] Farrer, *Lancashire Pipe Rolls and Early Charters*, 286.

[2] For examples see below, Appendix, Nos. 24, 47.

[3] For an example of such an address see *Facsimiles of Royal and other
Charters in the British Museum*, No. 33: 'Conanus dux Britannie et comes
Richemundie dapifero suo et camerario et omnibus ministris suis atque
baronibus et omnibus hominibus et amicis suis Francis et Anglis clericis et
laicis tocius Anglie salutem.' But Earl Conan sometimes omitted the
reference to his barons, as in the address of a charter printed by Round,
Ancient Charters (Pipe Roll Society, vol. x), No. 33: 'Conanus dux Britannie, comes Richemundie dapifero suo et camerario et omnibus ministris et
hominibus suis Francis et Anglis clericis et laicis.'

[4] *Mon. Ang.* iii. 520.   [5] Ibid.

charters of the Norman period. The custom by which a
lord of this date, when making an enfeoffment, commonly
addressed the record of it to his men and friends, gives a
general interest to the opening words of a typical feudal
charter. The 'barons' of more than one important honour
are only known under that designation because their lord
happened to address them collectively in one of his charters.
The second document which Madox printed in his *Formulare Anglicanum* gives a good illustration of this kind of
evidence. It records the confirmation by Earl Roger of
Warwick of an elaborate agreement between two of his
tenants, and it opens with the earl's address *omnibus baronibus suis, ministris, et omnibus fidelibus suis, Francis et Anglis,
tocius honoris sui.*[1] Similar formulas of address were coming
from most of the greater lords of the mid-twelfth century,
varying in detail but all conforming to the same general
type. A little before 1135, for example, Robert de Oilli
granted land in Oxford to a clerk by a charter addressed to
all his barons and to the burgesses of Oxford.[2] Early in
Stephen's reign William de Albini, as earl of Lincoln,
writes to all his barons and men, French and English, of
the honour of Arundel, informing them that he has confirmed Alan de Dunstanville's gift of Nyetimber in Sussex
to Lewes Priory,[3] and William de Roumara, who was
shortly to succeed William de Albini in the earldom of
Lincoln, tells all his barons and men, French and English,
of all England, of a gift which he has made to one of his
tenants.[4] Shortly after the accession of Henry II, Gilbert de
Gant, the third holder of the Norman earldom of Lincoln,
informs all his barons and men, French and English, that

---

[1] Madox, *Formulare*, No. II. The original of this charter, which Madox
derived from the records of the Augmentation Office, seems to have disappeared.

[2] *Cartulary of Eynsham*, ed. Salter, No. 65.

[3] Ancient Deeds, A. 14208; Appendix, No. 9. This charter is otherwise
important as one of the two original charters which prove that William
de Albini possessed the earldom of Lincoln before it was granted to William
de Roumara. It is quoted from the Lewes Cartulary in *Complete Peerage*,
vii. 667. See Round, *Geoffrey de Mandeville*, 325 and below, 233-4.

[4] Stenton, *Danelaw Charters*, No. 507.

he has given four carucates in Barton on Humber to William Basset;[1] and between 1138 and 1148 Gilbert earl of Pembroke notifies the barons and men of William de Mont-fitchet's honour, then in the earl's hand, that he has restored certain churches to the monks of Gloucester.[2] Even after 1166, Roger de Mowbray opens with the same address a writ releasing a tenant from half the knights' service which he formerly owed.[3] The addresses to feudal charters, even without other evidence, show that the great lords of the Norman and early Angevin time normally regarded their leading tenants as their barons.[4]

More interesting than these formulas of mere address are the passages which show a lord acting in the presence, or, as sometimes happens, with the advice of his barons. Such passages are more numerous than is always realized. At the very beginning of the twelfth century the widow and sons of Walscin de Douay, the first lord of the honour of Bampton, gave among other things the church of Bridgwater to Bath Abbey *consilio baronum suorum*.[5] In a charter of 1109 Simon I, earl of Northampton, and his wife state that they have confirmed to Daventry Priory a group of churches given by Robert son of Vitalis, *precatu suo et baronum nostrorum quos ipse obnixius precatus est ut nos imprecarentur*.[6] In 1127, while in attendance on Henry I

---

[1] *Sir Christopher Hatton's Book of Seals*, No. 297.

[2] M. M. Bigelow, *Placita Anglo-Normannica*, 154.

[3] *Coucher Book of Selby Abbey*, ed. Fowler, ii. 241.

[4] Among other Anglo-Norman lords who address charters to their barons may also be mentioned William Earl Warenne, *Mon. Ang.* v. 14; Richard de Redvers, earl of Devon, Cott. Tib. D. vi, (1) f. 72 b; Stephen count of Aumale, Farrer, *Early Yorkshire Charters*, 1318 (a specific address to the barons of Holderness); Robert 'Bossu', earl of Leicester, *Mon. Ang.* iv. 115; Roger earl of Hereford, *Gloucester Cartulary* (Rolls Series), ii. 152; Robert earl of Gloucester, ibid. ii. 89; Robert earl of Derby, *Mon. Ang.* iii. 393; John count of Eu, ibid. viii. 1171; Waleran count of Meulan, *Coucher Book of Selby Abbey* (ed. J. T. Fowler), ii. 260; Henry of Essex, *Colchester Cartulary*, i. 170. This list is merely offered in illustration of the frequency of these addresses, and is not intended to be in any way exhaustive.

[5] *Two Chartularies of the Priory of St. Peter at Bath* (Somerset Record Society), 39.

[6] *Mon. Ang.* v. 180. In this and other charters relating to the gift, these

at Eling, Hants, before a voyage to Normandy, Robert earl of Leicester by the advice of his wife and his barons confirmed a gift to Reading Abbey by one of his men.[1] A few years later Maud de Senliz, grandmother of the famous Robert fitz Walter, granted away a portion of her dower with the consent of Walter her son, in the presence of him and his barons,[2] and in 1142 Robert de Sigillo, bishop of London, put on record that Rannulf Peverel's gift of Abberton to St. Paul's Cathedral had been proved by an inquisition of the bishop's barons and the lawful men of his church.[3] In the next generation Humphrey de Bohun and his wife confirm the foundation of Farleigh Priory with the counsel and assent of their barons and men.[4] It has never been doubted that feudal custom required a lord to take the advice of at least his leading tenants before making any important grants from his fee. These passages, like the formulas of address which have just been quoted, show that these tenants were known as barons in the feudal language of the early twelfth century.[5]

churches are described as *ecclesiae terrae de Foxton'*. The latter place is in south Leicestershire, but the churches which were regarded as belonging to it were scattered over a wide area, and included those of Lubbenham and Gumley in south Leicestershire, Scalford in the north of the county, Braybrooke in Northamptonshire, and Bisbrooke in Rutland. The manors which they represent form, in fact, a typical fief of a great honorial baron.

[1] Egerton MS. 3031, f. 36.

[2] Harl. Chart. 55. G. 9.

[3] M. M. Bigelow, *Placita Anglo-Normannica*, 147.

[4] *Mon. Ang.* v. 26.

[5] Among other references made by tenants in chief to their barons may be mentioned Robert Malet's confirmation to Eye Priory of the gifts made by his barons and knights (*Mon. Ang.* iii. 405, an eleventh-century example); Ilbert de Lacy's confirmation of the tithes given to Pontefract Priory by the barons of his castlery (Farrer, *Early Yorkshire Charters*, No. 1492); Robert de Vere's statement that he and his wife consent to whatever gifts their barons or men shall make to Monks Horton Priory (*Mon. Ang.* v. 34, interesting because it comes from the mid-twelfth century and a lord not of the first rank is using the word); and the solemn renunciation of exactions which William de Albini, as earl of Chichester, granted to the churches of that diocese *in manu Hillarii episcopi Cicestriae, coram personis ecclesiae suae et baronibus meis* (*Mon. Ang.* viii. 1169). The fact that the barons of a fee regarded themselves as a group of *pares* is well brought out in a charter,

The nature of the materials for feudal history makes it almost impossible to penetrate behind the formality with which the lords of the twelfth century refer to their barons in their charters. A curious letter written by the third earl of Hertford soon after his succession in 1173 gives a slight touch of personality to the relations between the first lords of Clare and their barons.

'Richard de Clare, earl of Hertford, greets his dear friends master Staingrim and William archdeacons of the church of Norwich. I am assured by the true and certain testimony of my barons, and I make known to your weighty discretion by my present letters, without any ambiguity, that the tithes of Roger de Ginnei which are of my fee, those namely of Whitwell and Haveringland, with the church of blessed Clement the martyr of Norwich and all their appurtenances, belong and ought to belong to blessed John the baptist of Stoke, and have so belonged from the ancient time when the first Gilbert fitz Richard, after the conquest of England, appointed that the monks of Bec, brought into the church of blessed John, should be provided with rents and tithes and ecclesiastical benefices. For at that time all his barons, both Roger de Ginnei, grandfather of this Roger, and all his other barons, praising and making much of his devotion and alms, in their lord's presence and with the consent of the most noble Herbert bishop of Norwich, confirmed their tithes to the monks of that place for the health of their souls. And so, my dearest friends, secure in your faith and rectitude, I ask your help, and that you take thought for the assistance of my monks as befits your office, for Christ's sake, and that you may have me beholden to you in all things hereafter.'[1]

The Latin of this letter is stiff and artificial, but there is no doubt that the clerk who wrote it for the earl of Clare was only following the ordinary usage of his time in earlier than 1119, in which William of Bacton, an important tenant of the bishop of Norwich, states that he has made a grant *in presencia domini mei Herberti episcopi sub testimonio parium meorum baronum eius et quorundam hominum meorum* (quoted from a Norwich register, *Trans. R. Hist. Soc.* 1957, 17, by Miss Barbara Dodwell).

[1] Cott. MS. Appendix xxi, f. 28; Appendix, No. 22. The names of the archdeacons to whom the earl is writing show that the letter must be earlier than 1181. Staingrim and William have not been found together in any dated document later than 1178 (L. Landon, 'The Early Archdeacons of Norwich Diocese', in *Proceedings of the Suffolk Institute of Archaeology*, vol. xx, part i, p. 24).

his reiterated application of the word baron to the greater tenants on the earl's fee. Through all the involutions of his style he manages to give a definite impression of the barons of whom he speaks. They were clearly men of wealth and position, who could give tithes and churches to a monastery, and it was from them that their lord derived what he knew of the history of his honour. And all the other evidence which we possess about the honorial baronage agrees on these points with the earl's letter.

During the minority of a great lord, the collective memory of his barons could be called into action by the king himself. An early writ of Henry II orders Hugh II earl of Chester and Maud his mother to cause their barons of Lincolnshire to declare whether Arnulf son of Peter had lost the land of Honington by judgement in the court of King Henry I, and if so, to cause the nuns of Stixwould to hold the land as the gift of Earl Rannulf I of Chester and the countess Lucy, his wife.[1] The date of the plea in King Henry's court is unknown. But the fact that Earl Rannulf I had died in 1129 shows that the memory of a group of honorial barons could be expected to cover at least a quarter of a century.[2]

Less often than could be wished, though often enough to illustrate feudal custom, twelfth-century charters show the honorial baron in attendance at the honorial court. One of the earliest of these charters, which cannot be later than 1125, was printed by Round in *Feudal England* as evidence for the antiquity of scutage.[3] It is a notification by Count Eustace of Boulogne that one of his tenants has proved his right to certain lands in the count's court at 'Stanford', according to the wisdom of his barons. The Stanford of the charter was identified by Round with Stanford Rivers in Essex, of which Ongar was then a member,[4] and it is more than probable that the court in

---

[1] Bodleian Library, Stixwould Charters I.
[2] Earl Hugh was born in 1147.   [3] *Feudal England*, 270.
[4] This charter, of which the original is preserved in Westminster Abbey, was printed in the *Athenaeum* for 2 Dec. 1893. Its essential words run: 'Sciatis quod G. filius T. de Masseberia terram suam quam V. filius

which the count's barons gave their judgement was held in Ongar Castle, the head of his Essex honour. Some fifty years later, William Earl Ferrers recorded that his father's gift of Woodham Ferrers in Essex to Maurice son of Geoffrey had been 'recognized' in his court before himself, his barons, and his men,[1] and at about the same time, Earl Simon III of Northampton confirmed by charter an agreement formerly made in his court between Ralf of Hereford and the monks of Rufford touching certain land which had been adjudged to the monks before Philip of Kyme, the earl's *dapifer*, and the other barons of his court.[2] Like the count of Boulogne, the earls of Derby and Northampton belonged to the highest ranks in the baronage, but even in the reign of Henry II lords who had not reached the dignity of an earl or count could refer as a matter of course to their barons assembled in their courts. In a charter to Wardon Abbey, which cannot be much earlier than 1170, Simon de Beauchamp of Bedford speaks of land given and sold to that house before him and his barons in his court at Bedford.[3]

Bernardi super se calumniavit in curiam meam [*sic*] Stanffordie providentie [*sic*] baronum meorum derationavit ex quarte partu [*sic*] seruitii cuiusdam militis et ut ipse in quocunque loco milites mei fecerint faciat sive in nummis sive in exercitu sive in guarda.' Round identified this Stanford with Stanford Rivers and pointed out the significance of the identification in an article entitled 'The Honour of Ongar' printed in the *Essex Archaeological Society's Transactions for 1898* (vii. 142–52). The charter was obviously written by an illiterate clerk, and its bad grammar suggests that the rarity of early baronial charters of this type is chiefly due to the rarity of competent draftsmen in the Norman period.

[1] This charter, which apparently has never been printed, was discussed by Round in the *Essex Archaeological Society's Transactions*, vol. x. For Maurice son of Geoffrey see also below, 168.

[2] Harl. MS. 1063, f. 8 b. 'Sciatis me concessisse . . . monachis de Rufford' . . . pactionem quam [*sic*] olim facta est inter eos et Radulfum de Hereford in curia mea, scilicet de quadam terra in territorio de Eicring' (Eakring, Notts) . . . quam [*sic*] ipsis monachis coram Philippo de Chime dapifero et ceteris baronibus curie mee adiudicata fuit possidenda.' The bad grammar here is probably due to the bad scribe who wrote the Rufford cartulary. Most of Earl Simon's numerous charters are written very efficiently.

[3] *Wardon Cartulary* (Bedfordshire Historical Record Society), 135:

From the various passages which have just been quoted there emerges one essential element in the twelfth-century conception of a baron. Whatever else a baron may have been, he was his lord's counsellor.[1] There is no mistaking the significance of the phrases which show groups of honorial barons advising their lord, attending his court, approving what he has done, or giving an opinion as to events which have taken place on a fee in the past. As a class the barons of these charters were doubtless men of considerable possessions. Many of them must have been men of high birth. But the quality enabling a baron to play his distinctive part in the life of the honour to which he belonged was not derived from wealth or rank alone. It can best be described in modern terms as a sense of responsibility, the power of giving a reasoned opinion for his lord's guidance. The possession of this quality did not imply any special knowledge of law, nor even experience in administration beyond that which came in the Norman age to any man of position. It was essentially the power of using experience and elementary legal knowledge in the interest of a lord. In this lies one of the chief differences between the function of a baron and that of a mere knight in feudal society. The knight's opinion was not often

---

Hanc donationem et venditionem fecit . . . coram me et baronibus meis in curia mea apud Bedefordiam.

[1] The function of the baron as counsellor is very evident in the remarkable account given by Jordan Fantosme of the 'parlement' held by William king of Scots in 1174 (ed. Howlett, *Chronicles of the Reigns of Stephen, Henry II and Richard I*, iii. 226–31). The king had just received a letter from Henry, the young king of England, offering him Carlisle and Westmorland in addition to his Northumbrian inheritance in return for his support, and was inclined to threaten Henry II with a withdrawal of his 'faith and friendship' unless he received Northumberland immediately. In the following discussion Earl Duncan of Fife 'spoke like a baron' to the effect that it would be wise to approach the king of England with fair speech rather than with threats, and for the moment convinced the king of Scots and his other barons. In this passage, to speak like a baron evidently means to speak deliberately, and after careful thought. In the event the king disregarded this 'baron-like' speech and followed the advice of his knights, 'la gent juefne e salvage' who were eager for a declaration of war, but Jordan Fantosme thought him very unwise in doing so.

asked by his lord unless some military question was at issue. It was evidently thought strange that the duke of Normandy, when he had come into sight of London, asked his knights whether he should be crowned at once or wait until his wife should be associated with him. Haimer of Thouars, the spokesman of the army, observed that knights were rarely or never invited to a discussion of that kind.[1] On an individual honour there can rarely have been need for a lord to take his knights, as such, into counsel. The advice which he needed, in time of peace, was not the advice of a military entourage, nor of the knights whom he had provided with land sufficient for their maintenance alone, but that of tenants with a substantial interest in his honour, and responsibilities towards men enfeoffed under them. It was such tenants who formed the honorial baronage of the eleventh and twelfth centuries.

Nevertheless it is easy to overestimate the size of the fief which entitled a tenant to baronial rank within an honour. We may feel sure that a man who owed his lord the service of five knights or more would be regarded as a baron in his lord's court, but we have no warrant for making a fief of this exceptional size a minimum qualification for baronial status. The few early documents which refer by name to individual honorial barons suggest, on the contrary, that baronage, if the word may be used in this connexion, depended far less on the extent of a tenant's fee than on his general social position, his birth, and on the nature of his relations with his lord. It is at least certain that in the eleventh century the tenant of an estate which cannot possibly have carried the service of five knights could be described as a baron. In one of the early Norman charters of Westminster Abbey Abbot Gilbert recorded that Robert son of Swein of Essex, on the day of his father's burial, confirmed his father's gift of Wheatley in Essex to that house 'in the sight of his barons, Godebald,

---

[1] William of Poitiers, *Gesta Willelmi Ducis* (ed. Giles), 142: Is de-mirans, et urbane extollens modestiam inquirentem animos militum, num vellent dominum suum regem fieri: 'Ad disceptationem, inquit, hujus-modi, milites nunquam aut raro acciti sunt. . . .'

Thorald and his brother William, and many others'.[1] The
early date of this document makes it possible, for once, to
trace the holdings of a group of honorial barons in Domesday Book, and the result is suggestive.[2] William cannot
be identified there with any certainty, but he is probably
the 'W' who was holding three hides of Swein of Essex at
Basildon in that county. Thorald held of the same lord a
manor of seven hides at Wetherley in Huntingdonshire,
and two estates in Essex of a hide and thirty acres at
Hassingbroke and a hide and fifteen acres at Basildon.
Godebald, whose descendants held three knights' fees on
the honour of Rayleigh, the Domesday fief of Swein of
Essex,[3] was the founder of an important Essex family. His
son Robert founded Horkesley Priory, including among
those for whose souls his gifts were made, two brothers,
William and Thorald, who can safely be identified with
Godebald's fellow barons in the Westminster charter.[4]
But in 1086 Godebald's holding was small, consisting
only of a hide at Hockley, half a hide and thirty acres at
Black and White Notley, a hide and a half and thirty acres
at Horkesley and rights over thirty-seven free men, all in
Essex. In describing such men as barons, the writer of the
Westminster charter must have been using the language
of common speech, without any regard for the niceties of
terminology. To him a group of men, obviously persons
of condition, who stood beside their lord on a very solemn
occasion would naturally appear as barons. And his habit
of mind illustrates the conditions under which the word
baron first became naturalized in England.

But despite the indefiniteness of this early usage the

[1] Armitage Robinson, *Gilbert Crispin, Abbot of Westminster,* 135.

[2] For the identifications which follow see the *Victoria Histories of
Essex,* i. 482–91, and *Huntingdonshire,* i. 348.

[3] For the holding of Robert of Horkesley on the honour of Rayleigh see
Red Book of the Exchequer, ii. 738.

[4] *Mon. Ang.* v. 156. In the foundation charter of Horkesley Robert
speaks of the land which his wife Beatrice had received from Turold her
avunculus. He was probably identical with the Thorald who was to share
in the benefits of the foundation, and with the Thorald of the Westminster
charter.

language of Anglo-Norman charters, and in particular the contrast which they continually draw between barons and 'men', clearly points to a restricted use of the word *baro*. It is safe to assume that in the reigns of Henry I and Stephen the men who were described by their lords as barons were as a rule the leading tenants on the honours to which they belonged, men who individually owed to their lords more than the service of a single knight. It is more than probable that such a distinction was felt already in the eleventh century itself, though it is rarely, if ever, expressed in definite terms. It is at least certain that the detailed analysis of a great honour, as it is described in Domesday Book, will usually reveal the existence of two very different kinds of feudal tenant. On most honours of any size Domesday Book will record the names of a number of men of little consequence, generally holding, if later evidence may be trusted, by some form of sergeanty, or by some fractional part of a knight's service. But it will also bring out the presence of a group of tenants of far higher standing, lords of important manors and large fees. These men evidently represent under changed conditions the thegnly landholders of King Edward's day, and they are the predecessors of the honorial barons of the twelfth century. Between them and the king's own tenants in chief there was no distinction of any consequence. Many of them held larger fees than the lesser among the king's barons held of him, and as a class they were men of the same social standing. And the word baron denoted a man's place in society without reference to the position which he happened to hold in the tenurial scale.

Few of the greater honours of the eleventh century have been analysed as fully as the interest of their structure deserves. How various and complicated that structure might be can be gathered from the volume in which the late Dr. Farrer published the results of his work on the history of honours and their constituent knights' fees. It is only through such work as his that the history of the honorial baronage can ever be approached, and from this point of view it is worth while to follow his analysis of one

famous honour, that of Peverel of Nottingham.[1] The lands
which William Peverel received from the Conqueror lay
in six counties, and in the thirteenth century, as doubtless
in the eleventh, they answered for a *servitium debitum* of
sixty knights. The tenants whom William had enfeoffed
by 1086 form a miscellaneous body. They included seven
men bearing English names, of whom none held any
considerable estate at this time. Beside, but hardly above
them, came a small group of men whose later representatives in title appear as holding land of the honour by
sergeanty, and a slightly large group, whose members
seem to have founded local families holding by military
service. Ten individuals remain whose position was obviously different. One of them was Alfred the butler
of Robert count of Mortain; another was Eustace the
sheriff of Huntingdon; a third, Serlo of Glapwell, held
of Ralf fitz Hubert of Crich and Roger de Busli of Tickhill
in addition to his tenure on the Peverel honour; a fourth,
Robert de Paveilli, held Houghton Magna and Paulers-
pury in Northamptonshire immediately of William
Peverel, and South Wingfield in Derbyshire under Earl
Alan of Richmond, who himself held of William. Among
those who held of William Peverel alone, Robert de Heriz
held at Stapleford in Nottinghamshire, at Tibshelf, and
apparently at Bolsover in Derbyshire; a certain Warner
held at Shirland and Codnor in Derbyshire, Toton, and
Wollaton in Nottinghamshire;[2] 'Sasfrid' held at Baseford
in Nottinghamshire, Ashby Magna in Leicestershire,
Catesby in Northamptonshire, where his son founded a

---

[1] The details which follow are all derived from the section on the
honour of Peverel in *Honors and Knights' Fees*, i. 146–259. There is
nothing unusual about the structure of the honour, except that William
Peverel seems to have subinfeudated a larger portion of his fief than was
customary at this date. The honour gives a particularly good illustration
of the wide dispersal of the lands of which important mesne tenancies were
composed, but similar illustrations could easily be derived from other
honours.

[2] This mesne tenancy formed the nucleus of the later barony of Grey of
Codnor, though there is no family connexion between William Peverel's
tenant Warner and the fourteenth-century barons.

priory, and Empingham in Rutland;[1] 'Pagan' held at Barby in Northamptonshire, Lubbesthorpe in Leicestershire, Baseford in Nottinghamshire, and Tetchwick in Buckinghamshire; 'Drogo' held at Pinxton in Derbyshire, Ravensthorpe, Teton, and Cotton under Guilsborough in Northamptonshire, Stoke Goldington in Buckinghamshire, and East Horndon in Essex; 'Ambrose' held at Kelmarsh and Mollington in Northamptonshire, Tilsworth in Bedfordshire, Adstock in Buckinghamshire, and Bilborough in Nottinghamshire. It is men like Robert de Heriz, Drogo, Sasfrid, and Ambrose whom we should bear in mind when we are trying to form an impression of the honorial baronage of the eleventh century.

The number of these large mesne tenancies which can be traced on all the greater English honours[2] gives importance to the rights, and in particular to the rights of jurisdiction, which normally belonged to their holders. Early evidence on these matters is scanty. Apart from a few obscure allusions in Anglo-Norman law-books,[3] it is derived almost entirely from seignorial charters recording the enfeoffment of a tenant or the confirmation of his lands to his heir. Such documents are rare, many of them are only preserved imperfectly, and all of them are brief. Now and then, however, one of these charters will contain a clause indicating the rights of justice to be exercised over the land to which it relates, and the wording of these clauses is suggestive. In charters granted by the king's barons to their men, as in charters granted by the king to his own barons, rights of justice, if specified at all, are generally expressed in a famous phrase taken over from Old English

[1] For an enfeoffment by Sasfrid's son of a tenant to ride with him or his wife from Baseford to Ashby Magna see below, 130.

[2] Thus, to take one other example, the two knights' fees which Reginald de Gresley held of William Earl Ferrers in 1166 were shown by Round (*The Tenure of Draycote under Needwood*, Salt Society's Collections, N.S., vol. x) to represent the fief held in 1086 by Roger 'the huntsman' at Boyleston in Derbyshire, Frilsham and East Ilsley in Berkshire.

[3] On which see Liebermann, *Gesetze*, ii. 2, under *Gerichtsbarkeit*. The most suggestive of them is the reference in the *Leis Willelme* (2, 3) to the 'free man' who has soke and sake, toll, team, and infangenetheof.

law. The usual formula by which both the king and his barons grant jurisdictional powers is a statement that their recipient is to hold 'with sake and soke, toll and team, and infangenetheof'; ancient words, which are a curious blend of the general and the particular. By the early part of the eleventh century sake and soke had come to mean nothing more definite than the right to hold a court and take its profits. A grant of toll empowered a lord to take such payments as custom sanctioned on sales of cattle or other goods within his land.[1] A grant of team authorized him to entertain in his court pleas in which a person suspected of wrongful possession of cattle or other goods could vouch his warrantor, and as only those who could produce good witnesses of their purchases were admitted to this process, there was a connexion in sense as well as in alliteration between toll and team, for the payment of toll implied the due publicity of a sale.[2] The word

[1] This seems to be implied in the definition of *toll* given in the *Leges Eadwardi Confessoris*. See Leibermann, ii. 2, under *Zollabgabe*. But the word must certainly have covered another, and probably more ancient, form of toll, namely the right to take a payment in respect of cattle or other goods passing through an estate. Disputes about tolls of this kind occur in the earliest Assize Rolls. A case, for example, is recorded on the Northampton Assize Roll of 1202 (ed. D. M. Stenton, 10, 11) in which the local jurors presented that a lord was taking 'new customs . . . namely taking from a cart going through his land of Winwick with eels, a stick of eels, and from a cart of green fish, one green fish (&c) whereas he ought to take no custom from anything except from salt going through his land, namely from a cartload of salt one measure, and then ought the salter to have one loaf for that salt; and moreover if the salter's cart should be broken, the salter's horses ought to have pasture in ⟨the lord's⟩ land without charge, while he repairs his cart'. An arrangement of this kind has a very ancient appearance. But for the reason suggested in the text it is probable that a payment on sales is primarily meant when *toll* is associated with *team*.

[2] The most significant information about the process known as *team* in Old English law comes from certain passages in the code of Cnut, prescribing that no one may take advantage of the process unless he has good witness to the purchase on which he relies, and that no purchase of stock or goods shall be made to the value of more than four pence, either in a borough or 'upp on lande', without this witness (II Cnut 23–24. 2). The passages are particularly interesting because they prove the existence of trade in cattle and goods outside borough markets, as to which there is very little direct evidence in the Old English period. The definite reference to

of greatest moment in this series is infangenetheof, the power of doing justice upon a thief taken in possession of stolen property within the land of a lord thus privileged. How far these ancient words retained their original force in the Norman period is a hard question. In the thirteenth century seignorial jurisdiction in capital cases was closely watched by the king's justices. South, at least, of Northumbria and east of the Welsh march it was unsafe for a lord to do justice even upon a hand-having thief.[1] A

purchases made 'upp on lande' makes intelligible the inclusion of *team* among the jurisdictional rights which the greater Anglo-Saxon lords of the eleventh century normally possessed.

[1] A case which illustrates the narrow limits within which a lord could employ his privilege of infangenetheof in the thirteenth century is well recorded on the Berkshire Assize Roll of 1260 (Assize Roll 40, m. 27 d). Towards the middle of his reign Henry I gave to Robert Achard five Berkshire manors to hold for a knight's service with soke and sake, toll, team, and infangenetheof (*Calendar of Charter Rolls*, iii. 360, where the charter is printed in full). Under Henry III Robert's descendant exercised his undoubted right of infangenetheof, and the Assize Roll describes the sequel:

'Juratores presentant quod Petrus Achard et balliui sui ceperunt Aliciam de Hasel' de Fynchampsted' cum quodam equo furato et pannis furatis per sectam Henrici de Farenbergh' apud Fynchampsted', et ibidem imprisonata et postea in plena curia ipsius Petri ducta et per sectam predicti Henrici in eadem curia sine aliquo balliuo domini regis conuicta et suspensa super quamdam quercum ubi non recolunt aliquem alium ibidem antea esse suspensum, set nesciunt quo waranto. Ideo preceptum est vicecomiti quod venire faceret predictum Petrum ad ostendendum warantum suum etc. Post venit predictus Petrus et profert cartam domini regis nunc in qua continetur quod idem dominus rex concessit et carta sua confirmavit Roberto Achard filio Willelmi Achard et heredibus suis maneria de Aldirmaneston' Finchamsted' Colethorp, Speresholt, Chaulawe cum omnibus pertinenciis suis que Henricus rex auus Henrici regis aui domini regis nunc dedit predicto Roberto antecessori predicti Petri, cum soch et sach et infonginthef. Postea venit predictus Petrus et finem fecit per xl solidos per plegium Willelmi de Englefeld'.'

The real irregularity committed by Peter Achard was his exercise of the right of infangenetheof without seeing that a bailiff of the king watched the proceedings. But a privilege which could only be used under the eye of a royal officer cannot have been much use to its possessor, and infangenetheof was obviously becoming a dead letter when this case was heard. It was not by any direct challenge, but by insisting on their right of supervision that the Angevin kings reduced the higher judicial powers of the baronage.

rigorous insistence that toll could only be taken where and as it was allowed by a narrowly interpreted custom, threatened the financial profits which came to a lord from his traditional privileges. But it is easy to antedate the beginning of the royal attack upon feudal liberties, the law-books written under Henry I emphasize the reality of seignorial justice, and the reign of Stephen was not a period in which barons lost their inherited rights.

In any case the phrase is of great interest as a link between Old English and Anglo-Norman law, between pre-Conquest thegnhood and Norman baronage. Now and then the Norman kings themselves emphasize the reality of the link, as when Henry I grants three manors on the Mandeville fee to Eudo his dapifer, 'with the same customs with which Esgar the Staller best held them in King Edward's time, that is, with soke and sake, and toll and team and infangenetheof, and as Geoffrey de Mande-ville most quietly held them in my father's time'.[1] Long before the Conquest these words must have been current as a mnemonic summary of the privileges which belonged to the higher aristocracy and the greater churches. They were taken over by the Norman kings as applicable to the rights which their barons would expect to possess, and in this sense they passed from England to feudal Scotland. Even in the thirteenth century they were still felt to cover the essential nucleus of the complex of rights which formed a rough criterion of tenure by barony in that age.[2] It is

[1] *Colchester Cartulary*, i. 22.

[2] After what has been written on barony in recent years, and in par-ticular by Miss Rachel Reid ('Barony and Thanage', *Eng. Hist. Rev.* xxxv. 161–99), it seems clear that in the thirteenth century the possession of the rights covered by sake and soke, toll, team, and infangenetheof entitled a tenant in chief to the privileges, and subjected him to the burdens, of tenure *per baroniam*. It has also been argued that the rights of public justice covered by this formula gave to tenure in barony an official character from which most of its legal characteristics directly follow, and that in this respect the barons of Anglo-Norman and Angevin law are the successors in function of the Old English thegns, to whom these rights had also belonged. The twelfth-century evidence agrees, in general, with this view, but it also implies that in the Anglo-Norman period, these rights were not the criterion but the result of baronial status. The charters of this, and the

safe to say that under Henry I every tenant in chief of any consequence would have claimed to exercise these powers, however closely he might be watched by the king's justices in so doing. The question whether they came to him in virtue of a royal grant to a predecessor or as inherent in his position is, in the last resort, a matter of words rather than facts. We cannot easily imagine William the Conqueror giving an honour to one of his followers, laying a heavy burden of military service on him, but refusing him the right of doing justice on a thief caught in the act on his land.

Despite the rarity of early charters of enfeoffment, it would be possible to bring together a considerable number of texts in which a lord, holding of the king, grants to one of his tenants rights of justice extending as far as infangenetheof. Such a collection would illustrate early feudalism from many angles. In particular it would show that while most of the men who received powers of high justice from their lords were persons of condition, feudal custom allowed a lord to give these powers to anyone who had earned his favour. On this matter the charters of Rannulf II earl of Chester, are especially instructive. At the height of his power the earl was by far the greatest lord in England, and he obviously considered that rights of sake and soke, toll, team, and infangenetheof were his to give as he pleased. He gave them to Robert earl of Leicester with the castle and village of Mountsorrel in Leicestershire,[1] and to Henry de Lacy of Pontefract with the manors of Lowdham and East Bridgeford in central Nottinghamshire.[2] In Cheshire itself he was free to give away jurisdictional powers of every kind, and in this, his own palatinate, he

time immediately following, suggest that a man commonly received these rights from his lord because his social position entitled him to them, because, in fact, he was already a 'baron' as the word was understood in feudal society. The definition of baronial tenure belongs to a later age, and was naturally influenced by the fact that every tenant in chief who was regarded, socially, as a baron, actually possessed the rights traditionally described as sake and soke, toll, team, and infangenetheof.

[1] Lansd. MS. 415, f. 41 (Appendix, No. 47).
[2] *Duchy of Lancaster Misc. Books*, ii. 71 (Appendix, No. 23).

shows no sign of any feeling that infangenetheof and its associated rights should only be given to the tenants of large fees. In one curious charter he annexes these powers to an estate which is to be held by the service of half a knight until he shall see or hear what service the land can bear.[1] His attitude is illustrated still more clearly by charters relating to his great Lincolnshire fief. In one he grants a manor to his butler quit of service while he holds his office in the earl's court, and by the service of mewing a goshawk each year when he leaves the earl's court as a free man, with sake, soke, toll, team, and infangenetheof, and as freely as any of the earl's barons of Lindsey hold their lands.[2] The butler's office was always regarded as one of dignity. His colleague the cook is generally felt to be of humbler status. But he too could receive a grant of infangenetheof from the earl of Chester.

'Rannulf earl of Chester greets his constables, stewards, barons, castellans, justices, sheriffs, ministers, and bailiffs and all his men, French and English. Know that I have rendered to Wimund son of Herbert the cook all his father's land, and his office in my kitchen, that he may be cook there, with other matters, as his right and inheritance. Wherefore I will and command that Wimund and his heirs have the aforesaid tenure and right of me and my heirs in the kitchen and without (and the land) of Little Minting, in wood and plain, in meadows and pastures and in all other places, as well and freely as ever his father best had them, with sake and soke and toll and team and infangenetheof, and with all other customs and liberties.'[3]

This series of grants shows at least that infangenetheof was not the exclusive prerogative of wealth and rank. The earl of Chester grants this right impartially to a fellow earl, to the lord of a great castlery in the north, to a military tenant of no particular distinction, and to men who are serving him in the routine of his household. Of all these grants, that to Wimund the cook is certainly the most

[1] Ormerod, *History of Cheshire*, i. 659, from Sir Peter Leycester's *Antiquities of Cheshire*. I owe this reference to Professor Tait.

[2] F. M. Stenton, *Danelaw Charters*, 362–3.

[3] Add. MS. 35296, f. 411, one of a group of charters in the Spalding cartulary relating to Minting Priory (Appendix, No. 24).

remarkable. He obviously served in person in the earl's kitchen, and his holding in Minting is probably represented by the 'two and a half bovates of Wimund the cook' which the earl afterwards gave to Minting Priory.[1] There was not much opportunity for the exercise of higher criminal justice on a property of this size. The real interest of the case lies in its illustration of the relations between the earl of Chester and the members of his household. He had something of the royal power of giving honour to whom he chose. The rights conveyed by a grant of infangenetheof belonged to most, if not all, of his barons of Lindsey or Cheshire. No one in his court of Lincoln or Chester would have doubted that he could give to one of his hereditary servants whatever distinction a man received from possession of these rights, and no one would be interested to ask whether he would ever use them. The earl's gift of infangenetheof to Wimund the cook is one of the cases in which a grant of this privilege is evidence of a man's standing in his lord's court rather than a delegation of a lord's rights of justice.

No other lord of Stephen's time has left so many charters to the present day as Rannulf earl of Chester, and no one else writes so consistently in the language of independent feudalism. Nevertheless, grants of land with sake and soke, toll, team, and infangenetheof have come down from many of the earl's contemporaries. These words occur in what must be one of the earliest extant records of an enfeoffment for military service by a lay baron, a charter by which, before the end of 1122, William Peverel of Dover gave land in Huntingdonshire and Shropshire to his seneschal for the service of half a knight.[2] In Stephen's reign they were used by Gilbert de Gant, afterwards earl of Lincoln, when he confirmed to Seier de Arcelles, one of the English leaders in the crusade of 1147, his inheritance of Lusby in Lincolnshire for a knight's service.[3] Judicial rights could be granted in these terms

---

[1] *Mon. Ang.* vii. 1024.
[2] See below, 155–6 and Appendix, No. 29.
[3] Bardney Cartulary; Cott. Vesp. E. xx, f. 120 (Appendix, No. 25).

by lords of less than the highest feudal rank; as when
Richard Foliot, a tenant of Humfrey de Bohun, allowed
them to Maurice son of Robert fitz Harding in relation
to a group of Gloucestershire manors, soon after 1150.[1] A
little later, the ancient phrase occurs again in the following
charter, which shows the wide distribution of the estates
of an important mesne tenant as well as the rights which
he possessed over them. Like many of these early charters
of enfeoffment, it is only known through a late and imperfect copy.[2]

'Walter de Aincurt to all, &c. Know that I have restored to
Eliseus de Fanecurt the whole land which Gerard de Fanecurt, his
father, held of me, namely the fee of one knight in **Hickling** and
Kinoulton, and the fee of one knight in **Burnby**, and four carucates
of land in Scopwick and one carucate of land in Granby as half a
knight's fee in exchange for the land which he had in Timberland,
to hold to him and his heirs of me and my heirs, and as ever his
father best and most freely held of me in wood and plain, in fields,
in meadows, in waters, in mills, in ways, in paths, in all places, with
all free customs, with soke and sake and toll and team and infangenetheof.'

The date of this charter must fall between 1140 and
1166, and it probably belongs to the first part of this period.
The estate which it confirms amounted to no more than
two and a half knights' fees, but it lay in three counties.
One of the fees lay at Hickling and Kinoulton in south
Nottinghamshire, the other, at Burnby in the East Riding
of York, and although the half fee which the tenant received in exchange contained only five teamlands, one of
them lay at Granby in Nottinghamshire, and four at
Scopwick in Kesteven. This is a typical holding of an
honorial 'baron', and it is natural that it should be accompanied by a grant of infangenetheof. But the charter
shows that this privilege had been associated with the fee

---

[1] *Descriptive Catalogue of the Charters and Muniments . . . at Berkeley
Castle*, ed. I. H. Jeayes, 10, 11 (1892).

[2] Southwell Cathedral, Thurgarton Cartulary, f. 131 (Appendix, No.
26). The charter was known to Robert Thoroton, the seventeenth-century
historian of Nottinghamshire (see his *Antiquities of Nottinghamshire* (1677),
73), but does not seem ever to have been printed.

in a still earlier time. It is clear that Gerard de Fancourt, father of Eliseus, had possessed all the rights of jurisdiction which are here confirmed to his son. It can hardly be doubted that they had passed with the fee ever since the original grant to its first holder.[1]

It is rarely that charter evidence enables us to go beyond an indefinite statement of this kind. But the following charter, to which there can be few parallels, shows a non-military fee, at the moment of its creation subjected to the higher justice of its immediate lord.

'Hugh de Gurnai and Milesent his wife greet the bishop of Lincoln and the good men of Buckinghamshire, both clerk and lay, French and English. Know that we grant to Robert de Turri, my man, for his service, twenty *solidatae* of land at Bledlow, on which to dwell, namely the land which was Hemming's and that which was of Ailmer and Ailwin of Northgrave. And with this land we grant to the aforesaid Robert four pounds of pennies from my rent of Bledlow at four terms in the year, namely twenty shillings at Michaelmas, at the Purification of St. Mary, at Whitsuntide, and at the feast of St. Peter in Chains, until we shall give him four *libratae* of land. And we grant this to him and his heirs, to hold of me and my heirs, hereditarily, with sake and soke, and toll and team

---

1 The history of these lands shows the highly artificial character of this important military tenancy. In 1086 the land at Hickling and Kinoulton had been sokeland of the manor held by Walter de Aincurt, the first lord of the de Aincurt barony, at Granby. The land at Timberland, like the land at Scopwick given in part exchange for it, had been sokeland of Walter's manor of Branston, and that at Burnby had been sokeland of the royal manor of Pocklington. The whole Fancurt tenancy, apart from a single carucate at Granby, was made up out of scattered parcels of ancient sokeland. At some date, probably early, in the reign of Henry I the land at Burnby passed from the crown to the fee of the archbishop of York, of whom it was held in 1166 by Walter de Aincurt II, the grantor of this charter, as a mesne tenancy. In the *Carta* which he issued in this year as a tenant in chief Walter de Aincurt stated that 'Helias' de Fancurt held of him a knight's fee of the old enfeoffment, that is, the land at Hickling and Kinoulton, and half a fee of the new enfeoffment, namely the land at Granby and Scopwick. As Walter held Burnby, not of the king but of the archbishop, the fee held of him there by Eliseus is naturally not mentioned in his *Carta*. But the archbishop in his own *Carta* stated that Walter held two knights' fees of him of the old enfeoffment, and one of them was certainly the fee which Elias held of Walter in Burnby (*Red Book*, 380, 414).

and infangenetheof. We also grant to the said Robert and his heirs such customs and liberties as I have in that village, namely in woods, in plains, in pastures, in pannages, freely and quietly as regards me and my heirs, he giving to me (yearly) a sor sparrowhawk or two shillings.'[1]

This charter contains more than one feature which is remarkable in a document coming, like this, from the early part of the reign of Henry II. The address to the bishop of Lincoln and the good men of Buckinghamshire suggests that the charter was meant to be read at a meeting of the shire court, and there are few charters of this date which so clearly assume that the bishop will be present there. A yearly grant of four pounds of pennies from the revenues of a single manor illustrates the volume in which money circulated at the middle of the twelfth century. In its reference to baronial justice the charter agrees substantially with other documents of its kind. Here, at least, there is no doubt that the original grant of a fee was accompanied by a grant of infangenetheof over it. It is a remarkable fee with which this charter deals, consisting of no more than three small properties on which its lord may live and an annual gift of four pounds from his overlord. A grant of higher justice over this inchoate manor cannot have had much practical significance. But it shows that in the early years of Henry II powers of this kind would still be given, as a matter of course, to any tenant whose standing with his lord and his fellows was felt to justify the grant.

The results of this principle can be traced most clearly in the north of England, and above all in the greater franchises of this region, such as Richmondshire and the bishopric of Durham. Obscure as is the early history of these liberties, there is no doubt that in the twelfth century they included a very considerable number of fees to which the word barony was applied by contemporaries. No fewer than ten of these small baronies were in the hand of Bishop Hugh of Durham when he died in

[1] Ancient Deeds, C. 5895.

1196.[1] Their appearance in this number shows that the word carried as yet no sense of military or territorial power in the north. Later evidence proves, in fact, that in this country a barony meant little if anything more than a fee whose lord possessed the rights of sake and soke, toll, team, and infangenetheof.[2] The small baronies of Richmondshire and Durham, like those of the farther north and north-west, were certainly of diverse origin. Some of them represent estates of English thegns who had survived the Conquest and been secured in their possessions by their new overlords. Many families in northern England can be traced back to an ancestor of Old English name.[3] In such cases the rights of justice which caused a lord to be regarded as a baron and his fee as a barony presumably go back to pre-Conquest times. More often, no doubt, a northern barony of the twelfth or thirteenth century results from the bestowal of these rights on a foreign tenant, newly enfeoffed by bishop, earl, or king. In either case it was because of his position in the country or at his lord's court that a tenant received the rights which gave him baronial status.

It is very probable that a family connexion between an early tenant and his lord explains the appearance of some small fees over which a man of no particular importance has sake and soke, toll, team, and infangenetheof. Nothing

[1] Chancellor's Roll, 8 Richard I (Pipe Roll Soc., N.S., vii. 260–1).

[2] On these northern baronies see Miss Reid's article already quoted (above, 103–4, note 2) and Mr. J. E. A. Jolliffe's 'Northumbrian Institutions' (*Eng. Hist. Rev.* xli. 1–42). From among the baronies of the same type elsewhere in England there may be mentioned the Giffard barony of Fonthill in Wiltshire, and the Verdun barony of Alton in Staffordshire (*Red Book of the Exchequer*, 247 and 271), each of which was held for the service of a single knight.

[3] In view of their later importance the Nevilles of Raby are perhaps the most interesting of these families. Robert son of Meldred of Raby, who adopted his wife's surname of Neville in the thirteenth century, was son of Meldred son of Dolfin son of Uhtred. The names in this series are remarkable. Meldred, though an undoubted English compound name, is very rare, and apparently confined to Northumbria. Dolfin is one of many Scandinavian names which are well recorded in England but curiously rare in Scandinavia itself.

but the relationship indicated in the charter which follows will account for the grant of these rights to a tenant so far down in the scale of tenures as its recipient. The charter cannot be dated at all closely, but its extraordinary opening suggests a date not later than the first years of Henry II, and it may be upwards of a generation earlier. It relates to a village in Richmondshire, of which its grantor was one of the chief barons.

'Richard de Rullos greets all his men, French and English, present and future. O all ye who hear and see this, know that I grant to this Errald my *nepos* the carucate, formerly Godric's, in Skeeby, which I gave to Harsculf rufus for his service, with all appurtenances as Harsculf held it. And I grant that Errald may hold it of Robert son of Harsculf, to him and his heirs, saving my service, with sake and soke and toll and team and infangenetheof, with full liberty within the village and without, in water, in meadow, in pool, in mill, and in every pasture.'[1]

The wide phrases of this charter do not conceal the facts that the grant was small, and that two lords intervened between the tenant and the earl of Richmond, the chief lord of the fee. Errald is to hold of Robert, who holds of Richard, who holds of the earl. It seems plain that he owes the powers of justice which are here given him to the relationship—whatever its degree may have been—between him and Richard de Rullos, or rather that the relationship gave him a position within the honour which entitled him to such a grant. And many of his contemporaries may have gained similar powers in the same way, though the charters which might show the significant relationship have not been preserved.

Nevertheless, if they are regarded as a whole, the mesne tenants who in the twelfth century held their fees with sake and soke, toll, team, and infangenetheof appear as a body of very important men. There can be no doubt of their identity, as a class, with the honorial barons of twelfth-century charters. They were a miscellaneous class; for household duties, even more than the obligation of military service, brought a man into that direct personal

[1] Easby Cartulary, Egerton MS. 2827, f. 116 (Appendix, No. 27).

relationship with his lord which was the essence of a
baron's status. For various reasons it is hard to form an
adequate impression of the place of the honorial baron in
twelfth-century society. Before the end of the century
his powers of justice seem a mere obstacle to the establishment of a national system of administration under the
royal control. His lands appear in the records of the
Exchequer as nothing but groups of knights' fees from
which the king derived service or scutage. It is only
charter evidence which reveals anything material of his
position in the Norman time. The evidence is fragmentary,
and much of it is still unexplored. But it is already clear
that the honorial barons deserve recognition as an important element in the society which composed the Anglo-
Norman state.

They should, in particular, be remembered in any
attempt to answer what is perhaps the obscurest question
in Anglo-Norman history, the question of what really
happened at Salisbury on 1 August 1086. Few passages in
the *Anglo-Saxon Chronicle* are better known than that
which relates how King William 'came at Lammas to
Salisbury, and his council came to him there, and all the
landholding men of any account throughout England,
whosesoever men they were, and they all bowed to him and
became his men, and swore oaths of fealty to him that they
would be faithful to him against all other men'.[1] Here for
once it is unfortunate that the chronicler wrote in English.
Much discussion would have been saved if a contemporary
writer had set down the Latin equivalent of *ealle þa land
sittende men þe ahtes wæron ofer eall Engleland*. To
Florence of Worcester,[2] the first translator of this passage,
the 'land sittende men' were knights, who came with their
lords to Salisbury by the king's command in order to take

[1] Chronicle E, under 1085.

[2] Ed. Thorpe, ii. 19: 'Mandavit ut archiepiscopi episcopi abbates comites
barones vicecomites cum suis militibus . . . sibi occurrerent Searesbyriae;
quo cum venissent, milites eorum sibi fidelitatem contra omnes homines
jurare coegit.' There is no evidence that Florence, who died in 1118,
knew more about the meeting at Salisbury than he learned from a version
of the *Chronicle* closely resembling that which we possess.

the oath. But the language of the *Chronicle* is too in-definite for so precise a rendering, and in view of the modest position occupied by innumerable *milites* in Domesday Book we may doubt whether a contemporary annalist would have regarded an ordinary enfeoffed knight as a man of any account.[1] It must have been a very miscellaneous assemblage which appeared at Salisbury, but there is no doubt that to the chronicler its members were all men of some distinction.

The chronicler was only interested in the fact that a remarkable assembly came together to swear fealty and do homage to the king. He was not concerned with the precise condition of the individuals who appeared on that occasion. But his words begin to acquire a definite mean-ing when his landholding men of some account are brought into connexion with the honorial barons of Anglo-Norman society. If the *Chronicle* is read as meaning that King William at Salisbury exacted homage and an oath of fealty from all the barons of his tenants in chief, there is no longer any difficulty in taking this famous passage at its face value. An assembly for this purpose may have been without precedent, as indeed the chronicler's language implies, but it could easily have been brought together. The tenants on the great fief of William Peverel, who from this point of view were 'of any account', amounted at most to ten men, of whom one was also a household officer in the service of the king's half-brother, and another was himself a tenant in chief.[1] The oath of Salisbury was not exacted as a mere formality or for the purpose of display. There was good reason for the king to establish an immediate relationship between himself and every man of position in the kingdom.[2] He was on the point of leaving the country for a time. The king of France and the count of Flanders

---

[1] See below, 142–5.

[2] Although the situation in William's reign was much the more danger-ous, there is a real resemblance between the circumstances under which the oath of Salisbury was taken and the position in 1166, when Henry II, wishing to secure that all his barons' knights had done him fealty, ordered the famous 'Cartae' of that year to be made. On the motives which led Henry II to demand these returns see below, 137–8.

were hostile, and Edgar the Etheling, the heir of the Old English dynasty, was disaffected. The Scandinavian danger had been removed for the moment by the Danish rebellion which culminated in the murder of St. Cnut, three weeks before the gathering at Salisbury, but the events of the previous year had shown its reality. In this critical summer the king must have needed assurance of the loyalty, not only of his tenants in chief, but of the leading mesne tenants, men with military resources of their own, and the personal influence which birth and experience gave. It is to men of this kind that the chronicler's language most naturally refers. And the social custom of the time regarded such men as barons, 'whosesoever men they were'.

IV

THEGNS AND KNIGHTS

THERE is little need to emphasize the continuity of English rural society through the changes which followed the Norman Conquest. Its essential features, as they are revealed by Domesday Book and later records, are only intelligible in the light of Old English history. The Conquest did not obliterate the fundamental distinction between the rural economy of the Danelaw and that of Wessex and English Mercia.[1] Already before 1066 there had arisen in the south and west, and sporadically even in the northern Danelaw, the familiar form of social order by which the men of a village maintained their lord's household by rent or labour in return for his protection and for the justice done in his hall. In this village or that we may trace under its new rulers a tightening of seignorial control, a depression of the local peasantry. But in the south and west the French aristocracy of the eleventh century could ask for little more than Old English custom gave them, and in the Danelaw local conservatism prevented any general encroachment upon ancient liberties. To the author of the *Quadripartitus*, writing early in the reign of Henry I, the villeins of the society which he knew were the *ceorls* of whom he read in his books of Early English law.[2]

---

[1] F. M. Stenton, *The Danes in England* (Humphrey Milford, for the British Academy, 1927).

[2] This important identification comes out very clearly in the rubrics given in the *Quadripartitus* to passages in the laws which refer to men of this class, and in the Latin translations of the laws themselves. The *Quadripartitus*, for example, gives the rubric *si quis pugnet in domo villani* to the clause in Alfred's laws 'if any one fights in the house of a *cierlisc man*, let him make amends with six shillings to the *ceorl*', and translates by 'the oath of a *twelfhynd* man outweighs the oath of six *villani*' the passage in the tract on the oathworthiness of a thegn which reads *twelfhyndes mannes áð forstent vi ceorla áð*. References to these and other passages of the same kind are given by Liebermann, *Gesetze*, ii. 1, 234, under *Villanus*, and

The break came higher in the social scale. Nothing of all that happened after 1066 is more remarkable than the rapidity with which the thegnly class, all-important in the Confessor's day, became insignificant under the Norman kings. On the eve of the Conquest men of this rank had played an essential part in the maintenance of public order. They had administered law in the courts of shire and hundred, and as lords of what we can only call manors they had governed innumerable villages. They had been responsible for the military service, as for the other public burdens due by custom from the men of their estates,[1] and in addition to this responsibility they were themselves required to serve in the army when summoned by the king or their immediate lord. Twenty years after the Conquest, south at least of the Northumbrian border, they appear as anomalous survivals, outnumbered and wholly outweighed in local influence by members of a new aristocracy based on other principles. Many of them can only have been distinguished by their wergild of twelve hundred shillings from the higher ranks of the peasantry around them. Others derived consideration from some special service which they owed to the king. Some few of them were holding land of French lords by what later evidence shows to have been knight service. The class had, in fact, become disintegrated, and it was only in the farther north that the thegns of the eleventh century were able to preserve, for the complication of later law, the customs of land tenure characteristic of their order.[2]

other evidence pointing in the same direction is brought together by Liebermann in his Glossary under *Gemeinfrei* (*Gesetze*, ii. 2, 442).

[1] *Rectitudines Singularum Personarum*, 1. 'Thegenlagu is . . . thæt he threo thinc of his lande do: fyrdfæreld and burhbote and brycgeweorc.' The association of *fyrdfæreld* with *burhbot* and bridge work shows that the passage is not referring to the personal service of the thegn in war, but to his duty of seeing that the military service due from his property was done by its free inhabitants. On the passages in Domesday which refer to the thegn's military service see below, 119.

[2] Maitland, *Northumbrian Tenures* (*Collected Papers*, ii. 96–109); Reid, 'Barony and Thanage' (*Eng. Hist. Rev.* xxxv. 161–99); Jolliffe, 'Northumbrian Institutions' (ibid. xli. 1–42).

Few problems in Old English history are more obscure than the nature of the military responsibilities implied by thegnhood in the years immediately preceding the Norman Conquest. The few royal charters to private persons which have come down from Cnut and his three successors are unhelpful. Some of them expressly purport to be granted in return for service which an individual was already doing or had already done,[1] and none of them makes any precise stipulation for future service. Every land-book of this period contains, indeed, a clause implying that the land to which it relates is to bear the ancient burdens of fyrd service and the repair of bridges and borough defences. But fyrd service in such a context is plainly the duty of peasants, not of nobles. It was a territorial, not a personal obligation, and its apportionment was governed by custom.[2] The nature of this custom would be virtually unknown but for a single entry in Domesday Book which records that in Berkshire, if the king sent an army anywhere, only one *miles* went from every five hides of land, each of these five hides providing him with four shillings towards his food and payment for two months.[3] The

---

[1] Such, for example, as the grant of ten hides at Polehampton in Hampshire which Cnut made to Earl Godwine 'pro fideli obsequio quo michi fideliter obsecundatur' (*Cod. Dip.* 752). The phrase occurs with slight variations in earlier charters of this period, such as ibid. 692 by which Æthelred II grants land to the well-known Wulfric Spot, the founder of Burton Abbey, 'pro fidissimo quo mihi affabiliter obsecundatus est obsequio'.

[2] To borrow a convenient phrase from a twelfth-century charter, it may be said that the service owed by peasants to the fyrd before the Conquest 'went by hides and by hundreds' (*Danelaw Charters*, cxxvi).

[3] D.B. i. 56 b: 'Si rex mittebat alicubi exercitum, de quinque hidis tantum unus miles ibat, et ad eius victum vel stipendium de unaquaque hida dabantur ei iiii solidi ad duos menses. Hos vero denarios regi non mittebantur, sed militibus dabantur.' The sentence which immediately follows this passage and is sometimes taken in connexion with it—'Si quis in expeditionem summonitus non ibat totam terram suam erga regem forisfaciebat'—is shown by a comparison with entries in other local custumals to refer to the military service of the thegn, not that of the *ceorl*. See below, 119, note 1. But the whole character of the present passage shows that it is dealing with the service of peasants, and recording the traditional arrangements by which, in Berkshire, the rank and file of the fyrd had been brought

miles of this entry is clearly not a thegn, but one of a group of peasant landholders, whose responsibilities in regard to military service were determined by the amount of land which they held. Important as this passage is, it is dangerous material to use for the reconstruction of the Old English fyrd. The Berkshire hide was small,[1] and the country was one of the safest parts of England. During the Danish raids, early in the century, it was said that if the Danes ever reached 'Cwicchelmeshlæw', in the centre of the Berkshire Downs, they would never get to sea again.[2] It is unsafe to assume, as is often assumed, that in shires less happily placed the duty of serving in the fyrd was confined in practice to one man from every five hides. The passage is, in fact, chiefly valuable as proving that in the eleventh century the fyrd was still a true national levy. Of the conditions under which the peasants who answered this levy did their service we know little. There are passages in Domesday Book and elsewhere which

into the field and afterwards maintained. The use of *miles* for the selected peasant, which has sometimes led to a misunderstanding of this passage, does not offer any real difficulty. It so happens that one of the few passages in the Old English laws which refer to the peasant element in the fyrd shows that its members were mounted, at least when they left their villages for service. An isolated sentence in Æthelstan's laws (II Æthelstan 16) orders that every man in possession of a ploughland shall find two mounted men for this purpose. As the Berkshire custumal only demanded one *miles* from each five hides, there is no reason to suppose that the peasants sent from that country in 1066 would be less well provided for war than were their predecessors of the early tenth century. The men produced for service under this system must in many ways have resembled the lesser *cnihts* of contemporary society (on this class see below, 133–5) and it is not strange that the word *miles* should be applied to them.

[1] The evidence for a small hide is not so conclusive for Berkshire as for Wiltshire, but there is no doubt that the Berkshire hide approximated much more nearly to the 40-acre hide of Wiltshire (on which see Tait, *Eng. Hist. Rev.* xvii. 280–2) than to the 120-acre hide of the Midlands. The statement in the Domesday custumal of Malmesbury (D.B. i. 64 b) that when the king went on an expedition he either received twenty shillings from the borough or took one man with him *pro honore quinque hidarum*, is sometimes regarded as supporting the generalization of the Berkshire 'five-hide rule'. But it comes from the classical land of small hides.

[2] *Anglo-Saxon Chronicle, sub anno* 1006.

suggest that they would often serve under the lords of their village. But their obligation to service was of more ancient origin than manorial lordship itself.

The thegn's obligation was of no less ancient origin, but its basis was different. There is no doubt that in the eleventh century a king's thegn, when summoned to an expedition, must obey, under penalties which might amount to an entire forfeiture of his land. The same service was demanded from thegns who held of other lords than the king.[1] In either case, so far as we can see, the obligation was purely personal. There is nowhere any suggestion that a thegn's military service was due in respect of an estate which the king or any other lord has given him. It is a duty which follows from his rank, the expression of the traditions of an order which, as a class, represented the military companions of a lord, the *gesithas*, of ancient times. These traditions were still strong in the

[1] The essential information which we possess about the military responsibilities of the eleventh-century thegn is given by certain passages in Domesday Book. The most important of them occurs in a short custumal of Worcestershire (D.B. i. 172), and has often been quoted: 'Quando rex in hostem pergit si quis edictu eius vocatus remanserit, si ita liber homo est ut habeat socam suam et sacam et cum terra possit ire quo voluerit, de omni terra sua est in misericordia regis. Cuiuscunque vero alterius domini liber homo, si de hoste remanserit, et dominus eius pro eo alium hominem duxerit, xl solidos domino suo qui vocatus fuit emendabit. Quod si ex toto nullus pro eo abierit, ipse quidem domino suo xl solidos dabit; dominus autem eius totidem solidos regi emendabit.' It seems clear that the free man with sake and soke of this passage is a thegn, and that landowners of this class, whether they are the men of the king or of some other lord, will receive a personal summons when the king calls out his army. A shorter version of this information is given in a custumal of Berkshire (D.B. i. 56 b): 'Si quis in expeditionem summonitus non ibat, totam terram suam erga regem forisfaciebat. Quod si quis remanendi habens alium pro se mittere promitteret, et tamen qui mittendus erat remaneret, pro l solidis quietus erat dominus eius', and in the Oxfordshire survey (D.B. i. 154 b) there occurs the statement: 'Qui monitus ire in expeditionem non vadit, c solidos regi dabat.' These passages leave innumerable points of detail unexplained, but they agree in suggesting that there lay on the landed thegn of the eleventh century a military duty which was essentially a personal obligation to obey a royal summons, and entirely distinct from his responsibility for seeing that the free men upon his estate served in accordance with local custom.

century before the Norman Conquest. They are nowhere more clearly brought out than in the poem which relates the death of Byrhtnoth at Maldon in 991. The men who are most prominent in the poem are naturally the companions, the personal following of the earl, but they included landed Essex thegns and their close kinsmen.[1] The ideas which moved these men must have been common to the whole class from which they sprung. It is more than probable that many thegns of the eleventh century were country gentlemen, with no special aptitude for war. In most cases the estates of a thegn of 1066 must have come to him by inheritance, and not by the gift of a king or any other lord. But his obligation to military service represented the ancient duty of attending a lord in battle.

During the forty years which preceded the Norman Conquest a new element was incorporated into the English military aristocracy. The standing bodyguard of housecarles[2] which Cnut and his successors kept in their service is generally regarded from the standpoint of the king's household, where its essential duties lay. But many men who had served in this body received grants of land from the king, and ranked thenceforward among the landed thegns of their shires. It is impossible to estimate their numbers at all closely. Domesday Book, which is our chief source of information about them, was erratic in the manner of its reference to pre-Conquest landowners, and there is no doubt that it fails to indicate, as such, many housecarles who were lords of manors in 1066.[3] Even so, it shows that their number was considerable, and that

---

[1] See the note in *Crawford Charters*, 123, suggesting that Wulfstan son of Ceola, who guarded the bridge at Maldon according to the poem (lines 74–83), was father of the Essex landowner Leofwine son of Wulfstan whose will is printed in that volume.

[2] See Steenstrup, *Danelag*, iv. 150–4; L. M. Larson, *The King's Household in England before the Norman Conquest*, 152–66.

[3] For some reason the Domesday surveys of Hertfordshire and the neighbouring counties are particularly precise in the use of the term *huscarl*. The Buckinghamshire survey in particular shows that some landowners described elsewhere as thegns belonged to this class. See Round, *Victoria History of Buckinghamshire*, i. 219.

some of them had large estates. It also shows that other great lords beside the king kept a force of housecarles, and that some of these men might acquire land. A housecarle of Earl Leofwine held a manor at Willian in Hertford-shire,[1] and a housecarle of Earl Ælfgar, at Milton Bryant in Bedfordshire.[2] As a class these men certainly represent the retainers of Cnut and his leading followers. Even in 1066 nearly all the landowning housecarles mentioned in Domesday Book bore Danish names.[3] The settlement of such men began soon after the Danish Conquest, and more than one charter has been preserved in which Cnut appears as granting land to one of his housecarles. The clearest example is a charter of 1033, only known from a late copy, in which a certain Bovi receives an estate in Dorset from the king. It runs in the traditional form by which Cnut's predecessors had been accustomed to grant land to their thegns. In the body of the charter the king calls the grantee my faithful 'minister', the usual Latin rendering of the English 'thegn', and it is only a note, presumably derived from an endorsement, which describes him as the king's 'huskarle'.[4] From one point of view the local establishment of their retainers by Cnut and his succes-sors anticipates the enfeoffment of household knights by

---

[1] D.B. i. 140. [2] D.B. i. 213.

[3] e.g. Achi (ON. Áki); Alli (common in East Scandinavian); Anand (ON. Qnundr); Aschill (ON. Askell); Auti (common throughout Scandi-navia); Azor (ON. Qzurr) son of Toti (East Scandinavian); Brand (ON. Brandr); Gouti (ON. Gauti); Ingulf (ON. Ingólfr); Thori (common throughout Scandinavia); Tochi (ON. Tóki); Tovi (Old Danish Towi, Tufi, rare in ON.); Ulf (common throughout Scandinavia). Among the other names in this series, two (Golnil and Rotlesc) are obscure, Leuric represents OE. Leofric, and Burcard either OE. Burgheard or Old German Burcard. The Scandinavian element is strongly represented among the names of the ordinary king's thegns of 1066, even in the midland and southern shires. But the proportion of Scandinavian names among those of Domesday housecarles is far higher, and shows beyond question the northern extraction of most men of this class.

[4] *Codex Diplomaticus*, No. 1318. The note reads: *This ys ðæra vii hida landboc to Hortune the Cnut cining gebocode Bouige hys huskarle on ece yrfe.* The charter was taken by Kemble from the Sherborne Cartulary. A more famous housecarle of this period, though he does not happen to

Norman kings and barons after 1066. The essential
difference between these processes lies in the fact that a
housecarle who received an estate from his lord promised
no specific service in return for it. He may have been
expected to remain a member of his lord's bodyguard, but
to judge from all the evidence which we possess, his lands
were simply given to him in inheritance, without stipulation for service of any kind. Nevertheless, the housecarles
formed a distinctive element in eleventh-century English
society. Like the knighthood which superseded them,
they were specialized for war as was no other class. If
Harold had won the battle of Hastings, they would
certainly have played an important part in the history of
the following years. As it was, while thegnhood survived
for centuries in Northumbria, the housecarles were only
dimly remembered when Domesday Book was written.

Within a generation after the battle the Norman con-
querors had established in central and southern England,
and introduced into the region beyond Humber, a system
of military service which at every point ignored Old
English precedent. It is now nearly seventy years since
Round traced the history of English knight service back to
the unrecorded bargains by which the Conqueror fixed
the number of knights due for his service from each of his
greater followers.[1] The materials for the study of English

bear this title in any document of Cnut's reign, is Urki the founder of
Abbotsbury Abbey. He received an estate at Portesham adjoining Abbotsbury from Cnut in 1024 (*Cod. Dip.* iv, No. 741; *Ord. Survey Facsimiles*, ii,
Ilchester, ii), attests, as *minister*, Cnut's charter to Bovi, which has just
been quoted, and must have entered the personal service of Edward the
Confessor, who refers to him as 'Urk min huskarl' in a writ issued between
1053 and 1058 (*Cod. Dip.* iv. 871) and grants land to him as 'meo fideli
ministro' by a charter of 1044 (ibid. iv. 772). His name, though unique,
is certainly Scandinavian, and his wife bore the Danish name Tola (ibid.
iv. 841). He is best known as the founder of a gild at Abbotsbury, from
which has descended one of the few surviving sets of Old English gild
statutes (Thorpe, *Diplomaterium*, 605–8).

[1] In the articles entitled 'The Introduction of Knight-Service into
England' which appeared during 1891 and 1892 in the *English Historical
Review*, vols. vi and vii. They were reissued in *Feudal England* in
1895.

feudalism have greatly increased since 1891. Cartularies have been published, Domesday Book has been analysed, the outlines of the feudalism which the Normans knew in their own land have been established. This work has only confirmed Round's main position that the amount of knight service which King William demanded from his several tenants in chief bore no definite relation to the extent or value of their lands. It has also confirmed his more general argument that the feudal society which underlies English life in the centuries after the Conquest represents a definite break away from Old English tradition. The break, indeed, is far from absolute. The relationship between lord and man created by the tie of homage was common to the whole Germanic world. But the development of this relationship had been arrested in England, and only the most tentative of approaches had been made before the Conquest towards the great feudal principle of dependent tenure in return for definite service.

Here and there experiments which seem to tend in this direction have been noted by different scholars. In particular, evidence of a nascent feudalism in tenth-century England has been sought in the famous documents by which Bishop Oswald of Worcester granted out on leases for three lives[1] a considerable proportion of the ancient estates of his church in Worcestershire, Gloucestershire, and Warwickshire.[2] These leases, which in themselves give less information than many other documents of their

[1] The documents in this series which belong to Edgar's reign are printed in *Cart. Sax.* vol. iii, *passim*. The most recent edition of the leases which Oswald made between 975 and 991 is that of Kemble in vol. iii of the *Codex Diplomaticus*. The leases written in Old English were edited by Miss A. J. Robertson in her *Anglo-Saxon Charters* (1939).

[2] It is important to note that many of the estates with which Oswald dealt by lease lay outside the famous hundred of Oswaldslow, the court of which seems to have been in his hand, and in districts where he can have had no more influence than belonged in his time to any landowner of his rank. One at least of the estates was not even in the diocese of Worcester, namely the five hides of Golder in Pyrton, Oxfordshire, which he gave to his faithful man Leofward in 987 (*Cod. Dip.* 661).

class, become important when they are read in connexion
with a memorandum, addressed by the bishop to King
Edgar, and setting out the terms on which he has been
granting land to his men.[1] According to this memorandum
those who have taken land from the bishop were subject
to a great variety of duties.[2] They were bound 'to fulfil
the law of riding as riding men should', to pay whatever
was due to the church of Worcester, namely church-scot,
toll, payment for swine-pasture, and 'the other dues of
the church', and to swear that they would continue in
humble subjection to the bishop's commands. They were
also bound to apply themselves to supply the bishop's
needs, to lend horses, ride themselves, and apparently,
though here the bishop is obscure, to burn lime for the
work of the church[3] and for bridge-building. The memorandum goes on to state that they were to make the bishop's
deer-hedge when he wished to hunt, and it sums up their
relationship to their lord in the general statements that
they were liable to many other demands in the bishop's
name both in respect of the king's service and his own,
and that they were always to be subject to the bishop's

[1] *Cart. Sax.* 1136.

[2] These documents have become famous through the use which Maitland made of them in *Domesday Book and Beyond*, in the essay entitled
'England before the Conquest'. As a description of the terms on which a
great immunist of the tenth century could grant out his estates, Maitland's
discussion is a brilliant piece of historical reconstruction. But it is introduced as part of an argument intended to show that in Edgar's time the
greater English ecclesiastical lords were moving towards the organization
of their estates on feudal lines, and in following out this argument, Maitland attributed to Oswald a constructive policy which, to say the least, is
not suggested by his memorandum, and gave an unreal precision to the
vague language of the memorandum and the leases by his use of continental
and post-Conquest evidence for their illustration. The difference between
the indefiniteness of Oswald's leases and the precision of the twelfth-
century charter of enfeoffment represents a difference between the habits
of thought of two races, and to suggest, as Maitland suggested, that the
services described in the memorandum are all the more feudal because they
are miscellaneous and indefinite is to give to 'feudalism' so wide an extension that the word becomes almost meaningless.

[3] This was Maitland's suggestion (*Domesday Book and Beyond*, 306) for
'totum piramiticum opus aecclesiae calcis'.

lordship in respect of the loans which they had received from him and according to their amount. Failure to observe these conditions was to be punished by a money fine or by forfeiture of the holding, and on the expiry of the last of the three lives for which the lease was granted the bishop reserved the right of taking back the land into his own hand or of granting it out again. Whatever general interpretation may be given to this document, it is certainly a deliberate attempt to define the terms under which a great lord has been granting land to his men, and as such it is unique among Old English records.

But between these services and those which were imposed by enfeoffments of the eleventh and twelfth centuries there are two essential differences. The services for which Oswald stipulated were miscellaneous, and he left their exact nature vague. There is no trace in his memorandum of the feudal ideas that the services to be rendered for a tenement should admit of a close definition, and that if more than a single form of service is required from the same holding, the services with which it is associated should be of a cognate character. The services set out by Oswald form a very incoherent series of obligations. They range from hunting service to bridge-building, and at many points resemble the miscellaneous duties of the eleventh-century *geneat*, which are described in the *Rectitudines Singularum Personarum* as 'varying according to what is the rule on the estate'. It is more significant that Oswald made no attempt to define any of these duties. At every critical point in the memorandum its language shades off into vague assertions of general obligation. It is not the memorandum itself, but a comparison of it and other evidence, which shows that the famous 'law of riding' meant not military service, but the duty of escorting a lord from place to place.[1] This vagueness was due to the circumstances under which the memorandum was written. It was not intended as a precise formulation of rights and duties like a later feudal custumal. It was a retrospective document, drawn up to cover a number of grants already

[1] See below, 129–30.

made in still more general terms. Already before the earliest date at which it can have been composed, Oswald had been granting leases to his men,[1] and each of these leases must have been governed by its own set of implicit understandings. Oswald was clearly endeavouring to indicate in outline the relationship which he expected all who held loan-land of him to observe towards him and his church. A document written for such a purpose was not the place for exact definitions. But there can have been no real movement towards any conceptions which can properly be called feudal in a society where such a relationship needed to be clarified in such a way.

If, moreover, the opening words of the memorandum are read closely, they suggest that the bishop, far from attempting to extend his rights over his tenants, was afraid that they might take their lands altogether out of his obedience. He begins by expressing his gratitude to the king for granting a request he had made through Dunstan archbishop of Canterbury, Æthelwold bishop of Winchester, and the ealdorman Byrhtnoth. By the mediation of these men, he says, the king has received his complaint, and satisfied it according to the advice of his council, for the benefit of Oswald's church. Accordingly, with the king's leave, he and his three helpers have thought fit to state concisely how he has been endowing his faithful men with the lands subject to his authority, that his successors may know what to exact from them according to the covenants and promises they have made. In view of this preamble it is impossible to regard the text which follows as an arbitrary declaration of the bishop's rights over his tenants. There is clearly a plea in the background, in which the bishop has been the aggrieved party. He has brought his case before the king by the help of three

---

[1] This is clear from the language with which Oswald introduces his description of the services to be required by his successors from his tenants. It is unfortunate that the memorandum cannot be dated at all closely. The names which occur in it only show that it must have been written between the consecration of Æthelwold bishop of Winchester, in the winter of 963, and the death of Edgar in 975.

influential friends, and the memorandum which he has written by their advice was intended to secure the results of a decision in his favour. Beyond what may be inferred from the memorandum we know nothing about the incidents which were the cause of the bishop's *querela*, but its language leaves no doubt that some at least of his tenants had been refusing to observe the conditions under which, as he considered, they had taken land from him. The plea which lies behind the memorandum is, in fact, the first of a long series of suits caused by the vagueness of the pre-feudal relationship between free tenants and their lords. More than one of the great pleas of the Conqueror's time resulted in great part from these obscurities. When the Conqueror in a well-known writ commanded that those holding thegnlands which certainly ought to be held of the church of Ely should make agreement as best they could with the abbot, and that if they refused the lands should remain to the church,[1] he was dealing with a plea resembling in all essentials that of which Oswald's memorandum was the outcome.

It might be expected that a record drawn up under these conditions would say something definite about the military service due from the bishop's tenants. There can be no doubt that many of them were bound by their social position to serve in war. Most of the men to whom Oswald is known to have granted leases seem to have been thegns.[2]

---

[1] *Liber Eliensis*, ed. Stewart, 256.

[2] Most of these men are described by Oswald as *ministri*, and *minister* is the usual Latin rendering of *thegn* in charters of the tenth century. In *Cart. Sax.* 1181, 1207, and 1208 a lessee described as *minister* in the Latin body of the document appears as a thegn in an English note appended to it. A similar note added to *Cod. Dip.* 651 shows that a thegn could be covered by the still less definite word *fidelis*. Unfortunately, only a few of the leases have English additions of this kind. In a few documents written in English, e.g. *Cart. Sax.* 1233, the recipient of a grant appears as a *cniht* (for the position of the Old English *cniht* see below, 133–5), and a small group of leases were made to priests, e.g. *Cod. Dip.* 683, and to artisans, e.g. ibid. 678, one of the latest of all Oswald's grants. But as a whole, the persons who received these leases form a somewhat aristocratic body, differing essentially from the continental *ministeriales*, with whom Maitland was inclined to compare them (*Domesday Book and Beyond*, 313).

Two of them were his own brothers,[1] another was his *nepos*,[2] a fourth is more vaguely described as his kinsman,[3] a fifth is called *quidam inter primates huius regni nobilissimus*.[4] If need arose, such men would certainly be required to serve in the host with others of their class, and a passage in Hemming's cartulary which speaks of the *ductor exercitus episcopi ad servitium regis*[5] suggests that they would come under the command of an officer responsible to the bishop. It is therefore important to observe that neither the memorandum nor the leases which it helps to interpret ever imply that the bishop has given land to a tenant in order that he may do military service. The bishop no doubt expected his tenant to see that the men on the estate did the fyrd-service due by custom from its peasantry, but neither memorandum nor leases ever refer to the military service of the lessee as distinct from that of the peasants under him. If one of Oswald's tenants is of thegnly rank, he will serve because service is expected from a man of his class by a custom indistinguishable from law.[6] If he fails in this service, he must answer for it to the bishop, and the bishop to the king, but his service is a matter of personal duty, irrespective of the terms on which he has received land from his lord. None of all the documents which have come from Bishop Oswald offers any anticipation of the feudal principle by which a

[1] The Osulf of *Cart. Sax.* 1139 and 1204, and the Æthelstan of *Cod. Dip.* 623.

[2] The Ælfwine of *Cart. Sax.* 1205.

[3] This is the Gardulf to whom, as *cuidam consanguineo meo*, Oswald gave five hides at Lench in Worcestershire, *Cod. Dip.* 637. In connexion with Oswald's grants to his kinsfolk, there should be noted the lease of 966 by which Oswald granted to a woman named Ælfhild three hides at Hindlip in Worcestershire 'for the love of God and for our kinship' (*Cart. Sax.* 1180). Relationship of another kind between Oswald and one of his tenants is shown by ibid. 1182, which records a grant to a certain Eadric described by the bishop as his *compater*.

[4] *Cod. Dip.* 660.

[5] Ed. Hearne, i. 81.

[6] In the laws of Ine (*c*. 51) fyrd-service is required from the *gesith-cunð man*, even if he holds no land, though the penalty for his default is less than that exacted from the landowner of the same class.

man will take land from a lord in return for a definite amount
of military service to be rendered in respect of his tenure.

It is unlikely that the memorandum would ever have
been regarded as stipulating for military service had it not
been for its reference to the riding duties of the bishop's
tenants. In isolation a phrase like *omnis equitandi lex ab
eis impleatur quae ad equites pertinet* may well suggest the
duty of riding to the fyrd. But the phrase is immediately
followed in the memorandum by a statement that the
bishop's tenants are to pay in full whatever rightly belongs
to his church, and the payments mentioned obviously
represent, not public burdens, but ancient dues belonging
to the church of Worcester.[1] The real purpose of the
riding can, as it happens, be illustrated from a source little
later than the memorandum itself, and relating, like it, to
Edgar's reign. In the *Miracula Sancti Swithuni*, one of the
narratives which compose the work opens with an account of
an ealdorman, dear to King Edgar, setting out to inspect
an estate which the king has given him, 'attended by a large
mounted company, as is the custom among the Anglo-
Saxons'.[2] Whatever else the *lex equitandi* may have

[1] 'Ut omnis equitandi lex ab eis impleatur quae ad equites pertinet et
ut pleniter persolvant omnia quae ad jus ipsius aecclesiae juste competunt,
scilicet ea quae Anglice dicuntur ciric sceatt et toll, id est thelon' et tacc,
id est swin sceade, et caetera jura aecclesiae, nisi episcopus quid alicui
eorum perdonare voluerit.'

[2] *Miracula Metrica auctore Wulfstano monacho*, ed. Huber, 93:

> Consul erat quidam qua tempestate caducis
> Praepollens opibus regi dilectus eratque
> Eadgaro nimium. Multo comitatus equestre,
> Ut mos est Anglis Saxonibus, ire parabat
> Visere concessum regali munere vicum.

Ælfric's homily on Swithun gives what seems to be an independent
version of this story. It begins:

> Sumes þegnes cniht feoll færlice of his horse
> þæt him to-bærst se earm and se oðer sceanca
>
> .   .   .   .
>
> He wæs his hlaforde swyþe leof ærþan
> and se hlaford þa besargode swyðe þone cniht.

(Ælfric's *Lives of Saints*, Early English Text Society, i. 460.)

The description of the young mounted retainer as a *cniht* illustrates the
place of such men in tenth-century society, on which see below.

involved, its principal feature must have been the duty of escorting the bishop from place to place. Like every great lord he needed a retinue.[1] But neither he nor any other pre-Conquest lord ever seems to have made anything more than the vaguest of stipulations for this service when granting away a portion of demesne to a tenant. The times at which the tenant could be called upon and the limits between which he would be expected to ride are always left to custom or to an informal understanding between him and his lord. No lord before the Conquest ever approaches the precision with which his successors will define this and other like services. There is a fundamental difference between a statement that a tenant must fulfil the whole law of riding and a statement that he must ride with his lord or his lord's wife from Baseford to Ashby Magna.[2] And this new precision which governed relationships throughout the higher ranks of post-Conquest society is the most obvious illustration of the difference between the Old English social order and the feudalism which replaced it.

It is, in fact, something more than an illustration. The precise definition of service was a result of the feudal conception of society. English thegns of the eleventh century were familiar with the general idea of service rendered to a lord. They acknowledged the force of the tie of homage in binding a man to his lord, and admitted that failure in duty towards him might bring forfeiture on a defaulter. But

---

[1] For escort service in France and Norman England see below, 176–7.

[2] Historical MSS. Commission, *Report on the Manuscripts of Lord Middleton*, 11: 'Robertus filius Philippi omnibus amicis et hominibus suis tam futuris quam presentibus salutem. Certum sit vobis quod pater meus Philippus dedit et concessit Eustachio de Brocolvestou meo concessu quatuor bovatas terre . . . in feudo suo de Baseford in liberum conjugium cum sua filia, et etiam apud Magnam Essebiam unam virgatam terre . . . propter hominium suum et propter servicium suum, scilicet equitandi cum eo vel cum uxore sua de uno mansu ad alium mansum, scilicet de Baseford ad Essebiam.' W. H. Stevenson, who wrote this report, dated this charter *circa* 1175. But the arrangement which it records was already well established, and Philip of Baseford who made the original grant was son of Sasfrid, tenant at Baseford under William Peverel in 1086 (Farrer, *Honors and Knights' Fees,* i. 168).

they never came, in any effective degree, to the idea of the specialization of service. The social custom which they inherited allowed a man, even of thegnly rank, to engage himself in a remarkable variety of duties towards a lord from whom he took land. The rigidity of the Old English classification of society by wergilds meant that a free man's services bore little relation to his social condition. A thegn's place in society was secured by his wergild of twelve hundred shillings, irrespective of the duties which he might happen to owe to his lord. In this matter there is no indication that Old English society ever abandoned its traditional habit of mind. To the end it was little affected by contemporary movements on the Continent, of which the development of knighthood was the most significant, and the end, when it came, was catastrophic. Before the close of the eleventh century the conservative aristocracy of King Edward's time had been replaced, except in the far north, by a society organized essentially for war, in which the specialized knight was the central figure. To the men who introduced this society, the service of a knight was the most valuable return which could be made for a grant of land. But the specialization of a knight's duty must have reacted on the whole feudal conception of service. The idea that the service rendered for a holding should admit of a precise definition arose naturally in a society where the most important of all forms of service was the plain duty of attending a lord in war, mounted and equipped as a knight.

The French knights who followed the duke of Normandy in 1066 were not the first men of their class to appear in force in England. Castles of Norman type, implying garrisons of Norman knights, had arisen in England under Edward the Confessor, and a Norman military colony had been established in the earldom of Hereford, on the Welsh border.[1] Nevertheless, knighthood, in the technical sense, was alien to the whole character of Old English military tradition. Through her geographical isolation England

---

[1] See Round's essay on 'Normans under Edward the Confessor', *Feudal England*, 317–31.

had been unaffected by the forces which had created the trained cavalry of France and the adjacent states. The thegns and royal housecarles who formed the core of an English army in the eleventh century certainly used their horses in moving towards an engagement,[1] but they dismounted before action began. These conservative tactics gave no occasion for the training which produced the mounted knights of a feudal army. The essence of knighthood was the formal investiture with arms which marked the end of a youth's apprenticeship in a military household. It carried no implication of noble birth,[2] but it showed that a man had proved himself proficient in all that went to the art of fighting on horseback. The apprenticeship which preceded knighthood is the most significant fact in the organization of feudal society. The military class which it created possessed a solidarity which had never belonged to the Old English thegnhood. But it is easy to forget that the knighthood of the eleventh century was not in all respects the highly organized institution of the Angevin time, and that the rules about military tenure elaborated by the court of Henry II tell little about the conditions of the earlier period, when feudalism was still a matter of social custom rather than of law.

One curious anomaly comes at the very beginning of the history of knighthood in England. The application of the English word *cniht* to the French mounted soldiers who had formed the principal element in the Conqueror's army is very remarkable and stands in sharp contrast to the process which transformed *tunesmen* and *cotsetlas* into villeins and bordiers, and might easily have made *chevaler* an English word. The usage was not completely established in the Conqueror's own time. In 1083 any miscellaneous body of armed Frenchmen could be covered by the word *cnihtas*. The men thus described, who climbed to the upper floor of the abbey church of Glastonbury and

[1] On the mobility of the fyrd see Clapham, 'The Horsing of the Danes', *Eng. Hist. Rev.* xxv. 287–93, an article which gave a new starting-point for the history of the Danish wars of the ninth, tenth, and eleventh centuries.

[2] See below, 143–5.

shot arrows at the relics, were certainly not exclusively *chevalers*, knights in the technical sense of the word.[1] But the usage can be traced back into the generation of the Conquest. Already in 1088 the Old English chronicler writes of the *cnihtas* of Bishop Odo who formed part of the garrison of Tonbridge Castle.[2] Under the year 1094 he states that when Robert of Normandy took Argentan he captured Roger of Poitou, *and seofen hundred þes cynges cnihta mid him*, and knights in the Norman sense of the word are certainly included in the famous passage relating how three times a year there came to the Conqueror's court all the rich men in England, archbishops and bishops, abbots and earls, *þegnes and cnihtas*.[3] In any case the military significance of the word was well established by the beginning of the twelfth century, and its employment in this sense forms a most remarkable exception to the general prevalence of French social nomenclature in England. But it has a wider interest, for it affords a clue as to the way in which the native English population regarded the professional mounted soldiers of eleventh-century France. The class with which they were thus identified, the *cnihtas* of Old English texts, has received less than its due attention from modern students. It is rarely mentioned in the extant remains of Old English law. It is fortunate that numerous documents of the tenth and eleventh centuries refer to individual *cnihtas*, and give a general impression of the nature of the class to which they belonged.

They show, in particular, that the Old English *cniht*[4]

---

[1] *Anglo-Saxon Chronicle, sub anno* 1083.

[2] Ibid. *sub anno* 1087.

[3] *Sub anno* 1086. The two senses of the word meet in this passage. The Chronicler, writing as an Englishman, is describing an assembly composed almost entirely of Frenchmen, which had originally been organized on the English model and had never undergone a sudden transformation. His *cnihtas* no doubt include both knights in the strict sense and sergeants; and many of the latter must have been men of English birth, representing the lesser officers, the *cnihtas*, of the pre-Conquest royal household.

[4] For the use of *cniht* in Old English literature see the quotations in Bosworth-Toller, *Anglo-Saxon Dictionary*, and Supplement.

was essentially the retainer of some greater man. The cniht's place was in his lord's household or in attendance upon him as he rode about the country.[1] His service might well require him to fight by his lord's side. He was mounted and otherwise equipped for war. Ælfric abbot of Eynsham translates *portat miles gladium* by *byrð se cniht his swurd*. But his fighting was only an incidental part of his general duty to his lord, and the *cnihtas* of the tenth and eleventh centuries appear in our texts as servants rather than soldiers. In different Old English wills an ealdorman leaves five pounds to be divided between his *hired cnihtas*,[2] a bishop leaves forty pounds to the *cnihtas* whom his stewards know,[3] one wealthy lady leaves a 'band' of twenty mancusses of gold to four *cnihtas* whom she names,[4] and another leaves an estate between her chaplain, another named person, and the *cnihtas* who shall serve her best.[5] The connexion between the *cniht* and his lord's household is illustrated still more clearly by a comparison of two passages in the will of Æthelstan son of King Æthelred II. In the first he grants an estate at Chalton in south Hampshire to his father, except for the eight hides which he has granted to Ælfmaer his *cniht*; in the second he grants eight hides at Catherington to Ælfmaer his *discthegn*. As Catherington afterwards appears as part of the great manor of Chalton, it is evident that Ælfmaer the cniht and Ælfmaer the discthegn were identical.[6] It was natural that individual cnihts should receive land from their lords,[7] and more than one man of this class acquired property which must have given him an important place among the landed gentry of his shire. But the land in such cases was evidently a reward for past service, and it was only some special duty which drew the cniht permanently away from his lord's household. The gilds of cnihts which

---

[1] See the passage from Ælfric's homily on Swithun above, 129 and n.

[2] D. Whitelock, *Anglo-Saxon Wills*, 24.

[3] Ibid. 72.   [4] Ibid. 64.   [5] Ibid. 78.

[6] Ibid. 58, 60, and for the identification of the two Ælfmærs see Miss Whitelock's note, 170.

[7] More than one of Bishop Oswald's leases was made to a man of this class. See above, 127, n.

existed in Old English times at London, Winchester, and Canterbury are obscure bodies with a long history in which there was time for many changes to come over them.[1] But the name by which they were known becomes at least intelligible if the original cnihts who formed them are regarded as servants in charge of their lords' property in these towns. In any case there is no doubt that groups of cnihts could be settled on some outlying part of a great estate for its lord's convenience. Thurstan son of Wine, a great magnate in eastern England, leaves to his knights 'the wood at Ongar, apart from the park and the stud which I have there'.[2] In these cnihts we can safely see a group of hunt servants quartered by their master's park.

[1] The references to these bodies are collected in Gross's *Gild Merchant*, i. 183–8, but Gross hardly realized the peculiar difficulty presented by their name. Any satisfactory explanation of the name must take account of two facts—that the Old English word *cniht* meant a servant or minister, and that the members of the London *cnihtena gild* in the eleventh and early twelfth centuries were important persons. The simplest way of bringing these facts into intelligible relationship is to regard the original *cnihtas* who gave name to such gilds as the ministers of rural landowners, set in charge of their lords' burghal properties, and forming a link between their lords' upland estates and the borough market. There are many passages in late Old English charters which show burghal *hagae* attached to rural manors (e.g. *Cart. Sax.* 1040, Hereford; *Cod. Dip.* 705, Warwick; *Cod. Dip.* 1305, Cricklade), and it would be unsafe to lay much stress on the fact that no quite certain case of the kind seems to be found in documents earlier than the tenth century. The existence of a class of cnihts in one important ninth-century borough is proved by the attestation 'ego Æthelhelm et cniahta geoldan' (*sic*) to a charter of Æthelberht's reign relating to Canterbury (*Ordnance Survey Facsimiles*, i, Canterbury ix; *Cart. Sax.* 515), and whatever the meaning of the last word may be—it is mutilated in the manuscript—this passage makes it possible that associations of burghal *cnihts* similar to those which afterwards appear may have existed in the pre-Alfredian period. If the London *cnihtena gild* arose in this early period, and no town is so likely as London to have produced an ancient gild, there was abundant time for its character to change before the eleventh century when the first evidence of its existence occurs. Many factors in tenth-century history, especially the growth of English trade in this period, must have made for the development of cnihts' gilds from associations of other men's ministers into groups of independent merchants such as the first recorded members of the *cnihtena gild* of London.

[2] Whitelock, *Anglo-Saxon Wills*, 82, 'ic an mine cnihtes þat wude at Aungre buten þat derhage and þat stod þe ic þer habbe'.

Similar groups of cnihts probably lie behind the numerous place-names which contain an Old English *cnihta tun*. Most of them occur in the south and west, where estates were highly organized,[1] and the fact that settlements of this kind could give rise to place-names shows that they were exceptional. But there can be no doubt that the *cniht* with whom the English of the eleventh century identified the Norman *chevaler* was a retainer attached to the personal service of a nobleman.

The identification deserves to be taken seriously, for it represents the popular impression created by the knighthood of the Conquest. To the modern student, whose interest in early feudalism generally centres around the origin of knights' fees, there is something incongruous in the conception of a knight as a household retainer. Nevertheless, the conception agrees with various facts in the later history of knight service which should not be dismissed as mere anomalies, and it is certainly supported by the little that is known of the baronial retinues of the eleventh century. Many factors have combined to mask the personal character of the original relationship between a knight and his lord. In most parts of England subinfeudation had gone far before the Conqueror died, and the outlines of the feudal geography of England were drawn before the end of the next generation. The oldest records which we possess are far more closely concerned with the territorial units known as knights' fees than with the character of the service due from them. Before the end of the twelfth century the institution of scutage was beginning to give an air of unreality to the whole system of tenure by military service, and the king's court had imposed its jurisprudence upon feudal

[1] Of the seventeen Knightons mentioned in Bartholomew's *Gazetteer* (1887), none occur to the east of a line drawn due north from Portsmouth. Knighton outside Leicester is the most easterly of them. It is significant that only one of these places, Knighton in Radnorshire, is entered as an independent parish. Modern parishes are, of course, no certain guide to ancient arrangements, but the ecclesiastical dependence of nearly all the numerous Knightons suggests very strongly that they arose as settlements within pre-existing estates.

society. The rapidity with which feudalism became rooted in the soil means that there is little material to illustrate the conditions of the time when the tenant in chief brought the knights of his household to the king's service.[1]

Nevertheless, even a century after the Conquest, there were important barons who had not made full provision by enfeoffments for the military service which they owed to the king. In 1166 Henry II ordered his tenants in chief to tell him the names of the knights holding of them in virtue of enfeoffments made before the death of Henry I,[2] and the number of fees which each held, the names of those who held by later enfeoffments,[3] and the number of their fees, and the amount of knight-service to the king for which the tenant in chief had made no provision by the creation of knights' fees.[4] Whatever may have been the motive behind this demand,[5] it was obeyed by most of

[1] There is so little evidence to illustrate the personal service of the knight in the years immediately following the Conquest that a rarely quoted passage from the *Historia Monasterii Selebiensis* (*Coucher Book of Selby*, ed. Fowler, i [14]) deserves quotation. 'Contigit autem eodem tempore ut vicecomes Eboracensis Hugo scilicet, filius Baldrici, iuxta Selebeiam euectus nauigio pertransiret. . . . comitabatur autem eum non modica militiae multitudo, quia bellicae classis immanitate perdurante, non adhuc perfectae pacis tranquillitas ab armis et acie militem absoluerat.' As Hugh, though an important landowner in Yorkshire, was Sheriff of York, the men of other lords no doubt formed part of the *militiae multitudo* which attended him. But the passage illustrates the part played by retinues of knights in the establishment of Norman rule in England, and progresses of this kind were certainly not confined to the North in the early years of William's reign.

[2] Knights, that is, of the 'old enfeoffment'.

[3] Knights of the 'new enfeoffment'.

[4] 'Quot feoda militum sint super dominium uniuscujusque', as the archbishop of York expresses it (*Red Book of the Exchequer*, i. 412).

[5] On this see Doris M. Stenton, *Cambridge Medieval History*, v. 590. In his discussion of the *Cartae* (*Feudal England*, 236–46), Round argued that the king's purpose in demanding them was mainly financial, and that he wished to use them as the basis of a new and heavier feudal assessment. This is probable in itself, and there is evidence that in the following years the Exchequer in the light of these returns was endeavouring to take scutage in respect of the knights whom tenants in chief had enfeoffed in excess of their *debita*. But Round virtually ignored an important passage

those to whom it was addressed. The *Cartae Baronum* of this year[1] reveal for the first time the personnel of the higher English feudalism, and thenceforward the descent of fees can be traced, on the whole with singular certainty, down to the time when knight-service had become essentially a matter of finance. The number and the interest of the materials which illustrate the territorial side of feudalism in England have to some extent been allowed to obscure its personal aspect. The *Cartae* of 1166 show that the establishment of knight-service upon a territorial basis belongs in the main to the time before the death of Henry I. On most honours the fees of the 'new enfeoff-ment' form an insignificant addition to those which had been created before 1135, and on many honours no new fees had been created since that date. But the *Cartae* also prove that a large amount of the knight-service which the king could claim from his barons was still chargeable to the demesnes of individual tenants in chief. In particular, whatever the reason may have been, the process of sub-infeudation seems to have been proceeded much more slowly in the northern Danelaw than elsewhere.[2] Among

in the *Carta* of the archbishop of York which, after reciting the terms of the king's writ ordering him to return the number of his enfeoffed knights, reads, 'Omnium illorum nomina . . . sint in illo brevi scripta, quia vultis quod si aliqui ibi sunt qui vobis nondum fecerunt ligantiam et quorum nomina non sunt scripta in rotulo vestro quod infra dominicam primam quadra-gesime ligantiam vobis faciant'. This is the only direct evidence which we possess as to the king's object in demanding the *Cartae*, and it suggests very strongly that a political purpose lay behind the demand. The king was about to leave England for a considerable time, and it was natural that he should wish to assure himself that the knights enfeoffed by his tenants in chief had done allegiance to him before his departure. It would seem from the archbishop's language that the names of knights who had done alle-giance in the past were entered on a roll kept, presumably, at the Ex-chequer, with which the names of knights sent in by their lords could be compared. Unfortunately, no trace of this roll has yet been discovered.

[1] On which see above, 11.

[2] In Yorkshire innumerable estates suffered so heavily in the devastation of 1070 that it was long before they could support mesne tenancies, but in many of the less wasted parts of this county there had been remarkably little subinfeudation by 1086. Only one tenant, for example, had been enfeoffed on all the great fee which Roger de Busli held in the extreme

the barons of this region Walter de Aincurt, who owed forty knights to the king, returned a balance of eleven knights *super dominium*.[1] On the fee of Roger de Burun, from which ten knights were due, provision had only been made for six.[2] On that of Hubert fitz Ralf, who owed thirty knights, only twenty knights' fees had been created before the death of Henry I, and the solitary holding of two and a half knights' fees created *de novo feoffamento* on this honour formed a marriage portion for the sister of the tenant in chief.[3] Richard de Haia, with a *servicium debitum* of twenty knights, was himself responsible for the provision of five,[4] and Lambert de Scoteni, from whose small honour ten knights were due, provided only half of them through enfeoffment.[5] Robert fitz Hugh of Tattershall owed a *servicium debitum* of twenty-five knights, but only twelve and a half fees had been created on his honour before 1135, and only one and a half were added in the following twenty years.[6] Cases like these appear exceptional if England is regarded as a whole. Many tenants in chief had created more knights' fees than were required for the performance of their *servicia debita*, and many others had made an exact provision for this service. The interest of such returns as those of Walter de Aincurt and Robert fitz Hugh lies in the light which they throw on the organization of feudal service in the generations immediately following the Conquest, when a baron who had not created fees for all the knights due from his honour must make up the balance of his contingent with the knights of his own household.

south of the county near his castle of Tickhill, though he had created many tenancies on his adjacent fee in Nottinghamshire. Compare D.B. i. 319–20 with i. 284 b–285 b. Devastation, moreover, will not account for the under-enfeoffment which distinguishes many of the Lincolnshire honours, and it seems probable that in this part of England, peculiarly exposed as it was to Danish attack, many lords deliberately kept the knights at their disposal ready for instant service in their own households.

[1] *Red Book of the Exchequer*, i. 380–1.   [2] Ibid. 342.
[3] Ibid. 343–4.   [4] Ibid. 390–1.   [5] Ibid. 385–6.
[6] Ibid. 388–90. The *servitia debita* of these and other fees as reconstructed by Round are given in *Feudal England*, 253–6.

The household knight is an elusive person. As he held no land, he naturally does not appear in the records from which our knowledge of feudal organization is mainly drawn. Now and then a twelfth-century charter will mention the name of a knight in a context which is suggestive if not conclusive. When, for example, Hugh de Beauchamp of Eaton Socon granted land to St. Neots Priory 'for the soul of my knight Osbern de Meisil who has served me faithfully',[1] he was evidently thinking of a relationship between himself and his knight much more intimate than the ordinary connexion between a baron and his tenant. But the history of Hugh's barony is obscure, and Osbern may possibly have held land of his fee, although it cannot now be traced.[2] Here, as in many other twelfth-century charters, though the presence of a household knight may be suspected, it cannot be said that it is proved.

Now and then individual members of this class appear in the course of some historical narrative. The knight William whose settlement in the wilderness gave rise to the first abbey of Lanthony is described as belonging to the house and *familia* of Hugh de Lacy.[3] An incidental reference in the *Historia Fundationis* of Byland Abbey illustrates the position of such men more clearly. The little community of Cistercian monks from which the later abbey grew was originally established at Hood Grange near Byland under the patronage of the youthful Roger de Mowbray and Gundreda his mother. It quickly outgrew its quarters, and in a passage relating to the year 1144 the historian gives the reason for its expansion:[4]

'Certain veteran knights of good service belonging to the court and household of the lord Roger became lay brethren, and brought with them no small part of their worldly goods, with the help of which a grange was built at Wildon. Among these knights were

---

[1] Cott. Faust. A. v, f. 81.

[2] He does not, however, occur in Dr. G. H. Fowler's account of the Beauchamps of Eaton Socon in *Publications of the Bedfordshire Historical Record Society*, vol. ii, nor in the third volume of Farrer's *Honors and Knights' Fees*, which contains an account of the fees comprising this honour in so far as they once belonged to the fief of Eudo 'Dapifer'.

[3] *Mon. Ang.* vi. 129.   [4] Ibid. v. 350.

two of great reputation and discretion, namely Landric de Agys and Henry de Wasprey, and a third of equal discretion named Henry Bugge, guardian of the fabric of the abbey, who acquired much property for the house in course of time. For immediately after their entry it became known all over the country side that the new house had within a short time been wonderfully supported by noble gentlemen, and so the devotion of all hearing this turned to the aforesaid place.'

These sentences are interesting for their bearing upon the early history of what became an eminent monastery. They have a wider interest, for they form one of the few passages which refer unequivocally to the knightly retinue of a great Anglo-Norman baron. The knights who are mentioned here, men of good birth and high reputation, were not landholders. Their duty was to attend their lord in his court and household. They had obviously been the retainers of Nigel de Albini, the father of Roger de Mowbray, in the days of Henry I, and their presence in the *familia* of his son is particularly interesting when the history of his fee is considered. In 1166 the knights of Roger de Mowbray told Henry II that their lord had possessed eighty-eight *milites feodatos* before the death of Henry I.[1] Yet despite the number of Nigel's infeudations, a knightly element still survived in his household. Exceptional circumstances may well have contributed to its survival. The centre of the Mowbray fee lay in the north, and a baron whose chief seat was Thirsk Castle would naturally wish to have a force of knights ready in his court for immediate service against the Scots. But there is evidence of a different character which implies that the household knight was a normal member of feudal society in the early years of Stephen's reign.

A little before or after the death of Henry I a clerk in the diocese of Coventry wrote the law-book now commonly

---

[1] *Red Book of the Exchequer*, i. 418–20: 'Tot habuit milites feodatos in tempore Henrici regis, scilicet quater viginti et viii, scilicet lx de antiquo feodo. Et xx et viii istorum feodavit Nigellus de Albeneio de dominio suo.' According to Round (*Feudal England*, 253) the *servitium debitum* of the Mowbray fee was sixty knights.

known as the *Leges Eadwardi Confessoris*.[1] His work does not rank high among Anglo-Norman legal texts. He has been convicted of many errors in matters of fact, and his antiquarian tendencies do not inspire confidence. Nevertheless, he has preserved some historical traditions of great value, and his direct statements as to the law of his own time deserve respect. In particular his account of the system of frankpledge is of unusual interest.

'Moreover barons may have their knights and their own sergeants, namely stewards, butlers, chamberlains, cooks, and bakers under their own frankpledge, and they may have their esquires and their other sergeants under their frankpledge. So that if they do wrong, and the complaint of their neighbours arises against them, (their lords) shall have them to right in their courts, if they have sake and soke and toll and team and infangenetheof. . . . And those who do not possess these rights shall do right before the king's justice in the hundred or in wapentake or shire courts.'[2]

This passage is really an expansion, with reference to contemporary society, of the single sentence in which, a century previously, Cnut had ordered that every lord should be surety for his own household men.[3] Nevertheless, it should not be dismissed as mere antiquarianism. There is nothing incongruous in this picture of barons responsible for the conduct of their knights and of knights who must produce their esquires if right is sought from them. It is, in fact, strictly applicable to the early phase of feudal society in which the knights and household officers of a great man stood alike under his immediate, personal authority. There are few texts which illustrate this aspect of feudal life, but there is no reason for doubting its reality.

For although knighthood in the eleventh century implied military proficiency, it carried no social distinction.[4]

---

[1] For the date see Liebermann, *Über die Leges Eadwardi Confessoris* (Halle, 1896), 14–16.

[2] *Leges*, cc. 21, 21. 1, 21. 5.

[3] c. II Cnut 31. *Haebbe aelc hlaford his hiredmen on his agenum borge.* The passage was taken into Cnut's laws from I Æthelred 1. 10.

[4] It is suggestive that the word *miles* is rarely added as a mark of distinction to the names of individuals granting or attesting charters of the twelfth

Domesday Book was not concerned with the organization of baronial households, and the knights to whom it refers in innumerable passages are with hardly an exception knights who have already received land from their lords. Nevertheless, even from Domesday Book it is clear that the *milites* of the Conqueror's time formed a miscellaneous class. They included men of high social position, from whom important feudal families would descend. But they also included men of a very inferior condition, whose holdings were small, and whose names were not thought worth the recording. 'Goisfridus de Traillgi tenet de episcopo Constantiensi Giveldene. . . . In dominio sunt iii carrucae, et villani habent xi carrucas. Ibi xvii villani et unus miles et xii bordarii et i servus.' 'Goisfridus tenet Torlei. . . . Ibi v villani, et quodam milite et cum presbitero et ix bordariis habent iii carrucas et dimidiam.'[1] The *milites* of these passages have doubtless been treated hardly by the Domesday clerks, but it is evident, to say the least, that they were men of little social consequence. They represent, in fact, a large number of knights who were only distinguished from the rank and file of a baronial retinue by their skill in fighting on horseback and their possession of the simple equipment which the tactics of their time demanded. Men of this class always formed the bulk of the mercenary armies of the eleventh century. Knights *mediae nobilitatis atque gregarii* had formed an essential part of the army of Hastings.[2] They were dangerous servants,

century. In the course of the thirteenth century it becomes customary for the principal lay witnesses of a charter to be distinguished as *milites*, and to many clerks of this age knighthood entitled a witness to the prefix *dominus* in front of his name. But by this time knighthood had acquired a new legal and social significance.

[1] D.B. i. 210, 140. Giveldene is Yelden in Bedfordshire, which afterwards appears as the head of the Trailli fee. For the motte and bailey castle there see below, 199. Torlei is Thorley in Herts., held by Geoffrey de Mandeville.

[2] William of Poitiers, *Gesta Willelmi Ducis*, ed. Giles, 146. William's language throughout this work shows that to him the mere fact of knighthood gave a man no social distinction. As Spatz observes (*Die Schlacht von Hastings*, 27), 'Die Ritter Wilhelms können wir uns nicht roh und ungeschlacht genug vorstellen.'

and the Conqueror had disbanded his own mercenary army as soon as it had done its work.[1] But it was long before he or his barons could feel secure in England. It was only when the danger of an English rebellion was over, when the kings of Cnut's house had accepted the inevitable, and the eldest line of king William's own descendants was extinct, that the military retinues of the baronage ceased to be an essential factor in the defence of the land.

The conditions of this early time are reflected clearly enough in Domesday Book. There is no mistaking the significance of the small military tenancies which often appear in the immediate neighbourhood of a great baronial estate. The five *milites* who held fifty-eight acres worth twenty shillings in Hamo the Steward's Essex manor of Toppesfield[2] illustrate an early and interesting phase in the process of subinfeudation. They are obviously household knights who have been provided with small holdings around their lord's residence. They were available for immediate service if need arose, but to some extent, at least, they could thenceforward live of their own. Similar groups of tenants are found at many places where the residence of a great French lord is proved by the earthworks of an early Norman castle.[3] These tenants are not always described as *milites*. At Castle Bytham, for example, where a motte-and-bailey castle became the head of the Aumale fee in Kesteven, they are called *Francigenae*—a vague word, which will cover sergeants and household officers as well as knights and their squires.[4] The vague-

[1] Op. cit. 150; Ordericus Vitalis, *Historia Ecclesiastica*, ed. le Prevost, i. 199.   [2] D.B. ii. 55 b.

[3] The significance of these tenancies was continually emphasized by Round, notably in his article 'The Origin of Belvoir Castle', *Eng. Hist. Rev.* xxii. 508–10.

[4] D.B. i. 360 b: 'In West Bitham habuit Morcar ix carrucatas ad geldum. . . . Ibi habet Drogo (de Beurere) iii carrucas in dominio et xxiiii sochemannos de medietate huius terre et vii villanos cum viii carrucis. Ibi vii francigene habent ii carrucas et iii fabricas ferri de xl solidis et viii denariis.' This group of 'Francigenae' closely resembles the group of similar tenants at Bottesford in Leicestershire from which Round, in the article just quoted, inferred the existence of Belvoir Castle. Belvoir Priory was founded in the eleventh century, and the earliest document which relates

ness of Domesday Book only reflects the indefiniteness of
the social class to which the early Norman *miles* belonged.
His arms and armour were as yet by no means elaborate.[1]
Even a century after the Conquest, any well-to-do landholder was expected to possess the shield and helmet,
hauberk and lance, which formed a knight's essential
equipment.[2] His social position depended upon his birth
and reputation, but most of all, perhaps, upon the nature
of his relations with his lord. There was a fundamental
difference between the knight of gentle ancestry, his
lord's companion, perhaps his kinsman,[3] and the tutor of
youths under his guardianship, and the mere retainer,
hired for the king's service or for the defence of his lord's
castle or hall. In the end the higher conception of the
knight prevailed. In the perspective of English history the
landless knight only appears in times of crisis or confusion,
and is associated with feudal anarchy rather than feudal
order. But he had a respectable place of his own in
the life of the eleventh century, and it was of him that the
native English were thinking when they identified the
mounted soldier of Norman feudalism with the *cniht* of
Old English society.

A tradition to this effect still survived in the age of

to it refers expressly to the adjacent castle (*Mon. Ang.* iii. 288). If a religious
house had been founded near Castle Bytham in the Norman period, there
would probably be direct evidence for the existence of the castle in the
eleventh century.

[1] For the equipment of the knights in the army of Hastings the Bayeux
Tapestry is the fundamental authority. It can be studied most easily in the
edition published by the Phaidon Press in 1957.

[2] *Assize of Arms*, clause 1: 'Quicunque habet feodum unius militis
habeat loricam et cassidem, clypeum et lanceam.' Clause 2: 'Quicunque
vero liber laicus habuerit in catallo vel in redditu ad valentiam de xvi marcis
habeat loricam et cassidem et clypeum et lanceam.' Compare the Magna
Carta of Cheshire, c. 3: 'Unusquisque baronum dum opus fuerit in werra
plenarie faciat servicium tot feodorum militum quot tenet, et eorum
milites et libere tenentes loricas aut haubergella habeant et feoda sua per
corpora defendant licet milites non sint' (*Chartulary of Chester Abbey*, i.
103). Even in the earldom of Chester there seems no essential difference
between the equipment of the knight and the free tenant.

[3] A considerable proportion of the charters of enfeoffment which have
survived show a lord granting a fee to a younger son or a brother.

Henry II and Rannulf de Glanville. Early in the controversy between Archbishop Baldwin and the monks of Canterbury, Geoffrey the sub-prior of that church wrote a famous letter to the king, stating as part of his argument his conception of the origin of military tenure upon the estates of the metropolitan see. 'Now because there were not knights in England in King William's time, but "threngs", the king commanded that knights should be made of them for the defence of the land. Therefore Lanfranc made his "threngs" knights. The monks, however, did not do so, but from their portion (of the lands of their church) they gave two hundred *libratae* of land to the archbishop, so that he should defend their lands by his knights, and conduct all their business at the Roman *curia* at his own expense. Therefore there is still no knight on the whole of the monk's land but only on the land of the archbishop.'[1] The writer's history is bad, nor indeed can it be said that contemporary records support the story.[2] Most of the archbishop's tenants in 1086 were great men like Hamo the sheriff of Kent, Hugh de Montfort, and the count of Eu, and although the list includes a number of men bearing English names the amount of military service for which they were responsible was small. Nevertheless, it is hard to believe that the tale is a mere invention. We know nothing of the household knights of archbishop Lanfranc, as distinct from his tenants by military service, and no Kentish writer of the late twelfth century would of his own motion have used the word *dreng* for the predecessor of the Norman *miles*. The word is of Scandinavian origin,[3] and its currency in Kentish tradition, like the

---

[1] Somner, *A Treatise of Gavelkind*, ed. 2, appendix, 209, 210.

[2] The essential authorities are the section devoted in Domesday Book to the land of the archbishop's knights and the list of approximately 1096 headed *De militibus archiepiscopi* in the Domesday Monachorum of Christ Church, Canterbury. In the edition of this text by D. C. Douglas (London, 1944), the military tenures created by Lanfranc are used to illustrate the general subject of the introduction of knight-service into England.

[3] E. Björkman, *Scandinavian Loan-Words in Middle English*, part ii, p. 208. The original meaning of the old Norse *drengr* is 'young man'.

appearance of sokemen in the Kentish Domesday, points
to a Danish influence in this part of England of which
there is no direct record. The tradition should not be
rejected on this account. The *dreng* of the eleventh century
was the Scandinavian equivalent of the English *cniht*. He
was associated more closely than his English representative with the administration of his lord's estates,[1] but he
belonged to the same social class. The Kentish drengs of
Geoffrey's letter must have been servants of the archbishop, and Geoffrey may well be correct when he speaks
of their conversion into *milites*. We are certainly not entitled to deny the possibility that young Englishmen of
this type, in considerable number, may have undergone
the training, and acquired, if they did not already possess,
the equipment, which would entitle them to rank as
knights. Few of them can be identified in surviving records.
It is a mere chance that the writer of a very early Yorkshire charter, after setting down *Rodbertus filius Gamelli
et Rodbertus frater eius* in a list of witnesses, interlined
'clericus' above the first Rodbertus and 'miles' above the
second.[2] But some such process seems to lie behind the
few, but suggestive passages in Domesday Book which
refer to English *milites*[3]—in particular the curious entry
in the Middlesex survey which associates a single Englishman with a number of *Francigenae* in a group of tenants
described collectively as *milites probati*.[4] And according to

[1] On the 'drengages' of Northern England see Jolliffe, 'Northumbrian
Institutions', *Eng. Hist. Rev.* xli. 1. It is clear that drengage was essentially
a ministerial tenure.

[2] Hist. MSS. Comm. *Report on Hastings Manuscripts*, i. 165. The date
of this charter is 1101–8. The Scandinavian name Gamel (ON. *Gamall*) is
very common in pre-Conquest England and in the twelfth-century Danelaw, but seems to have fallen out of use in Normandy at an early date.

[3] As a rule we know nothing of the personal history of these English
knights, but in one case it is clear that the word *Anglus* should not be taken
literally. The Domesday description of the bishop of Salisbury's manor of
Potterne states that two 'Englishmen' were holding land there and that
one of them, a nephew of Herman, formerly bishop of Ramsbury, was 'a
knight by the King's command'. As Bishop Herman came from Lorraine,
his nephew cannot have been wholly English. D.B. i. 66.

[4] At Isleworth, Middlesex, under Walter de St. Valery. D.B. i. 130.

the Canterbury tradition, this process received the sanction of the highest authority in the land.

Nevertheless it was a process which might easily lead to trouble in the future. A contingent of English drengs, whatever their equipment may have been, cannot have fitted at all neatly into the organization of a feudal army in the eleventh century. It is, in fact, hard to avoid the conclusion that the drengs whom Lanfranc converted into knights were really the cause of the first, and one of the most famous of all controversies about knight-service in England. It cannot be a mere coincidence that eight years after Lanfranc's death the knights of the see of Canterbury proved highly unsatisfactory to William II in the Welsh expedition of 1097. The plea which the king brought against their lord on this account is familiar, for it forms a notable episode in the career of Archbishop Anselm, and is carefully described by his biographer.

'The king on his return from France sent disturbing letters to the archbishop, saying in them that he owed the archbishop the reverse of thanks for the knights whom he had sent to his host, for as was said, they were neither properly equipped nor were they suitable persons for warfare of that character, and he ordered that the archbishop should be ready to do right to him according to the judgment of his court whenever he should choose to implead him there.'[1]

The king was undoubtedly angry. William II was an expert in all that belonged to a knight's training and equipment. But we have no reason to think that he was judging Anselm's knights by an impossible standard. His language, as it is reported by Eadmer, is curiously precise and there is no reason to believe that he was trying to find ground for a charge against the archbishop. The facts of which he complained, that the archbishop's knights were unsuitable for an expedition like that of 1097, and that they were not properly equipped, deserve, at least, to be

---

[1] *Historia Novorum*, ed. M. Rule, 78. Cf. *Vita Anselmi*, ibid. 377: 'Rex a Gualis victor regressus, renovata ira propter milites quos, sicut falso a malignis dicebatur, male instructos in expeditionem Anselmus direxerat, contra ipsum turbatus est.'

taken seriously in view of the Canterbury tradition about Lanfranc's converted drengs.

It may seem strange that William the Conqueror should have been a party to such an arrangement. He was himself a knight, with all a knight's training and instincts, and he can have had no illusions as to the value of a body of Englishmen required to adopt the military methods of a foreign race. The truth is that he could not afford to neglect any means of providing knights for the defence of the land. For nearly twenty years after the battle of Hastings the chances were against the survival of the Anglo-Norman monarchy. The resources at the king's command were doubtless equal to the suppression of any purely English rising, but disaffected Englishmen were in touch with the courts of Swegn Estrithson and his sons, who had made the Danish kingdom a formidable power after a long period of eclipse. The danger of a Danish attack upon England has received less than its due of attention from historians because it never materialized on a scale comparable with the invasions of 1014 and 1066. Nevertheless, the appearance of two hundred Danish ships off the English coast in 1074[1] would have seemed remarkable if it had not been overshadowed by greater events in the immediate past, and ten years later, King Cnut of Denmark, in association with King Olaf of Norway and Count Robert of Flanders, planned an invasion which might well have changed the whole course of English history. The plan led to a catastrophe which seems to have convinced subsequent kings of Denmark that a direct attack on England was no longer practicable. The Danish fleet which had been brought together in the Limfjord dispersed while the king was absent in Schleswig, and the penalties imposed on defaulters caused a rebellion which ended in the king's murder. But the measures taken in England to meet this projected invasion show more clearly than any other evidence how inadequate were the military forces at the disposal of the king and his barons. 'When William king of England, who was then dwelling in

[1] *Anglo-Saxon Chronicle*, E, *sub anno* 1075; D, *sub anno* 1076.

Normandy... heard this, he passed over into England with such a force of horsemen and footmen from France and Brittany as had never sought this land before, so it was wondered how the land could feed all that army. But the king distributed the army among his men over all the land, and they fed the army, each according to the amount of his land.'¹ An independent tradition of these preparations is preserved in the life of St. Cnut written by Ægelnoth, a monk of Canterbury, who seems to have left England for Denmark in 1085, the year of the proposed invasion. He describes how William 'duke of the southern Northmen' surrounded castles with walls, ditches, and foreworks, repaired the walls of towns and set guards on them, and appointed persons to keep the sea ports. He then relates that William brought over an army of Frenchmen, Bretons, and Manceaus, which filled the houses of the English towns so that there was no room left for their inhabitants.²

---

¹ *Anglo-Saxon Chronicle, sub anno* 1085. It is interesting to note that the annal which records the distribution of the king's mercenaries among his tenants in chief passes almost immediately into the famous passage relating how the king held very deep speech with his council 'about this land, how it was settled, and with what men'. It is, in fact, highly probable that the difficulties which must have been found in carrying out this distribution formed one of the reasons for the taking of the Domesday Inquest in the following year. In 1085, although the king and his ministers may have known well enough what lands had been granted to each tenant in chief, they can have had little precise information as to the proportion of those lands which each baron had kept in his demesne, and without this knowledge it cannot have been easy to divide out a force of mercenaries among the king's barons according to the amount of their lands.

² *Ælnothi Historia Sancti Canuti Regis*, c. xii (Langebek, *Scriptores Rerum Danicarum*, iii. 349, 350): 'Rumore expeditionis eorum Brittanniam usque velificante, atque universum Anglorum orbem cursitando replente, Willelmus, arte tuitionis, utpote bellicosus heros, non imperitus, castra et oppida munire, muris et fossatis cum propugnaculis castella circumcingere, urbium muros renovare, et eis vigilantiam adhibere, diversosque ad portus nauticas custodias deputare, exercitu vero conducto tam a Gallis et Brittonibus, quam a Cenomannis aggregato, ita urbium aedes replebantur ut vix suis domestici focis assidere viderentur.' There is a touch of fiction in the words which follow to the effect that William ordered Englishmen to shave their beards and dress themselves like Normans for the deception of the Danes. But the passage as a whole certainly represents the account of William's preparations which came across to Denmark, and as the reference

In view of these passages there can be no doubt of the great size of the army brought over from France in 1085. It was the largest army remembered by a writer who had lived through the invasions of England by Harold Hardrada and William of Normandy. In a great emergency the knight-service due to the king from his tenants in chief was obviously unequal to the defence of the land.

to the Manceaus shows, it is independent of the source represented by the *Anglo-Saxon Chronicle*. The date of Ægelnoth's work cannot be fixed closely. It is dedicated to Nicholas I, king of Denmark, from 1105 to 1134, and there can be little doubt that it belongs to the earlier part of this period.

V

KNIGHTS' FEES AND THE KNIGHT'S SERVICE

THE direct evidence which we possess as to the place of the knight in Anglo-Norman society comes in the main from literary sources, which tell little as to the extent of his normal endowment in land or the nature of the service to be done in return for it. The essential materials for the study of these questions, as, indeed, for the whole history of military tenure in England, are the charters which explicitly record enfeoffments for knight service. The series begins in the reign of the Conqueror himself, and is continued by a gradually increasing succession of documents down to the period when feudal history can be illustrated from the abundant national records of the thirteenth century. As sources of historical information, these charters have many defects. By the beginning of the reign of Henry II they have already assumed a stereotyped form.[1] Even at an earlier time, their writers seem preoccupied by the wish to find the shortest possible expression for the facts which they were attempting to record, and few of them allow themselves the freedom of the letter, from which, in the last resort, the charter of enfeoffment is derived. Nevertheless, any charter of enfeoffment written in the century which followed the Conquest is an important historical record. The extreme value of these charters for feudal genealogy has always been recognized, and it is from this standpoint that they have generally been studied in the past. But they also provide the best evidence now to be obtained as to the internal history of the honours of the Anglo-Norman period, and it is here that their chief interest lies. Almost alone, they connect the elementary arrangements intended to

[1] See below, 156–8.

secure the original Norman settlement with the elaborate organization of knight-service which prevailed under the early Angevin kings. And in this connexion even the recurrent formulas which give monotony to a long series of feudal charters become significant. For the words and phrases which found general acceptance in the age when feudal organization was in the making came by that very fact to influence the course of social history.

It is not remarkable that we possess very few contemporary records of enfeoffments made in the eleventh century. Few private charters of any kind have come down from this period, either in their original form or in later copies. Most of the earliest Anglo-Norman charters of which the text has survived are records of benefactions to religious houses, expressed in solemn and formal language and closely resembling contemporary French documents. The records of enfeoffment for military service characteristic of the twelfth century have a very different character. Essentially, they are writs rather than charters, addressed to the men and often also to the friends of the persons in whose names they run. Like the royal writs which they closely resemble in form, these documents were ultimately derived from Old English models. Informal writs in English, of a type which first appears under Æthelred II, were issued in considerable numbers by the Conqueror. Latin writs, obviously modelled on these Old English prototypes, had become the normal method of communication between the king and his subjects long before the Conqueror's death, and by the early twelfth century the king's greater tenants in chief were beginning to imitate the general style of his chancery. But it was not until the reign of Henry I was well advanced that documents of this form were at all commonly used to record grants of land for knight service, and it is highly probable that the earliest grants for this service were usually made without any written record by a lord in the presence of his leading tenants. In the last resort, the charter of enfeoffment was only a substitute for the memory of the peers of a fee. It would seem that the need for this substitute was only impressed, very gradually, on the lay baronage by the increasing complexity of tenures within their honours, and the disappearance of the knights who could give evidence as to the provisions of the original enfeoffments made by their predecessors.

Nevertheless, two records of enfeoffment made in the Conqueror's time have already been discovered and printed. One of them, of which there is no text earlier than the late thirteenth century, recites the conditions under which a certain Peter, a knight of King William, became the 'feudal man' of St. Edmund and Baldwin, abbot of his house.[1] It is an ill-drafted record, and at more than one crucial point its language suddenly becomes obscure. But it gives a valuable illustration of early feudal conditions, for in addition to other curious provisions it stipulates that Peter, when duly summoned on behalf of the king and the abbot, shall serve within the kingdom 'with three or four knights' at his own cost, and that he shall 'provide' a knight for the abbot's service within and without the kingdom when the abbot shall wish. If more records of this type had survived it would be unnecessary to argue back from later evidence as to the undistinguished, stipendiary knighthood of the Conqueror's reign. The second record, of which the original has been preserved, recites the terms by which Robert Losinga, bishop of Hereford, granted the manor of Holme Lacy to Roger de Lacy for the service of two knights, as Roger's father had held it.[2] The peculiar interest of this record, which is dated 1085, lies in its provision that if Roger shall die or become a monk the bishop may take the land again into the demesne of his church without hindrance from Roger's mother, wife, sons, brothers, or kin in general. It is no doubt dangerous to generalize from two isolated documents as to the general character of pre-Domesday enfeoffments for military service, but it is remarkable that

[1] D. C. Douglas, 'A Charter of Enfeoffment under William the Conqueror', *Eng. Hist. Rev.* xlii. 245–7.
[2] V. H. Galbraith, 'An Episcopal Land-Grant of 1085', ibid. xliv. 353–72, and facsimile.

each of these records conflicts with one of the most persistent features of tenure by knight-service as it was understood in the twelfth century. Already in Stephen's reign it seems to have been universally accepted that land held by this service should descend to the tenant's heirs, and that the amount, though not the conditions, of this service should be certain and definite. It is therefore interesting to see that in the two earliest English records of enfeoffment for knight-service, one leaves indefinite the number of knights whom the tenant must provide, and the other creates a life tenancy of the estate with which it deals. There could hardly be a clearer illustration of the danger of assuming that the conception of military tenure which prevailed under Henry II had existed ever since the introduction of this form of tenure into England after the Norman Conquest.

There can be no doubt that a general clarifying of feudal conceptions occurred in that time of rapid but obscure social development, the reign of Henry I. It is naturally reflected in the increasing precision shown by the feudal documents of this period, and in particular by those which record grants of land for knight-service. The following charter, which has already been quoted in another context, shows that the general style and many of the formulas of the later charter of enfeoffment were already established by the year 1122.[1]

'Willelmus Peverel de Dour' Hamundo Peverel fratri suo et Willelmo Peverel nepoti suo ac omnibus fidelibus suis hominibus Francigenis et Angligenis necnon et amicis tam futuris quam presentibus salutem. Sciatis me donasse Turstano dapifero meo et heredibus suis Geddingam et Daiwellam pro seruicio suo de me et heredibus meis tenendas in feodo et hereditate et sacha et socha et

---

[1] Appendix, No. 29. Copies of this charter, which have few material variations, are entered on Curia Regis Roll 88, m. 12 (*Curia Regis Rolls*, vol. xii, case 1033) and *Cartae Antiquae* (ed. J. Conway Davies, Pipe Roll Society, N.S. vol. xxxiii, no. 478). It was printed by Eyton, *Antiquities of Shropshire*, xi. 35. That it is not later than 1122 is shown by a writ of Henry I confirming the grant, issued at Bridgnorth in 1121 or 1122 (ibid.).

tol et theam et infangenethef in nemoribus et planis in uilla et uico et campis et pratis in aquis et omnibus aliis locis pro seruitio dimidii equitis. Teste Waltero de la Haia et Waltero de Marisco et Hugone de Girund' et Pagano de Suruia Ærnulfo sacerdote de Ketelestan Waltero filio Traulf Roberto capellano Rogero filio Wimundi Roberto filio Walteri Reginaldo Lagud.'

There are several features in this charter which would seem anomalous in a similar document of the next generation. The use of *eques* instead of *miles* is curious,[1] the grant of sake and soke with their associated privileges suggests the Norman rather than the Angevin period, and it is worth noting that an independent copy of the charter says that the land is to be held by the 'services', not the 'service', of half a knight.[2] Nevertheless, at all essential points the charter anticipates the typical formulas of the late twelfth century. It is addressed to persons interested in its provisions—the grantor's men and nearest kin. The land with which it deals is given in fee and inheritance to be held of the grantor and his heirs, and the service to be done in return for it is defined in the manner customary in later times. The charter shows, in fact, that the normal formulas of a grant of land for knight-service were current at a time when many of the younger knights who appear in Domesday Book must still have been alive. It is therefore clear that we can carry back to the time of the 'old enfeoffment'—the period before 1135—phrases and conceptions which are familiar from their occurrence in charters of the late twelfth century, that there is no important break in the development of feudal tenure between the death of Henry I and the accession of Henry II. Here, at least, the disorders of Stephen's time made no permanent impression on English society.

[1] *Eques* is occasionally used in this sense in royal writs of this period, as, for instance, in a writ of Henry I confirming to Archbishop Gerard of York the rights belonging to his Nottinghamshire estates *de equitibus et de sochemannis* (*Calendar of Patent Rolls, 1381–1385,* 57).

[2] For the significance of the grant of sake and soke see above, Chapter III, and for the implications of the reference to 'services', below, 171 et seqq.

Some twenty years after the date of this charter the
nephew of its grantor, the William Peverel who appears
in its address, enfeoffed one of his own tenants for the half
of a knight's service. The original text of his charter has
been preserved, and may stand as typical of such records
of enfeoffment as have survived from the early part of
Stephen's reign.[1]

'Willelmus Peuerel de Duure omnibus hominibus suis et amicis
Francis et Anglicis salutem. Sciant tam presentes quam futuri quod
ego Willelmus Peuerel dedi Hamoni Pichard pro seruitio et humagio suo dominium ecclesie de Morduna et curiam meam et
molendinum et prata mea et totam demeniam meam que est in
manu mea in Morduna, et homines meos, et Moram et homines de
Mora et terram et prata cum omnibus pertinentiis suis que pertinent ad Moram in pratis et in pascuis, et unam uirgatam terre de
Obernestun quam Hetwi tenet cum omnibus pertinentiis suis.
Hanc predictam terram do Hamoni Pichart et heredibus suis
tenendam de me et heredibus meis pro seruitio dimidii militis, libere
et quiete et honorifice et in omni libertate sicut ego unquam liberius
eam tenui uel antecessores mei, et hoc presenti ista mea carta confirmaui.'

Except that it is more loosely written than is the normal
feudal charter of Glanville's time, there is little in this
charter to suggest an early date. Yet its grantor, who had
been a prominent figure on the Welsh border in the early
wars of Stephen's reign, disappears soon afterwards,[2] and
the charter can hardly be later than 1145. So few documents of this type and date have yet been printed that it is
perhaps dangerous to generalize about them. But it is safe
to say that while the charters of enfeoffment which belong
to the middle decades of the twelfth century vary much
from one another in details, they are all, like the present
example, formal records, through which there runs a well-
established phraseology. The charters of this time which
have an intrinsic interest, apart from their subject matter,
are not records of enfeoffment for military service, but

[1] Harl. Chart. 54. G. 46 (Appendix, No. 30).
[2] For the Peverels of Dover see Eyton, *Antiquities of Shropshire*, ix.
62–70.

records of grants in frankalmoign, where the draftsman's individuality continually breaks through the restraints of set composition.

Nevertheless, the language of these early records of enfeoffment has a quality of its own, and in regard to one important matter their formulas are remarkably consistent and suggestive. It is only on rare and special occasions that one of them will use the familiar phrase *feudum militis*. These early charters are conclusive evidence against any theory that knight-service in England was originally based on territorial units of uniform, or even approximately uniform standard. They imply, on the contrary, that the *feudum unius militis* is a conception which gradually developed as the process of subinfeudation went on, and the need was felt for some general term to denote an estate charged with the service of a single knight. It is with the knight's service, not with the knight's fee, that they are concerned, and as a group they do not suggest that a man who undertook this service inquired at all closely into the extent or value of the lands which he received from his lord. He certainly paid curiously little regard to the geographical distribution of the lands which were to form his fee. Now and then a lord will grant a single village for the service of a single knight, but the deviations from this ideal, if ideal it was, are numerous and striking. It is entirely ignored, for example, in each of the two charters which have just been quoted. The lands which Thurstan the steward took from William Peverel of Dover for the half of a knight's service lay at Gidding in Huntingdonshire, and Daywell, a hamlet of Whittington, in north Shropshire, places which lie more than a hundred miles apart in a straight line. The lands which William Peverel the younger gave to Hamon Pichart for the same service lay at Guilden Morden in Cambridgeshire, Osbaston and Moortown near Ellesmere. These are early cases, but fees of an even more obvious artificiality could be created in the reign of Henry II, when Ingeram de Dumart gave the quarter of his land in each of four Northamptonshire villages to Walter Duredent, his *nepos*,

for a knight's service.[1] The lands comprising a knight's fee
are not often dispersed with this deliberate symmetry. But
the evidence of charters, inconclusive as it is on many
points, at least disproves the existence of any general idea
that the land which provided a knight's service should form
an economic unit, or that manor and knight's fee should
be identical.[2]

The evidence suggests, on the contrary, that many of
the knights' fees which appear in the great thirteenth-
century feodaries are artificial creations, which had only
acquired their permanent shape in the course of time. Now
and then a lord can be seen increasing his tenant's fee from
his own land. Earl Alan of Richmond, who died in
1146, says that he has given a small wood to one of his
Nottinghamshire tenants to increase the knight's fee which
he has there beyond Trent.[3] Archbishop Thurstan of
York, the earl's elder contemporary, adds a spinney to the
land which his steward was holding of him for the third
of a knight's service.[4] More interesting, because they
show knights' fees in the making, are the charters in which
a lord when enfeoffing a tenant for the fractional part of a
knight's service states that he will increase the holding at
some future date. In 1163, for example, Ernald de Bosco

---

[1] Harl. Chart. 49. F. 53; Appendix, No. 32. The villages in question
are Faxton, Mawsley, Walgrave, and Moulton. The first three of these
places lie close together near Kettering, and the fourth is only a few miles
to the south-west. For Ingeram de Dumart see Round's note in his edition
of the *Rotuli de Dominabus* (Pipe Roll Society, vol. xxxv), 23.

[2] The distribution of knight-service over the lands of bishoprics and
abbeys was sometimes governed by the details of their pre-Conquest assessment to public burdens. The original knights' fees created by the bishops
of Worcester were based on the principle that a fee should consist of five
hides (on which see Marjory Hollings, *Eng. Hist. Rev.* lxiii. 453–87).
They reflect, in fact, the traditional assessment of the normal Anglo-Saxon
village to taxation and public duties in terms of a five-hide unit. It is a
remarkable example of continuity. But the barony of the bishops of
Worcester represented an ancient and highly organized ecclesiastical estate,
within which a manorial system of English origin could be adapted with
exceptional ease to the Norman demand for military service.

[3] Harl. MS. 1063, f. 94 b.

[4] Southwell Cathedral, White Book, f. 26 b.

gives all his land in three Lincolnshire villages to Philip de Dive as seven *libratae terrae* for two parts of a knight's service, promising that under certain conditions he will make up the holding to ten *libratae terrae* from his own inheritance in the future.[1] A few years earlier Gilbert earl of Lincoln gives four carucates in Barton on Humber to William Basset for the half of a knight's service, until he shall give him ten *libratae terrae* from his own inheritance,[2] and another document of the same period raises so many points of interest that it deserves to be quoted at length.

'Hugh de Bayeux greets clerks and laymen, Frenchmen and Englishmen, and all his good men. Know that I have given and granted to Robert Rabaz and his heirs in fee and inheritance half the fee of one knight in Maidwell and Kelmarsh which his father Richard son of Bernard and he himself held of Rannulf my father, for the same service which he and his father used to do to Rannulf my father, and I will that he hold that land as he and his father held it best and most freely of Rannulf my father, until I shall fully make up for him the fee of one knight. Know also that he will make for me one perch in the wall of the castle of Welbourne in return for my confirmation and acknowledgment to him of the aforesaid land.'[3]

The date of this intensely feudal document can be fixed with some precision. It was obviously written very soon after Hugh de Bayeux had succeeded to his inheritance, and Hugh appears in the Pipe Roll of 1158 as paying twenty marks for his land.[4] Under these conditions the reference to the work on Hugh's castle of Welbourne becomes interesting, for it shows a private castle in course of erection in a time of general peace, some four years after the accession of Henry II and the wholesale destruction of the castles of Stephen's time. It is also interesting

[1] F. M. Stenton, *Danelaw Charters*, No. 471.

[2] *Sir Christopher Hatton's Book of Seals*, No. 297. The arrangements described in this, and the charter previously quoted, suggest very strongly that when the ten *libratae terrae* were made up they would carry a full knight's service. On knights' fees of this amount see below, 168–9.

[3] Add. Chart. 6038 (Appendix, No. 31).

[4] The Great Rolls of the Pipe for the second, third, and fourth years of King Henry II (ed. Hunter), 137. There is no trace of this payment on the roll of 1157, the first roll of Henry II which has survived in full.

to see a tenant undertaking to build some eighteen feet of castle wall in return for a confirmation of his hereditary fee from his new lord. It does not seem to have been customary for an English lord to exact a relief from his tenants on his own succession, but individual charters of confirmation were often granted at such a time, and a substantial payment was often made for them.[1] The return which Robert Rabaz made for his lord's confirmation was remarkable for its nature rather than its occasion. Apart from these matters of general interest, the charter is noteworthy as one of the earliest private documents to speak expressly of a knight's fee as distinct from a knight's service. And while it suggests that Hugh de Bayeux and his tenants had already reached a definite conception of what a knight's fee should be, it proves that the distribution of Hugh's land in knights' fees among his men was still to some extent a matter under his own control.

In view of the number of tenancies, obviously military from the beginning, which can be traced from the Conqueror's time through the reigns of his sons, there is no room for doubt that knights' fees were in fact normally hereditary from the time of the first enfeoffments.[2] But the regularity of their descent does not mean that the original precarious character of the military benefice was forgotten. Late in the reign of Henry II it was still very unusual for a charter granting land for knight-service to contain a clause of warranty.[3] Moreover, although nearly

[1] See next page.

[2] For a charter creating a life tenancy of a military fee see above, 154.

[3] Two charters in a private collection in Northamptonshire show in a very curious way that the absence of this clause was considered unsatisfactory in the early thirteenth century. Between 1180 and 1189, William Mauduit, chamberlain to Henry II, granted a manor to his brother Robert *per seruicium dimidie partis feodi unius militis* without any clause of warranty. Early in the reign of Henry III someone, presumably in the interest of a descendant of Robert Mauduit, was at pains to fabricate an improved version of this charter, authenticating it with William Mauduit's seal, keeping all the witnesses and nearly all the wording of the original document, but inserting a clause: 'Ego vero predictus Willelmus Mauduit et heredes mei predictum manerium de Scaudeden' predicto Roberto Mauduit fratri meo et heredibus suis contra omnes homines et feminas warentizare

all the earliest charters of enfeoffment which we possess were made to a tenant and his heirs, it was evidently wise for an heir on his succession to obtain from his lord a new charter restoring or confirming his father's land to him. Charters of this kind have survived in considerable number from the third quarter of the twelfth century onwards, and although lords in such charters seem generally to use the verbs *concedo et confirmo* usual in an act of mere confirmation, and may even acknowledge that the tenant is to hold the land as of right,[1] they could also use the *do et concedo* proper to a new and original gift.[2] Moreover, although there seems no English evidence that a military tenant paid anything that can strictly be called a relief when his lord was succeeded by an heir, he might well obtain a new charter from his new lord, and it is unlikely that such charters were often granted for the mere asking. This practice was not confined to the lower ranks of English feudalism. In a charter which Madox selected for his *Formulare* as a typical deed of confirmation,[3] Gerard de Limesi granted to Richard de Lucy the manor of Chigwell for a knight's service, as Gerard's father had given it to Richard and confirmed it by his charter, receiving from Richard three marks by way of recognition of his lordship, and a golden ring from Richard's son, who became his *affidatus*. If one who may already have been joint justiciar of England thought it wise to obtain a new charter under these conditions, the practice must have been well

debemus.' The absence of such a clause from the original charter was undoubtedly the reason for the forgery (F. M. Stenton, *Facsimiles of Charters from Northamptonshire Collections*, Northamptonshire Record Society, Nos. XXXIII (a) and (b)).

[1] As in the example given in the Appendix, No. 34.

[2] Thus Maurice de Craon, some years before 1166, writes: 'Sciatis me dedisse et concessisse Tome filio Willelmi in feodum et hereditatem sibi et heredibus suis totam terram quam pater suus Willelmus tenuit de patre meo et de me, scilicet in Salebeia et in Thorestorp, ipse et heredes sui tenere de me et de heredibus meis pro seruicio unius militis.' Add. Chart. 20591; *Genealogist*, New Series, xviii. 163.

[3] *Formulare Anglicanum*, No. LXXV. Comparison with other documents in this collection (LXXIX and CCLXXXVIII) shows that this charter must be earlier than 1163.

established. More than ceremonial business must often
have been done in those assemblies at which the tenants
of a fee came together to do homage to a new lord.[1]

The payments made by way of relief, in the proper
sense of the word, must have varied according to the
special circumstances of each case. The 'relief' paid by the
holder of a knight's fee on his own succession is often
regarded as a definite sum—the hundred shillings prescribed for the relief of a vavassor by the *Leis Willelme*[2]
and of a knight by Glanville.[3] But there is little early
evidence as to the amounts which military tenants were
actually paying for their reliefs.[4] Charters of confirmation
rarely mention the sum which a tenant has given for his
relief, as too often they fail to mention the service by
which he is to hold of his lord. But the little information
which lies to hand certainly does not suggest that the
normal relief on a knight's fee was nearly as high as the
hundred shillings of the *Leis Willelme*, nor indeed that it

[1] A good example of such an assembly is given by a charter in the
Boarstall Cartulary, published by the Oxford Historical Society (No. 21).
Geoffrey Marmion grants to William Marmion his brother land previously
given him by Robert Marmion son of Milisent *coram illis qui homagium
fecerunt Roberto filio Roberti filii Milisent*. This particular assembly seems
to have been held when an heir came of age in his father's lifetime, but it
illustrates the character of these meetings. A more dramatic ceremony of
the same kind took place in June 1155 at Bridgnorth, where Henry II,
after suppressing the rebellion of Hugh de Mortimer, restored to William
fitz Alan the lands which he had lost during the Anarchy. In gratitude,
William gave the church of Wroxeter to his abbey of Haughmond *die . . .
qua homagium ab hominibus suis apud Brugiam suscepit, adunata multitudine
baronum et militum coram omnibus . . . pro salute domini regis, qui terram
suam sibi reddiderat*. Eyton, *Antiquities of Shropshire*, vii. 312.

[2] See above, 23.   [3] ix. 4.

[4] A clear case in which a hundred shillings are given *de relevagio* in
return for the confirmation of a knight's fee occurs in Add. Chart. 20454, a
Herefordshire charter printed below, Appendix, No. 41. But the circumstances are exceptional. The fee was given by a tenant to one of his own
younger sons, with the consent of his heir, his other sons, and Ralf de
Toeni, his lord. Thereupon the son in question, who was to hold thenceforward immediately of Ralf de Toeni, gave him a palfrey, did him homage,
et pro relevagio suo dedit ei centum solidos. An unusual transaction like this
is obviously no proof that the heir of a knight's fee normally gave a hundred
shillings to his lord on succeeding to his inheritance.

was determined by any general rule. At the middle of the twelfth century, for example, Gilbert de Pinkeny states that after investigation he has 'restored' to Robert de Pinkeny certain lands to hold for the same service by which his father held of Gilbert's father, 'namely for the service of a knight and a half, quit of relief and of all other matters which were formerly between us for five marks which he has given to me'.[1] This charter cannot be regarded as indicating the normal relief for a knight's fee on the Pinkeny honour. It reads like the settlement of a plea in Gilbert de Pinkeny's court, and the five marks for which Robert de Pinkeny was quit obviously form a round sum satisfying various claims by his lord, of which that to relief was only one. But it shows clearly enough that on this particular honour reliefs must have been taken at a considerably lower rate than a hundred shillings on the knight's fee, and it suggests that each case of a relief was decided separately as it arose. This undoubtedly was the intention of those who drew up the coronation charter of Henry I, with its provision that the men of his barons should relieve their lands from their lords with a just and lawful relief. 'Legitima' in such a context certainly does not mean 'statutory'.

Early feudal custom was equally indefinite in regard to more essential matters than the amount of the relief on the knight's fee. Much of the obscurity which attends the history of English knight-service is due to the fact that no general conception of a knight's fee itself can ever have prevailed throughout the whole of England, nor even throughout those southern shires where the magnates of the eleventh century planted their knights in greatest number. The smallness of the fees created on some honours, notably on that of Robert count of Mortain, came to be recognized by the king's court itself, and their holders received special treatment on this account when a scutage was taken. Such variations were only natural, for in the early phases of English feudalism there was no need for a general uniformity of knights' fees. The king had no

1 Add. Chart. 2201; Appendix, No. 35.

interest in attempting to enforce it, for it was the tenant in chief and not the enfeoffed knight whom he held responsible for the performance of the military service due to the crown. Even within the individual honour, though frequent debate in the lord's court must have tended to create a common interest among all his men, there was room for wide variation in the scale of their individual fees. In the last resort the extent and value of any knight's fee were closely connected with the social position of the man who first received it, and the knights of a great Anglo-Norman honour in the eleventh century must have included men of very diverse condition. On every honour many years must have passed before any real advance could be made towards the establishment of a standard knight's fee, and on most honours it is probable that nothing approaching uniformity was ever achieved. It is not surprising that the twelfth century was far advanced before the clerks who wrote charters for feudal magnates allowed themselves the free use of the words *feudum militis*.

In the middle years of that century charters defining the land charged with a knight's service were beginning to appear in considerable number. The definition is rarely as precise as we could wish. Generally, such an estate is defined in terms of hides or carucates, and its value, which mattered far more to its recipient than its agricultural content, can only be inferred from later evidence. Sometimes, however, a charter will itself estimate the value of the land with which it is dealing in *solidatae* or *libratae terrae*[1] and through the study and collection of

---

[1] It is impossible to offer any satisfactory translation of *librata* or *solidata terrae*, but the meaning of the phrase is clear. Like the earlier *Valet* of Domesday Book, the description of an estate as so many *libratae terrae* represents an estimate of the amount of money which it ought to bring in, yearly, to its lord under normal conditions. There is so little early evidence as to the way in which a grant in terms of *libratae*, *marcatae*, or *solidatae terrae* was carried out, that a clear twelfth-century case, given in the Christchurch cartulary, may be described. Richard del Estre, an important landowner in the Isle of Wight, gave a *marcata terrae* there, at Nyton, to the canons of Christchurch. The following document describes the way

these estimates it may some day become possible to understand the various conceptions of the knight's fee which prevailed in the twelfth century. Their importance lies in the material which they afford for the comparison of knights' fees in different parts of England. The value, like the acreage, of the hide or carucate varied greatly between place and place. The mere statement, for example, that Bernard son of Miles held two and a half hides at Mixbury in north Oxfordshire for half a knight's service, of Bernard de St. Valery, tells little of the value of the knight's fee on the St. Valery honour. But the *librata* or *solidata terrae* was uniform throughout England. It was a deliberate estimate of yearly value expressed in the simplest of phrases.[1] The charters recording enfeoffments in terms of this unit deserve to be taken very seriously into account in any discussion of the questions which centre round the meaning of the twelfth-century knight's fee.

It should be said at once that they are unlikely to afford any simple solution of these questions. Whatever may have been the case in an earlier time, and there is no reason to believe that simpler conceptions then prevailed, the knights' fees of the mid-twelfth century certainly varied in value as widely as they varied in extent. But they did not vary indefinitely, and two distinct types of fee stand

in which this *marcata terrae* was made up: 'Notum sit omnibus quod ego Willelmus filius Osb' et Willelmus Auenel et Symon filius Rogeri del Estre, precepto Ricardi del Estre, tradidimus canonicis Christi ecclesie terram quam ipse Ricardus del Estre dedit predicte ecclesie cum corpore suo, cum hominibus et uxoribus et pueris suis qui terram illam tenent; scilicet Sefare palmarium qui reddet .xxxv. denarios. Iuonem qui reddet .xlv. denarios, Ricardum qui reddet iii solidos et unum denarium, Willelmum Derby (*sic*) qui reddet .xxi. denarios et obulum, Willelmum filium telarii qui reddet xxi. denarios et obolum, Gunore que reddet .vi. denarios de domo quam tenet. Hanc tradimus terram predictis canonicis sacramento hominum de Nywetun' qui iurauerunt quantum de gabulo . de operibus de cherset terra illa ualere potuit. Hec terra liberata est coram omnibus hominibus de Nywetun' quorum sacramento notum fuit quantum valere potuit ut dictum est scilicet unam marcam argenti' (Cott. Tib. D. vi, part i, f. 104 b). The figures do not add up neatly to a mark, but the nature of the arrangement is plain.

[1] See preceding note.

out clearly enough in the earliest charters of enfeoffment. One of them has long been recognized. The baronial *Cartae* in 1166 give little information about the value of individual fees, but they contain three passages which point unequivocally to a fee of twenty *libratae terrae*.[1] Before 1159 William earl of Gloucester, at Bristol, in the presence of many of his feudal tenants, gave 12 *libratae terrae* at Great Gransden in Huntingdonshire to Rannulf son of Gerold, with the stipulation that Rannulf should do him the service of one knight for this land and for 8 *libratae terrae* at Toppesfield in Essex.[2] Traces of the same equation can be found in charters of an earlier time. The land at Ibstone in Buckinghamshire, which Henry de Oilli gave to Henry of Oxford for half a knight's service by a charter made before 1163, was estimated at ten *libratae*.[3] A less obvious instance of the twenty *libratae* unit occurs in a charter in the unpublished cartulary of Stoke by Clare, by which Earl Roger of Hertford gave fifty *solidatae* of land at Crimplesham in Norfolk to William de Cunteville for the eighth of a knight's service.[4] The extent to which this unit underlay the enfeoffments of the eleventh century is a difficult question. That some knights of unusual personal distinction received fees upon this scale is probable. But a manor which produced twenty pounds a year was a rich endowment for a knight at any time before the standard of knightly equipment was raised in the thirteenth century,[5]

---

[1] These passages are quoted by Vinogradoff, *English Society in the Eleventh Century*, 48, and are there associated with an entry in the *Carta* of the honour of Clare: 'Willelmus de Hastinges tenet xx libratas terre et unum militem feodatum de quibus non facit servitium nisi unius militis.' But the original *Carta* of this Honour read *servitium i militis et dimidii* instead of *servitium unius militis* (*Red Book*, 405). The entry does not really give any definite information as to the value of the knight's fee.

[2] *Sir Christopher Hatton's Book of Seals*, No. 213. The charter is addressed *suo dapifero. omnibusque suis baronibus . et hominibus atque fidelibus. Francis Anglis.*   [3] Salter, *Early Oxford Charters*, No. 42.

[4] Cott. MS. Appendix xxi, f. 21 b.

[5] In view of the moderate values which Domesday Book assigns to a large number of important manors and the still lower value which they often bore when the Conqueror gave them out, it is difficult to believe

and the charter evidence, confused as it often is, shows at least that fees formed upon a far lower scale were known already in the earliest years of Henry II.

It would seem, indeed, that a fee of ten *libratae terrae* was really commoner than one of twenty in the central years of the twelfth century. Persons of high rank were prepared to take fees of this value. Between 1160 and 1163 Robert earl of Leicester, then Justiciar of England, formally acknowledged by charter that he held of the bishop of Lincoln ten *libratae* in the bishop's manor of Knighton by Leicester, for a knight's service.[1] Between 1139 and 1162 Robert de Ferrers, earl of Derby, gave ten *libratae* at Stebbing in Essex for the same service to his man Maurice son of Geoffrey—an important tenant who founded the Cistercian abbey of Tilty in Stephen's reign and twice served as sheriff of Essex in that of Henry II.[2] Shortly after the middle of Henry's reign Robert Marmion granted a hundred *solidatae* at Checkendon in Oxfordshire to a certain Geoffrey Marmion for the service of half a knight.[3] An earlier Oxfordshire charter by which Thomas de Druval confirms sixty *solidatae* of land at Goring to his uncle for the quarter of a knight's service points to a knight's fee of twelve, not ten, *libratae terrae*, but it certainly does not suggest the general prevalence of a large fee of twenty *libratae*.[4] Fees of or closely approximating to the ten *libratae* standard were created by Henry II himself. During his visit to Nottingham in the spring of 1155 Henry granted to Guy le Strange, for half a knight's service, the manor of Alveley in Shropshire, which formerly rendered 110 shillings *in firma*.[5] The

that knights' fees of as much as 20 *libratae terrae* were common in the age of the first Norman enfeoffments. It cannot have been usual for a lord to give, in return for a single knight's service, an estate which was more valuable than his own *caput honoris*, and many of these estates were worth much less than £20, even in 1086.

[1] *Registrum Antiquissimum of Lincoln Cathedral*, ed. C. W. Foster, ii. 5.
[2] Hist. MSS. Comm., *Reports on Various Collections*, vii. 310.
[3] *Boarstall Cartulary*, ed. Salter, 12.
[4] Harl. Chart. 83. H. 5. See additional note, 190–1.
[5] Hamon le Strange, *Le Strange Records* (1916), 28 and plate V.

grant is interesting, for the king is evidently attempting a rough equation between the traditional render of the estate and the amount of knight-service which he proposed to exact in return for it. It is probable that many of his barons followed a similar practice, that the knights' fees of the twelfth century were often framed in accordance with the local renders of an earlier time. That many lords regarded an estate of twenty *libratae terrae* as a fitting return for a knight's service need not be doubted, but the evidence for a knight's fee of half this value certainly deserves more consideration than it has generally received.

A charter which comes from the middle of Stephen's reign shows one of these small fees in the process of creation. Soon after 1142 William de Roumara, earl of Lincoln, gave ten *libratae terrae* in Lincolnshire to Peter of Goxhill for a knight's service.[1] The land lay in two portions, each estimated at precisely five *libratae*. One portion was situated at Hundleby near Spilsby, on the border of the Lincolnshire Marsh. The other portion lay more than thirty miles away towards the north-west, at Hemswell and Aisby, between the Lincoln Edge and the Trent. To say the least, there is no attempt in this charter to frame a knight's fee which will be an economic unit. The unity of the fee is not economic but feudal, and in this there can be no doubt that it is fairly representative of the estates which were created for a similar purpose in the earlier phases of subinfeudation. The interest of this particular fee lies in its value rather than in its local distribution. How many of Earl William's contemporaries were endowing their men with fees of ten *libratae* will always be an open question, for it is only by chance that a charter defining a knight's fee in terms of *libratae terrae* comes in the way of the inquirer. But until these charters have been collected we can never hope to trace the varying standards of endowment which prevailed in different honours.

There is nothing strange in the variation of the knight's fee between honour and honour, and from time to time. It is much more remarkable that many years passed before

[1] F. M. Stenton, *Danelaw Charters*, 356–7.

the conception of a knight's service assumed a definite form. To the end, indeed, many important issues were never settled by royal authority. From every standpoint it is remarkable how little we really know about the nature of military service in the century after the Conquest. The length of time for which a knight must serve, the conditions under which he or his lord might find a substitute, the system by which the king's barons found garrisons for his castles, and the circumstances which entitled them to take an aid from their men are all involved in obscurity. We are, in fact, driven to conclude that the organization of military service was essentially the business of the great baronial courts; that so long as a due contingent of suitable knights answered the king's summons, he was not concerned with the arrangements which produced them. Even Henry II, whose legislative activity colours the whole history of his time, attempted no more in this direction than a brief definition of a knight's equipment.[1] Charters of enfeoffment, which might be expected to illustrate the detail of knight-service, are disappointing materials for this particular study. With few exceptions they are composed on the assumption that those who hear them will understand what is meant by the service of a knight, and that disputes about this duty will be settled by the peers of the fee and not by the terms of any written document. It is significant that most of the exceptions occur among the earliest charters which we possess. No lawyer of the Angevin period would have felt happy in construing the memorandum which recites that Peter, King William's knight, must come to the service of the abbot of Bury 'with three or four knights, and at his own cost'.[2] But its provisions are natural enough if they are regarded from the standpoint of the Conqueror's reign, when men were still free to make experiments in forms of military tenure.

Now and then a dispute about the terms of an early enfeoffment produced a later recital of its provisions. Early, it would seem, in Stephen's reign, it was found necessary to set down in writing the conditions under

[1] *Assize of Arms*, clause 1.   [2] See above, 154.

which Noel, the ancester of an important line of Staffordshire barons, had received an estate at Ranton and Cooks-
land in that county from Nicholas of Stafford in the time
of William II. After observing that written testimony is
always necessary for the settlement of disputes, the
memorandum which was then produced makes known
to all the men of the honour of Stafford that Nicholas of
Stafford, and Robert his son after him, gave this land to
Noel *in feodo et per servitium dimidii manerii et dimidii
militis et ad servitium proprii clypei domini Nicolai et ab
omni custodia et operatione castelli . . . liberam.*[1] Many points
are left unexplained by this memorandum, in particular the
curious equation of the service of half a knight with the
service due from 'half a manor'. But it undoubtedly
represents the terms of an enfeoffment made in the earliest
age of English feudalism, and its very incoherence is
significant. It emphasizes, what few records of enfeoffment even express, the duty of the man to serve in person
beside his lord in war, and it brings out very clearly the
importance of castle-guard and the maintenance of castle
defences in the early time to which it refers. In doing this
it also raises the question of the interpretation which
should be put upon the earliest grants of land for the
service of half a knight. It is usual to assume that a man
who received such a grant was bound to co-operate with
some other tenant in the provision of a knight, or, as at a
later time,[2] to find two sergeants for the king's service.
In most cases this interpretation is doubtless correct. But
it is also possible that the men of the eleventh century were
sometimes thinking of the various duties which made up a
knight's service when they enfeoffed a man for a fractional
part of it. Nicholas of Stafford, for example, certainly
thought that castle-guard was a part of a knight's service
which need not necessarily be combined with his obligation
to serve in the field, and many other lords of his generation
may well have taken a similar view. Many forms of duty
were included in the service of a knight in the age when

---

[1] *Salt Society's Collections,* ii. 219.
[2] Pollock and Maitland, *History of English Law* (2nd ed.), i. 256.

knight-service was a military reality, and it was for a lord to decide how they should be apportioned among his men.

Our clearest information as to the nature of these duties comes, as it happens, not from charters recording the enfeoffment of knights, but from charters granting to religious houses exemption from the military services incumbent on lands which they have lately acquired. In the twelfth century a donor will often state that the lands of his gift are to be free thenceforward from all forms of military obligation, and he sometimes describes them in considerable detail. Between 1148 and 1166, for example, Walter de Aincurt states that certain lands in Lincolnshire which have been given to Kirkstead Abbey shall be free *de exercitu et warda et scutagio et equitatione et opere et omni servitio quod ad militem pertinet.*[1] Despite the vagueness of its last words this passage is a careful attempt to indicate the various duties which might be exacted from a tenant by knight-service, and it comes from a source of high authority. Walter de Aincurt was lord of an honour which owed to the king the service of forty knights, and his analysis of a knight's duty deserves respect.

Before these services are discussed in detail it should certainly be noted that only two of them, the feudal *expeditio* and the scutage which was its commutation, were peculiar to tenure by knight-service in the strict sense. The personal service of a knight implied by the word *expeditio* stands, indeed, apart from all the other services in the list, for even scutage appears in many early charters as a mere occasional addition to a tenant's other rent or service.[2] But apart from *expeditio*, all the services in the list could be combined in the twelfth century very much as a lord chose, and he was perfectly free to associate any of them with an enfeoffment for which the principal return was a money rent. The result is that tenures which seem highly anomalous, and indeed are so when compared with

[1] Cott. MS. Vesp. E. xviii, f. 32; Appendix, No. 36. Innumerable charters of the twelfth century grant exemptions of this kind, but very few of them go into so much detail.

[2] See below, 184–5.

the neat tenurial categories of Bracton's day, were continually arising in the Norman age and even under Henry II.
One example which is described in unusual detail may be
quoted here at length. Early in the reign of Henry II,
a knight named Waleran, of Sulgrave in Northamptonshire, gave his land there to St. Andrew's Priory at
Northampton, and in 1183–4 a dispute between his lord
and the monks produced the charter which follows.[1]

'Let all men, present and future, know that I, William son of
Richard, have given and granted to the monks of St. Andrew's at
Northampton the service of the land which Waleran held of me in
Sulgrave, that is, thirty acres of inland[2] to be sown each year and
five yardlands in addition, to hold of me and my heirs for the same
service which Waleran used to do to me; namely for eight shillings
of yearly rent, and five pence towards watchman's fee,[3] and the
other services which my free men do to me, that is, if need shall
arise they shall help to redeem my body and to make my eldest son
a knight, and to give in marriage my eldest daughter. And if my
free men shall give me a common aid, the monks shall give me what
is appropriate to their holding. Moreover I have granted to them
that I will not summon them to my pleas except for default in my
service, and therein I will set them a day at Culworth or at Sulgrave. Moreover I and my heirs will acquit the monks in every way
in respect of castle-guard at Windsor,[4] as to which I formerly began
a plea against them because they had never done it, and for this
acquittance Henry the prior of St. Andrew's has given forty shillings

[1] Royal MS. 11 B. ix, f. 43; Appendix, No. 33. William son of Richard,
held 2½ knights' fees of Gilbert de Pinkeny in 1166 (*Red Book*, i. 317).
There seems no means of dating Waleran's original gift of the land at all
closely. The present agreement can be dated to 1183–4 by the statement
that it was made 'when Ralf Morin was sheriff of Northamptonshire', and
it implies that Waleran's gift is some distance in the past.

[2] The charter by which Waleran originally gave the land reads *xxx
acras de dominio* instead of *xxx acras de inlanda*. The use of 'inland' for
demesne is characteristic of, though by no means confined to, Northamptonshire documents.

[3] *V denarios de waita*. On payments for this purpose, which have sometimes been confused with payments for castle-guard, see Round, 'Castle
Watchmen', *Eng. Hist. Rev.* xxxv. 400-1.

[4] The Pinkeny barony, of which William son of Richard was a tenant,
was one of the honours which are known to have owed castle-guard at
Windsor, according to the system described below, 212–13.

to me and two bezants to Robert my son and heir. Moreover the monks have given me security that they will keep faith with me in respect of my fee, and will not seek device or invention by which I or my heirs may be deprived of our fee. To this, Henry son of Ernewi and Hugh son of Ermeburg have pledged their faith on the monks' behalf, and Hugh of Culworth has pledged his faith on mine. This agreement was made when Ralf Morin was sheriff, in the sight of the shire court of Northampton.'

Although Waleran of Sulgrave described himself as *miles* in the charter which he originally gave to St. Andrew's Priory,[1] the fact that he was a knight was clearly irrelevant to the form of tenure by which he held. To his lord, writing retrospectively, he was only one of a group of 'free men', and the essential obligation which his tenure involved was a rent of eight shillings a year. On the other hand, he was bound to regular payments towards castle-guard at the royal castle of Windsor and towards the wages of a watchman, presumably at the same castle, and he was subject to 'aids' which, though not peculiar to tenure by knight-service, are of strictly feudal character. It is in its definition of these aids that the chief interest of this charter lies. The three aids for the knighting of a lord's eldest son, the marriage of his eldest daughter, and the ransoming of his person are famous because they are associated in the Great Charter of 1215, but they are very rarely mentioned in earlier private charters, and, indeed, this seems to be the first occasion on which they occur together in an English document. They are so prominent in the modern conception of a knight's duty to his lord that it is interesting to see them laid, as here, on a group of men who certainly as a whole were not tenants by knight-service. But English feudal custom always allowed a lord to take reasonable aids from his free, non-military, tenants, and never seems to have associated any particular type of aid with tenants of any particular class.[2] It certainly never arrived at any exhaustive list of the occasions on which a lord might seek monetary help from his *libere tenentes*. Glanville himself remarks that nothing certain

[1] Royal MS. 11 B. ix, f. 42 b.   [2] *Rotuli de Dominabus*, Index *s.v.* Auxilium

had been appointed touching the giving or exaction of aids, except that they should be 'reasonable',[1] and the little evidence which exists about these payments bears him out. In 1125 William Fitzherbert received Norbury from the priory of Tutbury so that 'if the lord of Tutbury shall redeem his body from capture or give his eldest daughter in marriage or redeem his honour, and the prior shall give an aid for these occasions, then William or his heir shall tender a suitable aid to the prior, proportionate to his fee'.[2] The precision of the Great Charter has some-what obscured the variety of the occasions on which in early days a lord might ask his free tenants to help him with their money.

By their very nature, aids were only occasional imposi-tions, extraneous to the services which made up the essen-tial body of the enfeoffed knight's duty, and from which Walter de Aincurt so explicitly freed the monks of Kirk-stead. The list which he gave is a curious mixture of the familiar and the obscure. Service in the feudal army, scutage, and castle-guard are obvious and essential parts of a knight's obligation. The nature of the services described as 'work' and 'riding' is less evident, and it is not easy to find passages which illustrate them in Anglo-Norman charters. That 'work' in such a context meant work upon a lord's castle is probable in itself, and is made virtually certain by comparison with the exemption from *operatio castelli* which Nicholas of Stafford granted to Noel of Ranton according to a charter which has already been quoted.[3] The same conclusion is suggested by the language of a charter of William Martel, King Stephen's *dapifer*, granting to Eye Priory the land of one of his tenants in a Suffolk village 'free from the third part of a knight's service and from all other *consuetudines* which he used to do for me and my predecessors at Eye or at Thorndon, in work or in other services'.[4] The nature

---

[1] ix. 8.   [2] *Mon. Ang.* iii. 394.   [3] Above, 171.
[4] Add. MS. 8177, p. 134 b. William Martel was an important tenant on the honour of Eye of which Eye Castle was the head. Thorndon seems to have been his chief residence in Suffolk.

of this work is left uncertain by early charters, and it probably varied from honour to honour. In most cases it probably comprised the necessary repair of walls, banks, and palisades. Definite references to such a service occur in documents of the thirteenth and fourteenth centuries, and it is doubtless of ancient origin. In other cases the work must have covered the repair of the houses maintained in many important castles by the tenants who owed castle-guard there.[1] Whatever its precise nature, it was essentially a feudal obligation, undertaken by the military tenant as part of his duty to his lord and wholly unconnected with the *burh bot* of Anglo-Saxon law.

The riding which was part of a knight's duty is often mentioned in twelfth-century charters. The context in which it occurs sometimes leads to a suspicion that *equitatio* is merely a synonym for service in the feudal army, intended to emphasize the knight's mounted duty in the field. But the key to the real meaning of the word is given by its identity in sense with the Romance-Latin *chevalchia*, the French *chevauchée*.[2] It seems certain that the *chevalchia* of French documents denoted, not military service, but the duty of escorting an immediate lord or the king from place to place, and the same meaning can safely be given to the *equitatio* of English documents, as when the Pipe Roll of 1197 records the disseisin of a certain William Luvel *quia dicebatur non fuisse in exercitu regis et in equitationibus suis in Normannia*.[3] The word *chevalchia* itself is found occasionally in English documents of the twelfth century. It appears in the *Carta* of Richard de Chandos of Snodhill, who states that one of his tenants owes him the full service of a knight *in exercitu et chivalchia et custodia*—a phrase which brings together the duties of serving in the lord's array,

---

[1] For work on castle walls and on houses within castles see, for example, the references collected by Ballard, 'Castle Guard and Barons' Houses', *Eng. Hist. Rev.* xxv. 712–15.

[2] I am indebted to Mr. Lewis C. Loyd for many references to this service in French documents, showing its difference from military service in the strict sense.

[3] Pipe Roll Society, n.s. viii. 233.

acting in his escort, and helping to guard his castle.[1] The fact that a knight might be required to serve in the escort of the king as well as in that of his lord is well brought out in a charter of Haket de Rideford, a tenant of the earl of Chester, freeing certain lands *ab equitatu tam regis quam comitis*.[2] Of the circumstances under which this service must be done, charters say nothing. But it is safe to assume that they were normally a matter of custom, determined by the special conditions of each honour, and in particular by the geographical distribution of its lord's demesnes.

There is no doubt as to the nature of the service described by the word *expeditio*. It can be defined in general terms as the duty of the military tenant to serve in person when the king summoned his lord to bring the knights whose service he owed to the royal muster. The solitary writ of summons which has survived from the Norman period[3] lays unequivocally upon the lord the responsibility for the due appearance of his knights, but neither it nor any private charter of the earliest feudal age tells anything of the conditions of their service in the feudal host. It is probable that each knight was required to serve for forty days at his own cost, though it is Norman rather than English evidence which fixes this period.[4] The best English evidence on the subject comes from a charter of Stephen's reign,[5] by which John son of Gilbert grants Nettlecombe in Somerset to Hugh de Ralegh for the service of a knight 'so defined that if there is war he shall find me an equipped knight for two months, and if

[1] *Red Book*, i. 285.

[2] F. M. Stenton, *Danelaw Charters*, 181.

[3] This is the famous writ by which William I commanded Abbot Æthelwig of Evesham to summon all who held within his jurisdiction 'quatinus omnes milites quos mihi debent paratos habeant ante me ad octauas Pentecostes apud Clarendunam' (*Feudal England*, 304; Stubbs, *Select Charters*, 9th ed., 97).

[4] On the forty days' service required by Norman custom see Haskins, *Norman Institutions*, 20, 21.

[5] *Collectanea Topographica et Genealogica* (1835), ii. 163, where it is printed in record type from an original.

there is peace, for 40 days, for such service as the knights of the barons of the land reasonably ought to do'. The historical importance of this charter is greater than appears on the surface. John son of Gilbert had served Henry I and Stephen, and was to serve Henry II, as marshal. No one could speak with more authority about the proper duration of a knight's service. The careful phrases of his charter may fairly be allowed the weight of an official definition.

It is also certain that the king could call on his tenants for the service of their knights outside the kingdom of England, in Wales, or Scotland, and no king of this period would have doubted his right to demand service beyond the Channel. It is suggestive that Hugh son of Richard, late in the reign of Henry I, frees a Warwickshire manor given to Kenilworth Priory 'from every *expeditio*, within or without England', as well as 'from pennies for knights, when or in whatever way they may be demanded'.[1] At the present time it is easy to underestimate the frequency with which the feudal army was summoned by the Norman kings. Chronicles record but few *expeditiones* during this period, and the fact, now well established, that scutage goes back at least to the end of the eleventh century, tends to minimize the importance of the actual feudal array. It is well to remember that no chronicle professes to enumerate all the occasions on which the feudal army was called into being, and that for most of the Norman period no financial records exist to supplement the literary authorities. Even in the reign of Richard I it was possible for a general summons of the feudal army to escape the notice of a whole group of singularly well-informed chroniclers. It is only the Pipe Roll of 1193 which records that the feudal army of all England was summoned to Gloucester in the previous year for the relief of Swansea.[2]

Among the few extant charters recording early enfeoff-

[1] Harl. MS. 3650, f. 15.
[2] Pipe Roll Society, n.s., vol. iii, p. xiv, where the references are collected.

ments for knight-service, there has survived one document which shows a lord requiring the tenant to compound
for the whole complex of duties involved in military
tenure by an annual payment in money. At a date which
can hardly be later than 1125, Peter of Studley, son of
William son of Corbucion, granted Wolverton in Warwickshire to William son of Reinfrid, in fee and inheritance,
for the third of a knight's service, with the express provision that William shall 'redeem his whole service' by a
payment of 20 shillings each year.[1] There is no hint in
the charter that the 'redemption' of military service by
an annual payment was unusual at the time when the
charter was made. The feature which makes the charter
remarkable is the insertion of an unemphatic clause to this
effect by a lord who was the son of a Domesday tenant in
chief.

In any case, the idea that the military service due from
a tenant to his lord could on occasion be discharged by a
monetary payment was current throughout feudal society
by the year 1125. The institution of 'scutage' is generally
regarded by historians from the king's standpoint. The
view that the initiative in the introduction was his has
always been stressed, and many reasons have been found
for his action. Some of them will not bear any real examina-
tion. The idea that kings, mistrusting the loyalty of their
barons, wished to abolish the feudal army is contradicted
by all the facts which we possess. In the year 1100, when
the first reference to scutage occurs, Henry I was urgently
in need of all the resources which his barons could bring to
his help, and in the thirteenth century the king was still
using the feudal army as a military reality.[2] But the
difficulty of enforcing this personal military service on a
general scale was very great, and it is not surprising that
scutage can be traced back in England to the last year of
the eleventh century. It is not always remembered that

[1] Printed, with facsimile and notes, in *Sir Christopher Hatton's Book of
Seals*, No. 528.
[2] See, for example, the references collected by J. E. Morris, *The Welsh
Wars of Edward I*.

the interests of the feudal aristocracy were tending in the same direction. A lord who owed the king the service of thirty knights or more was faced by heavy personal responsibility when the king called up the feudal array. He must often have been uncertain whether individual tenants had made adequate provision for their military duties. He must always have been aware of the possible consequences to himself of any default on their part, of the ease with which the king's *malevolentia* could be incurred, and the difficulty of buying its remission. The Pipe Roll of 1197 affords two striking examples of this. Otuel of Sudeley is recorded as owing forty marks 'for having seisin of his land whereof he had been disseized because his knight was not found in his constabulary in the March', and Gerard de Camville was finding pledges for a hundred pounds 'for having seisin of his land whereof he had been disseized because his knight was not found in the king's service'.[1]

In 1921 Professor W. A. Morris showed that a payment called scutage was included among the burdens from which Lewes Priory obtained exemption from Henry I in the year 1100.[2] His discovery made unnecessary any further search for evidence to prove the use of the word later in the reign, and gave a new precision to certain passages in very early charters which speak of pence given by a tenant to a lord for knights.[3] In itself, however, the discovery threw no new light on the nature of the payment denoted by the word or on the way in which it was regarded by the king and the feudal aristocracy. It is highly probable that already in 1100 scutage denoted a payment taken by the king from his tenants in chief as a

[1] Pipe Roll Society, N.S. viii. 128, 114.

[2] *Eng. Hist. Rev.* xxxvi. 45–46.

[3] Round, *Feudal England*, 270; *Studies on the Red Book of the Exchequer*, 6. Another reference to the commutation of knight-service under Henry I was pointed out by Round in 1905 (Hist. MSS. Comm., *Report on the Manuscripts of the Duke of Rutland*, iv. 58). William de Insula grants land in Beckenham to the canons of Holy Trinity, Aldgate, for half a knight's service with the provision: 'Quod servicium ego et heredes mei ab ipsis canonicis in eadem ecclesia semper repetere debemus.'

substitute for the personal service of the knights with whom they should have answered his summons to the feudal array. But for information as to the methods by which this payment was assessed before the reign of Henry II, we still depend in the main on the fragments of evidence supplied by private charters, and the charters which give such information are few.

Scutage is not mentioned by name in the Pipe Roll of 1130. Now, as when Round wrote his essays on the origin of knight-service, only one charter of Henry I is known which makes any illuminating reference to scutage. This charter is the well-known writ of 1127 in which the king releases to Hervey bishop of Ely forty out of the hundred pounds formerly due from his church when scutage ran through the king's land of England.[1] In itself this release proves little, but it is certainly connected, as Round connected it, with an entry on the Pipe Roll of 1130 which states that the bishop owes £240 for a quittance *de superplus militum episcopatus* and for a remission of the wardpenny due from Chatteris Abbey.[2] When brought together, the writ and the Pipe Roll entry suggest very strongly that the bishop or the abbots, his predecessors, had enfeoffed more knights than were needed for the service which the Conqueror had imposed on that church, and that the king had been exacting scutage, not only in respect of the knights' fees created for the performance of this *servicium debitum*, but also from those created in excess of this amount—the *superplus militum* of the Pipe Roll. As the Pipe Roll entry shows that it was the king's wish to release his right to scutage on this excess, the sixty pounds with which his writ leaves the bishopric charged to scutage ought to represent the amount of scutage due from the knights' fees of the *servicium debitum* when this payment was taken at its usual rate. As there is no doubt that the see of Ely owed a *servicium debitum* of forty knights, we seem entitled to conclude that scutage was

---

[1] Printed in Bentham's *History and Antiquities of the Conventual and Cathedral Church of Ely* (1771), appendix, No. xxi, and in *Feudal England*. 268.   [2] Ed. Hunter, 44.

normally taken under Henry I at a rate of thirty shillings on the knight's fee.

There are, however, two difficulties in accepting this conclusion. In the first place a scutage of thirty shillings on the knight's fee is extremely heavy in view of the fact that the heaviest scutage taken under Henry II amounted to only two marks on the fee. In the second place a payment of a hundred pounds when scutage was taken at thirty shillings on the knight's fee implies that $66\frac{2}{3}$ fees had been created on the lands of the bishopric before the date of the writ, or at least that the fees then created approached so closely to this number that a hundred pounds could be taken as a round sum in respect of them. But in 1166 Bishop Nigel of Ely showed with convincing detail that his existing fees of the old enfeoffment amounted to no more than $56\frac{1}{4}$.[1] No scutage that could have been borne in the reign of Henry I would have produced a hundred pounds from $56\frac{1}{4}$ knights' fees. The possibility has therefore to be faced that the sums of money mentioned in the writ bear no close relation to the number of knights' fees held of the bishop—that, in fact, the sums which Henry I exacted as scutage from his tenants were fixed arbitrarily, in large, round figures, at the king's mere will. And this would mean that the scutages levied by Henry I were based on a principle wholly different from that which governed the earliest scutages taken after 1154.

It may ultimately be necessary to accept this view. New evidence may show that the first scutages took the form of large, round sums of money demanded by the king from his individual tenants in chief without much inquiry into either the amount of their several *servicia debita* or the number of their actual enfeoffments. But we are not yet compelled to this conclusion. In the first place evidence quite independent of the Ely writ suggests that scutages were being taken under Henry I at thirty shillings on the knight's fee. In a letter addressed to Bishop Roger of

---

[1] The *Carta* of Bishop Nigel (*Red Book*, 363–6) is unusually elaborate, indicating the different counties in which his fees lay as well as making the customary distinction between those of the old and new enfeoffments.

Salisbury, Bishop Herbert of Norwich complained that
he had recently been required to find the sum of sixty
pounds *pro militibus*.[1] It can hardly be a mere coincidence
that the *servicium debitum* of the bishopric of Norwich was
exactly forty knights.[2] In the second place the fact that
only 56¼ of the fees acknowledged by the bishop of Ely
in 1166 had been created by 1135 is no proof that a larger
number of fees had not existed on the episcopal lands
earlier in the reign of Henry I. Between 1127, the date of
the king's release of scutage, and 1135, when the period of
'old enfeoffment' ended, there falls the accession to the
see of Bishop Nigel himself in 1133. Among his first acts
as bishop was an inquiry into the state of the possessions of his see *in dominio, in censu, aut in milite*, and in
a great plea, held before the men of nine hundreds, he
recovered a large number of manors which had been
wrongfully alienated in the past.[3] The recent history of
these manors is not recorded, but, to judge from the
experience of other religious houses, it is safe to conclude
that some, if not many, of them had been unnecessarily
granted away for knight-service by the bishop's predecessors. It is therefore probable that in 1127 the fees
existing on the lands of the bishopric may have approached
very nearly to the number of 66⅓, which would have
brought in to the king the sum of a hundred pounds on a
scutage of thirty shillings. And, if so, there is no need to
assume that the scutages levied by Henry I differed
materially in the manner of their assessment from those
levied in the time of his grandson.

Beyond this we can hardly go at present, for it is not
until Stephen's reign that references to scutage become
numerous. Most of them, it is true, are mere statements
that a particular piece of land is to be exempt from this

---

[1] Quoted in *Feudal England*, 270, as evidence of the antiquity of scutage,
from the letters of Herbert Losinga (ed. R. Anstruther, 50–52).

[2] This is the figure given by Round on the evidence of the Pipe Rolls
(*Feudal England*, 249). The *Carta* of Bishop William (*Red Book*, 391, 392)
only accounts for 33¾ fees of the old enfeoffment.

[3] *Anglia Sacra*, i. 619.

payment. Nevertheless, they show that scutage was a familiar burden before the accession of Henry II, and that, contrary to what is often stated, it was being levied on lay as well as ecclesiastical tenants in chief. The clearest of these passages occurs in a charter of Gilbert, the first earl of Pembroke, confirming certain lands to Southwark Priory, 'free from all service except scutage, so that when it shall happen that a knight gives twenty shillings, that land shall give two shillings, and if a knight gives one mark, it shall give sixteen pence, and this by the favour of the lord Talbot to whom the service of that land is due, and who holds it of me'.[1] As Round pointed out,[2] this charter shows that scutage under Stephen was already being levied in the manner made familiar by the records of the next reign, and the terms in which this information is given imply that this method of assessment was well established when the charter was written. All the early evidence which we possess suggests, in fact, that under Henry I a lord holding of the king by military service must pay scutage when he is called upon to do so, and King Henry's writ in favour of the church of Ely shows that in the case of his ecclesiastical tenants he had held himself free to exact scutage in respect of knights enfeoffed in excess of *servicia debita*. The earl of Pembroke's charter just quoted shows that a payment definitely called scutage was being taken from mesne tenants by their lords in the period immediately following the king's death. It would also seem that even at this early date the individual holders of knights' fees were distributing this burden among their own agricultural tenants, imposing definite portions of a knight's scutage upon the various holdings of which their fees were composed. In a charter which apparently comes from the last years of Henry I, Walter Croc, one of a family important in Wiltshire and the

---

[1] *Facsimiles of Royal and other Charters in the British Museum*, No. 17. The charter is there dated 1138–48, perhaps 1138–40.

[2] *Studies on the Red Book of the Exchequer* (1898), 8. Apparently, Round was not acquainted with this charter when he wrote the section on the Antiquity of Scutage in *Feudal England*.

neighbouring counties, grants a mill to Farleigh priory 'free and quit of everything as free alms, except the scutage of a knight and so much Danegeld as is due from the mill', and promises to induce his lord, and his own wife, son, and brothers to confirm the gift.[1] To the man who wrote this charter scutage seems to have appeared in the light of an occasional supplementary rent.

In the thirteenth century the lord's right to take scutage was narrowly restricted by the king's officers. He could only take scutage by authority of the writ *de scutagio habendo* authorizing him to recoup himself in whole or in part for the sum exacted from him by the king. The Pipe Rolls of the late twelfth century give many examples of this writ.[2] But the development of the principle underlying the writ was the result of many years of strong government. In the feudal charters of the reign of Stephen and the earlier years of Henry II, the lord seems at least as much interested as the king in the profits of a scutage. Whatever may have been the case under Henry I, both political conditions and the language of charters suggest that in Stephen's reign many scutages were being levied on the initiative of individual lords. A charter from the Register of Monks Horton Priory points very clearly to the existence of baronial scutages in this period.

'Be it known to all the faithful of Holy Church that I, Robert of Aldglose, and Hamo my son give and grant to God and St. John of Horton and the monks serving God there that half *virgata* of land which Robert de Vere held of me by hereditary right, and the service of Cola son of Lanter, with all the liberties, customs, and honours with which Cola himself and his ancestors served me and my ancestors. We give these things, I say, in perpetual and free alms, to hold as ever my father Osbert held most freely, and I after his decease, saving the king's right to carrying service, for which the monks shall answer to me and my heirs and Cola shall answer to the monks, and the service of my lord, namely scutage, in respect

---

[1] P.R.O. Ancient Deeds, B. 11642; Appendix, No. 37. Walter Croc figures somewhat frequently in the Pipe Roll of 1130.

[2] Pipe Roll 1195, Chancellor's Roll 1196, Pipe Roll Society, n.s., vols. vi and vii. See under *Scutagium* in Index Rerum.

of which the monks shall render the fourth penny when my lord shall take scutage in his land.'[1]

The exact interpretation of this charter is not easy, and, in particular, the reference to 'the fourth penny' of scutage is ambiguous. But there is no ambiguity about the contrast which the charter draws between the king's claim to carrying-service and the lord's claim to scutage, 'when he shall take scutage in his land'. These words are irreconcilable with the existence of any law or custom that a lord may only take scutage from his men when the king has taken a scutage from him. The king's interest in scutage is not so much ignored as implicitly denied by the writer of this charter. Scutage to him is a form of feudal service. And the same idea undoubtedly lies behind the remarkable exemption given by a contemporary lord to a monastic estate 'from all worldly services, that is, from royal as well as military services'.[2]

Phrases so definite as these are rarely found in private charters after the close of Stephen's reign. But it is certain, at least, that the greater lords of the next generation, after a scutage had been taken from them, felt themselves fully competent to levy scutage from their men without waiting for the king's authorization. Some of them frame their charters in a way which shows the survival, far into Henry's reign, of the ideas about scutage

---

[1] Stowe MS. 935, f. 17 b; Appendix, No. 38. The distinction between the king's service and the lord's scutage comes out no less clearly in a charter of Hamo son of Robert confirming his father's gift *quietam de omnibus rebus preter servicium regis et scutagium dimidie virgate terre* (ibid.). The lord to whom the scutage belonged was William Patrick of Patrixbourne, who confirmed the gift, with the reservation of his service, doubtless the scutage in question (ibid. and Stowe MS. 924, p. 196). Of the other persons mentioned in the charter, Robert de Vere was the founder of Monks Horton Priory and constable to King Stephen (Round, *Geoffrey de Mandeville*, 326–7), and Osbert, father of Robert of Aldglose, was probably the Osbert who held the village in 1086 (D.B. i. 10 b).

[2] Ancient Deeds, B. 8361: 'ab omnibus servitiis terrenis, tam regalibus videlicet quam militaribus, donis quoque et debitis et auxiliis et exactionibus denique universis.' The charter records a confirmation by Warin de Aula to Quarr Abbey of land at Shalfleet in the Isle of Wight, and its date is approximately 1145–50.

current in the earlier age of feudal autonomy. William Earl Ferrers, late in this reign, goes so far as to include scutage among the 'services' which belong to himself, as distinguished from those which are due to the king.[1] At the date of this charter we seem far from any general idea that the taking of a scutage was a matter for the king alone. But the king's power was now re-established over the feudal world and the way was clear for the development of scutage into the constitutional imposition which bore that name in the thirteenth century. Beside the charters which speak of scutage as the service of a feudal lord, there may be set in contrast a charter from the early years of Henry III in which a small Lincolnshire landowner makes a grant to another of his kind 'for one penny to scutage, that is, when scutage is given in the kingdom by the common counsel of the kingdom'.[2]

By themselves the explicit references to scutage in documents earlier than 1154 would give a misleading impression of the extent to which these payments were really being made. Already in the reign of Henry I lords can be seen granting out portions of their estates to be held by minute fractions of a knight's service—fractions so small that the service which they represent can only have been discharged by a money payment. Later in the century the service involved by these tenancies amounts to little more than a contribution to a scutage imposed by the king. Tenure by the twentieth part of a knight's service means essentially an undertaking to pay the twentieth part of the sum at which a knight's fee may be assessed to scutage from time to time, though some small payment towards castle-guard may also have been required from the tenant. The idea that the obligation to pay a single halfpenny as scutage exposed a tenant to all the incidents of military tenure belongs to the thirteenth century, not the twelfth, and certainly cannot be carried back to the small military tenancies, if such they can be called, of the Norman time. If the language of the *Cartae Baronum* can

[1] F. M. Stenton, *Danelaw Charters*, cxxvii and 308.
[2] *Duchy of Lancaster Misc. Books*, ii. 258.

be trusted, tenancies of this kind had been created in considerable numbers before the death of Henry I. It is true that most of the tenancies created by tenants in chief in the time of the 'old enfeoffment' required from their holders at least the whole of a knight's service, and that most of the remainder had been granted for the service of half a knight, a service which then, as later, could possibly be discharged by sending a sergeant to the royal array. But there are more cases than is always realized in which a baron will return among his fees of the old enfeoffment tenancies carrying a very small part of a knight's service: a fifth, a tenth, or even a twentieth. In some cases a baron may have been mistaken as to the date of one of these small tenancies, and in others he may be recording the results of the partition of a knight's fee between coheiresses. It is unlikely that many of these small tenancies should be thus explained away, for the essential purpose of the *Cartae* was to record the tenancies created before the death of Henry I, and the whole tendency of the time was towards maintaining the integrity of the knight's fee. There is no need, for example, to mistrust the accuracy of Alfred of Lincoln, who states that he owes the service of twenty-five knights 'of the old enfeoffment', accounts for twenty-four knights' fees, and then records that 'a certain old woman' holds the sixteenth of a knight's fee, that Thomas de Chamflur and 'the widow of Bockham' each hold a quarter, and that Robert son of William and Alfred the Frenchman each hold the fifth of a fee.[1] These are small tenancies for the period before 1135, but they are kept well apart in the *Carta* from their lord's fees of the new enfeoffment and it is hard to conceive any method by which they can have arisen through the division of a larger holding.

The general accuracy of the *Cartae* in regard to this matter is confirmed by the existence of a small number of charters which actually record enfeoffments for a minute fraction of a knight's service in the reign of Henry I. One of them, which has never yet been printed, may be

Red Book, 215.

translated here. It relates to the neighbourhood of Kingsbury in the north of Warwickshire, and was drawn up by a man little practised in writing.

'Osbert of Arden greets Osbert his son and Philip and Peter and all men, present and future. Know that I have given to Gerard and Nicholas sons of Thomas, in fee and inheritance, to them and their heirs to hold of me and my heirs, all the park of Brockley, except Hennecroft and Clippescroft, and la Haie and Sichplode and fifty acres by Essebroc and the assart of Serich and the assart of Grimbald with the meadow, and Longesleie and the land of Richard the steward, free and quit with every liberty for the twentieth part of a knight's service, and twenty-four acres in fee for three shillings of service to Hedric the priest, Farewell.[1]

Another charter, which cannot be later than 1142, records the gift of a tenant's service by a great baron to a third party. It is interesting because the service in question, which includes the duty of 'making up the sixteenth part of a knight', must have been fixed far back in the reign of Henry I.

'Let all present and future know that I, Robert de Oilli, grant to Richard de Brai the service of Richard of St. Edmunds, who shall hold of him, freely and quietly, as he held of my father and of me, and by the same service, that is, for his tenure he shall make up the sixteenth part of a knight, and in addition, if his lord wishes, he shall send him once a year all the way from Oxford to Shenstone, and all the expence shall be his lord's.'[2]

---

[1] Cott. Chart. xxii. 2; Appendix, No. 39. This charter is assigned to the reign of Henry I in the *Index to the Charters and Rolls in the British Museum* (vol. i, under 'Brocheleie'). For other references to Osbert of Arden see the notes to plate IX in the *Facsimiles of royal and other charters in the British Museum*, where another charter of Osbert is reproduced. Towards the year 1150 all these parcels of land, except the assarts of Serich and Grimbald, the meadow of Longesleie, and the final twenty-four acres, were confirmed to Gerard and Nicholas by Robert son of Walter and his wife, daughter of Osbert de Arden the younger, for the twenty-sixth of a knight's service to the earl of Warwick (Cott. Chart. xxv. 25).

[2] Add. Chart. 20461; Appendix, No. 40. Printed from a copy in the Great Coucher of the Duchy of Lancaster in *Transactions of the William Salt Archaeological Society*, xvii. 240. Robert de Oilli, the grantor of this charter, died in 1142 (Salter, *Eynsham Cartulary*, i. 73). It may be added

Each of these charters has its own curious feature. In the first a number of parcels of land, some of which have obviously been recently reclaimed from woodland, are being granted out for a fraction of a knight's service which can have involved little more than the payment of one or two shillings when a scutage was taken. In the second charter a riding service which would afterwards be classified as sergeanty is combined with a fraction of knight-service in a way which was not usual, at least in central England, at a later time. It is more important to note that each of these charters stipulates for a small fraction of knight-service in a manner which shows that the discharge of this service by a money payment was a well-established custom when they were drawn up. In view of this contemporary evidence that grants of land for the sixteenth and even the twentieth of a knight's service were possible before 1135, the references to such enfeoffments in later records such as the Cartae of 1166 clearly deserve respect. There can, in fact, be no doubt that the introduction of scutage was affecting the system of tenure by knight-service long before the death of Henry I. The Yorkshire knight of the mid-twelfth century who said that a tenant's ancestors had held land of his ancestors for the sixteenth of a knight's service since the Conquest of England cannot be taken quite literally, but he may not have been very wide of the mark.[1]

Note to pages 167–9. After this chapter was written, that, as Shenstone is nearly seventy miles from Oxford, Richard of St. Edmunds would be occupied in going and returning for at least four days each time this riding service was required from him.

[1] Add. Chart. 20507. 'Ego Alexander de Santona reddidi Willelmo cognato meo...foedum suum... Et sciendum est quod predictus Willelmus et heredes sui tenebunt . . . predictam terram . . . faciendo liberum seruicium scilicet sextam decimam partem seruicii unius militis sicut antecessores sui tenuerunt de antecessoribus meis de conquestu Anglie.' The charter can at most be only a few years later than 1154, and may well be earlier, so that it stands apart from the numerous later documents which refer, almost as a matter of common form, to tenures coming down from the Conquest. 'Santona' is Sancton in the East Riding of Yorkshire.

another early charter implying a knight's fee of ten *libratae terrae* was published by Sir Cyril Flower in *Curia Regis Rolls*, v. 317–18. Robert de Gant, after granting certain lands at Irnham, Lincolnshire, to Alfred of Pointon, adds that if Alfred gives him his father's land he will make up for Alfred a hundred *solidatae terrae* for the service of half a knight.

VI

CASTLES AND CASTLE-GUARD

AMONG the various forms of a knight's duty, his service in the field and the payments which at a later time were made in lieu of it have naturally attracted most attention from modern scholars. The knight's service 'by his lord's shield' was the most obvious expression of the feudal relationship,[1] and the development of scutage forms part of the general history of English taxation. But it is at least an open question whether the services which may be comprised under the name of castle-guard were not originally more onerous. The feudal army of England was only brought together for some especial purpose, and scutage was only an occasional imposition. But the conditions of feudal society demanded the continual presence of knights in the castles of the eleventh and early twelfth centuries, and there are some early charters granting land for a knight's service which make castle-guard the essential part of the tenant's obligation. Soon after the middle of the twelfth century Robert of Ewias gave the village of Upton Scudamore to Godfrey 'Escudamore' for his homage and service and for one white destrier, *faciendo inde annuatim servicium unius militis ad castrum de Ewias, scilicet ad wardam castri super custagium suam.*[2] Under Stephen a Herefordshire landowner speaks of the land which Ralf de Toeni, his lord, had given him 'for the service of one knight when it ought to be done at Clifford'.[3] Ewias Harold and Clifford were border castles, but the normal conditions of life within a castle must have been much the same everywhere. Only men of some position

---

[1] It was part of the duty owed by a man to the lord of whom he was *ligius*. See above, 30.

[2] M. Gibson, *A View of the Ancient and Present State of the Churches of Door, Home-Lacy, and Hempsted*, 56.

[3] Add. Chart. 20454; Appendix, No. 41.

could maintain order among the miscellaneous sergeants and men-at-arms who inhabited the castles of this early time. The household knights of a great baron were essentially his personal attendants, who followed him over the country from place to place. The knights who were required for the permanent garrison of a baronial castle would naturally be drawn in the first instance from the ranks of a baron's *milites feoffati*. Little is known of the method by which this service was organized, but the evidence suggests that a rotation of duty was originally established among the knights of an honour, and that in course of time, when the private castle lost its first military importance, this duty became commuted into a system of monetary payments.[1] Even at an early date many barons may have preferred to hire knights for this purpose.[2] No lord could be sure that all his knights would punctually keep their terms in the rota, and the problem of the super-annuated knight confronted the baron as well as the king.

It is easy to misconceive the place of the baronial castle in the twelfth century. It is generally regarded from the standpoint of Stephen's reign, when for a short time it formed an obstacle to the maintenance of public order. In reality the baronial castle was the expression of ideas which underlay the social custom of the whole French-speaking world, and passed rapidly into the consciousness of the Anglo-Norman people of every race. To the king himself the baronial castle was long necessary for the defence of the land. It was not until the death of William son of Robert of Normandy in 1128 that the Anglo-Norman monarchy at last became secure. For more than sixty years after the Conquest it had depended in the last resort on the loyalty of individual barons and the knights of their honours. In different ways the Conqueror and his immediate successors were each on the defensive in England, and their financial resources were unequal to

[1] See below, 209–11.

[2] The low rate at which 'castle-guard rents' are generally fixed suggests that they were stabilized at an early period, when knights could be hired very cheaply.

the business of national fortification upon a scale sufficient to meet invasion which might have come from France or Flanders, Norway or Denmark. Within a generation from the death of William Clito the military situation had changed. The events of Stephen's reign had shown how easily the private castle might become a centre of revolt. Henry II was compelled to a policy of military centralization. With few exceptions the baronial castles of the midlands and south had lost their military significance before the end of his reign.[1] By the end of the century, except along the Welsh and Scotch borders, national defence had come to turn essentially on the king's own castles and the mercenary soldiers in his service. The baronial castle had become an anachronism.[2]

It is chiefly for this reason that the *castellaria*, the district organized feudally for the defence of a particular castle, is so rarely mentioned in English records. In its broadest sense the word denoted a group of fees owing service at the castle from which it took its name by finding knights or sergeants for its defence, or by contributing money for this purpose.[3] But the castlery of the earliest Anglo-Norman records appears as a territory rather than a mere group of fees, as a well-defined district within which the whole arrangement of tenancies was primarily designed for the maintenance of the castle. The clearest evidence of this usage comes from the statement in the Summary of the Yorkshire Domesday that Earl Alan has 199 manors in his *castellatus*, of which his men hold 133, and that apart from his castlery he has 43 manors, of which his men hold 10.[4] The distinction thus carefully drawn shows that the

[1] On the temporary importance of baronial castles in the reign of Richard I see below, 205, note 3.

[2] A new basis for the study of the English castle under Henry II and his sons is provided by R. Allen Brown's *List of Castles, 1154–1216* (*English Historical Review*, lxxiv. 249–80), 1959. It covers 'all those castles in the Angevin kingdom of England in active existence at any time within the period 1154–1216 to which contemporary or near-contemporary written reference has been found'.

[3] This seems to be the meaning of the *castellaria* of Nottingham discussed below, 215.   [4] D.B. i. 381.

original castlery of Richmond was the large and compact
fee afterwards known as Richmondshire, the 'Honour of
Richmond' in the narrow sense of the phrase. It definitely
excludes from the castlery the fees which the earl's men
held of him elsewhere in Yorkshire, and in England south
of the Humber, although later records show their successors charged with payments for castle-guard at Richmond.[1]
The rapes of Sussex, which have been described suscinctly
as 'self-contained feudal castellanies',[2] illustrate the
territorial aspect of the *castellaria* no less clearly, and the
five marcher castleries mentioned incidentally in Domesday, Caerleon on Usk,[3] Richard's Castle,[4] Ewias Harold,[5]
Clifford,[6] and Montgomery,[7] obviously have the same
character. Even the castlery of Dudley, the one *castellaria*
in central England to which Domesday Book refers
explicitly, seems to have belonged to the same type. Its
boundaries cannot now be neatly drawn like those of Richmondshire and the rapes of Sussex, but there can be little
doubt that the eleventh-century castlery of Dudley consisted of the compact group of manors held by William
son of Ansculf, its lord, in the country where Staffordshire,
Warwickshire, and Worcestershire meet.[8] Later records
throw little light on the structure of the first Norman
castleries. A notification by William II that he has
granted to Ilbert de Laci 'the custom of the castlery of his

---

[1] In the survey of the Richmond Fee in the *Calendar of Inquisitions,
Miscellaneous*, i. 168–71, the fees owing castle-guard at Richmond are
divided into three groups: 'Richmondshire', to which the earl's more
southerly Yorkshire lands seem to have been annexed by this time, 'Hol-
land', covering his fees in Lincolnshire and Nottinghamshire, and a district
broadly described as 'between Well Stream and the Norman Sea', em-
bracing the earl's fees south of the Welland.

[2] By Professor Tait in *Place-Names of Sussex* (English Place-Name
Society), i. 9. Lewes and Hastings definitely appear as the head of castleries
in Domesday.   [3] D.B. i. 185 b.

[4] Ibid. i. 185.   [5] Ibid. i. 181 b, 184, 185.
[6] Ibid. i. 183.   [7] Ibid. i. 253 b.

[8] Ibid. i. 177. The nature of this *castellaria* is disguised by the fact that
the lands which once formed it were, and are, divided between three
counties, and by the modern industrial development of this country, which
has obscured ancient boundaries.

castle' as he had it in the time of the king's father and of
Odo bishop of Bayeux, shows that Pontefract was the
head of another of these early *castellariae*,[1] and the
distribution of Ilbert's lands in south Yorkshire shows
that it belonged to the compact type of which the castlery
of Richmond is the great example. The ancient rural deanery of 'Castillar' in the archdeaconry of Derby probably
preserves the memory of a Norman castlery of Tutbury
of the same kind, for nearly all the manors in this deanery
were of the Domesday fee of Henry de Ferrers, and his
castle of Tutbury is only separated from this district by
the river Dove.[2] But before the end of the twelfth century
the word was certainly being used in a less restricted
sense, to cover the whole complex of fees which contributed to the maintenance of a lord's chief castle or of
a castle belonging to the king.[3] It became an occasional
synonym for *honor*, which could be used when a writer
was chiefly thinking of the castle at the honorial centre.
The *castellaniae* of Eye and Berkhamstead, of which Ralf
de Diceto states that Thomas Becket once had possession,
were really the honours to which these castles had given
name.[4]

At present it is impossible to give even an approximate
list of the castles which existed in England in the first half
of the century. Domesday Book is most erratic in its
record of castles, and the Pipe Roll of 1130 only mentions
a private castle when its upkeep for some reason had
become a charge upon the king. The Mowbray castles of
Kirkby Malzeard, Burton in Lonsdale, Thirsk, and Brinklow only appear in the roll because the land of Roger de

---

[1] Farrer, *Early Yorkshire Charters*, No. 1415. The castlery of Pontefract appears again when Ilbert de Laci II confirms to Pontefract Priory
terciam partem decime quam habebant monachi de dominio castellanie and the
various gifts made by the barons of the same 'castellania', ibid., No. 1492.

[2] *Taxatio Papae Nicholai*, 247; Bacon, *Liber Regis*, 173.

[3] For a castlery of Nottingham which seems to have belonged to the
latter type see below, 215.

[4] *Historical Works of Ralf de Diceto*, ed. Stubbs, i. 314. Becket's custody
of the honour of Eye is proved by the Pipe Roll of 1163 (Pipe Roll Society,
vi. 34).

Mowbray was in the king's hands, and it was for him to pay the porter and watchmen of each castle.[1] No list of early castles will ever be more than approximate, for many unimportant castles seem to have been deserted by their lords at an early date. Before 1148 Earl William of Lincoln, when confirming the gifts of Peter of Goxhill to Newhouse Abbey, mentions among them the *capitalis curia* where Peter's castle was.[2] Between 1140 and 1153 Earl Simon of Northampton granted to Odo de Dammartin land, 'as much as the site of the castle comprises', at Boughton in Southoe near St. Neots.[3] There seems no other record of this castle, and the earl's language suggests that it was derelict when he wrote. At any moment a newly discovered charter may reveal another early baronial castle. The evidence which carries Kenilworth Castle itself back into the reign of Henry I comes, not from any chronicle, but from the charters by which Geoffrey de Clinton granted to his monastery of Kenilworth all the open land of that place, excepting that which he had retained to make his castle and park.[4] The castles of Ascot d'Oilly in Oxfordshire and Oversley in Warwickshire, each of which was certainly in being before the accession of Henry II, are carried back to this early time through the charters by which Roger de Oilli

---

[1] Pipe Roll of 1130, ed. Hunter, 137, 138. This early reference to Brinklow Castle is important, for it shows that this castle, a typical motte and bailey fortress of the type discussed below, 198–201, had arisen long before the wars of Stephen's reign.

[2] *Facsimiles of royal and other charters in the British Museum*, No. 24.

[3] Add. Chart. 11233. A later twelfth-century reference to a deserted castle occurs in a charter in the Wardon cartulary, dated by Dr. Fowler, its editor, *c.* 1180–1200. A certain William son of Wigain grants to Wardon Abbey *quicquid habui al baille ueteris castelli apud molendinum de Risingeho* (*Bedfordshire Historical Record Society*, xiii. 125). A mound still known as Risinghoe Castle stands by the Ouse some miles below Bedford, and is doubtless the 'mota' which is mentioned in another charter in the Wardon cartulary relating to this place (ibid., 131). Unfortunately, these passages do not show whether Risinghoe Castle was first occupied before or during the wars of Stephen's time.

[4] *Mon. Ang.* vi. 220–1.

gave the chapel in the castle of Ascot to the canons of St. Frideswide,[1] and Ralf Pincerna, when founding a monastery at Alcester, gave it the chapel in his castle of Oversley.[2] Grants of this kind show that the castles to which they relate were something more than places for temporary defence upon a sudden emergency. The existence of a chapel within a castle implies at lea st th occasional presence of its lord. The castle of Ascot d'Oilly has now been brought to light by excavation and that of Oversley by observation from the air.[3]

Evidently, the extent to which the Anglo-Norman aristocracy had given itself to the work of castle-building cannot be determined by written evidence alone. The remains of its castles still exist in every part of the country and in great number. For the past thirty years it has been generally recognized that the common type of earthwork consisting of a mound, girt with a ditch, and overlooking a base court—the motte and bailey of archaeological literature—represents a French castle of the eleventh or twelfth century.[4] Individual students had long been aware of the curious uniformity of plan shown by the earliest Norman castles in England. But the demonstration of the French origin of the motte and bailey earthwork belongs to the earliest years of the present century, and for the first time made possible an estimate of the place of the castle in Anglo-Norman society. For the number of these earthworks which have survived time and change is very great. That they should occur in large numbers along the Welsh border might be set down to the special conditions prevailing on a military frontier. The numerous mottes and baileys of the Midlands are more remarkable. In the single county of Warwick, castles of

---

[1] *Cartulary of the Monastery of St. Frideswide*, ed. Wigram, ii. 242.

[2] *Mon. Ang.* iv. 175.

[3] E. M. Jope and R. J. Threlfall, *Antiquaries Journal*, xxxix. 219–73.

[4] Among the books and articles which have established this view there may be mentioned Round's paper, 'The Castles of the Conquest' (*Archaeologia*, vol. lviii, 1902), Mrs. Armitage's 'Early Norman Castles of England' (*Eng. Hist. Rev.* xix. 209–45 and 417–55), and her book *The Early Norman Castles of the British Isles* (published in 1912).

this type are found at Kineton and Brailes in the south, at Brinklow in the centre, at Hartshill, Castle Bromwich, Seckington, and Tamworth in the north.[1] From every standpoint these fortifications deserve study. The scores of earthworks in the heart of England which we now know to represent castles built between the battle of Hastings and the death of King Stephen are the most authentic memorials remaining of the age of militant feudalism. They stand for an organization of feudal service in which the defence of the private castle was at least as important as the provision of knights for the king's armies. They show that the process of castellation was one of the cardinal facts of Anglo-Norman history, and they raise in a concrete form the whole question of the relations between the Anglo-Norman baronage and the king. The feudalism of the twelfth century is described for us by the law books which that age produced, but they reveal, at most, only one side of a highly complicated society. Beneath the *imperium regiae majestatis* on which they insist, the private castle stood for the liberty of the individual baron.

A large proportion of these motte and bailey castles have no recorded history. Now and then excavation or chance discovery brings to light evidence suggesting a prolonged occupation of such a site in the Norman period; as when a trench through the outworks of the motte and bailey at Yelden in Bedfordshire produced many traces of stone buildings, including one fragment bearing a moulding of Norman character.[2] Generally there is nothing but indirect evidence as to the date or purpose of these early castles, though this evidence is sometimes convincing enough. When one of them is situated in a place known to have been the centre of a feudal honour the castle can hardly be other than itself the *caput honoris*, the fortified residence of the lord. Many motte and bailey castles are known to have been the centres of fees which bore their names— Tutbury, Haughley, Cainhoe, and Eye are four clear

[1] For plans and descriptions of these motte and bailey castles see *Victoria County History of Warwickshire*, i. 355–406.
[2] *Associated Architectural Societies' Reports for 1882*, 261–3.

instances—and the significance of others is only con-
cealed by the informality of feudal nomenclature. There
can be no doubt, for example, that the large motte and
bailey earthwork at Laxton or Lexington in Nottinghamshire was really the head of the fee for which Robert de
Cauz acknowledged the *servicium debitum* of fifteen knights
in 1166,[1] but the name of the castle was only occasionally
annexed to his barony. Few castles in England are more
famous than the motte and bailey at Fotheringay, but its
recorded history does not begin before the thirteenth
century,[2] and it is only a somewhat elaborate argument
which leads to the conclusion that it formed the head of
the vast honour of Huntingdon.[3] It would be premature
at present to speculate as to the number of motte and
bailey castles which can be connected with the centres of
important fees. The number is certainly considerable, but
the feudal geography of England is a new science, and its
elements have hardly been established as yet.

The uncertainty is unfortunate, for the question has a
direct bearing on the general history of England in the
twelfth century. Should these motte and bailey castles
be regarded as natural results of the feudal organization of
Anglo-Norman society or as the outcome of the disintegra-
tion of royal authority which marks the reign of Stephen?
In other words is it probable that the 'adulterine' castles
of Stephen's reign, in so far as they have survived at all,
should be sought among the extant earthworks of this
class? Now and then an unusual combination of evidence

---

[1] *Red Book of the Exchequer*, i. 343. This fee represented a portion of the
large fief held in 1086 by Geoffrey Alselin. The larger part of the fief,
which carried a service of twenty-five knights, was held in 1166 by Ralf
Alselin. Its head was Shelford in Nottinghamshire, where there is no
evidence of any early castle. The great size of the motte and double bailey
at Laxton, for which see the *Victoria County History of Nottinghamshire*,
i. 307, suggests that it was built before the division of the Alselin fee, and,
if so, it cannot be later than the reign of Henry I.

[2] The existence of the castle is virtually implied by the fact that Earl
Simon of Northampton held his court at Fotheringay immediately after
he obtained the honour of Huntingdon in 1174 (above, 44), but there
seems to be no definite reference to the castle before 1212 (Farrer, *Honors
and Knights' Fees*, ii. 396).   [3] *Ibid.* ii. 300.

suggests the identification of an existing motte and bailey with a castle built during this period. The foundation history of Welbeck Abbey, for instance, recites that Thomas of Cuckney, the founder of that house, was brought up at the court of Henry I, and after his father's death held his land 'until the old war, and then he made for himself a castle in the aforesaid land of Cuckney'.[1] The authority of this as of most similar narratives is poor, but it is suggestive that the church of Cuckney in Nottinghamshire stands within a small earthwork which has been badly mutilated but preserves the essential features of a motte and bailey castle.[2] The essential facts which point to an earlier origin than this for the majority of motte and bailey castles are the large scale on which they tend to be planned and the evidence of deliberation in design which most of them show. A highly developed castle of this type, like Cainhoe in Bedfordshire or Castle Bytham in Lincolnshire,[3] could not have been raised under the conditions which were inevitable in a time of feudal anarchy. It was easy to dig a ditch and throw the upcast into a mound sufficiently solid to bear an encircling stockade. It was a different task to choose a site which would command its environment, to plot out the elaborate defences of water and earthwork which often distinguish the motte and bailey castle, to raise a mound compact enough to carry substantial buildings of timber or even stone, and at the same time steep enough to check a direct assault. The general character of these castles suggests very strongly that most of them were planned under conditions which allowed a lord to choose his ground deliberately, and gave the time necessary for its modelling into a permanent defensive work. It was under very different circumstances that the innumerable castles of Stephen's reign arose.

---

[1] *Mon. Ang.* vii. 873.

[2] The outline of the plan is indicated on the six-inch Ordnance Map of Nottinghamshire, Sheet xviii, NW.

[3] Cainhoe, as has just been observed, formed the head of a barony, and Domesday Book suggests, though it does not state, that a castle had already arisen at 'West Bitham' by 1086. See above, 144–5.

That these castles differed widely from one another in scale and type is more than probable. Other forms of castle than the motte and bailey were familiar in the twelfth century. Geoffrey de Clinton relied on water rather than earthwork for the external defences of his castles at Brandon and Kenilworth. Other lords were content with defences of extreme simplicity. The castle near Solihull in Warwickshire which formed the head of the important Limesi barony consisted essentially of a simple enclosure of earthwork.[1] In the twelfth century, *castellum* was a vague word, and it could be applied to fortifications whose defensive value, to say the least, was small. A plea roll of 1194, reciting an appeal which had arisen from Count John's recent rebellion, makes the appellator allege that the appellee 'was against the lord king in the castle of Kingshaugh'.[2] Kingshaugh in central Nottinghamshire may have been a centre of local rebellion, but the 'castle' was itself no more than a moated hunting-lodge, over-looked by rising ground immediately behind it. That some adulterine castles were intended to be permanent is probable enough. The castle which Thomas of Cuckney built 'in the old war'[3] would have been a suitable residence for a small baron. But the extreme difficulty of identifying any considerable number of these fortifications suggests that most of them were only intended to serve a temporary purpose—to interrupt lines of communication, to command a stretch of country during the continuance of the war, or to form a defensible warehouse for plunder. It is highly significant that the castles which determined the general course of the war, with hardly a single prominent exception, were castles which are known to have been in existence before the troubles began.

That the castles of the Anarchy were rarely, if ever,

[1] Brandon, Kenilworth, and the entrenchments at Solihull which mark the *caput* of the Limesi-Odingsells fee are described in the article already quoted in the *Victoria County History of Warwickshire*, vol. i.

[2] *Rolls of the King's Court* (Pipe Roll Society, vol. xiv), 23. For a plan of the earthworks at Kingshaugh see *Victoria County History of Nottinghamshire*, i. 301.

[3] See previous page.

castles of stone is beyond dispute. It would seem that some of them were not even castles of earthwork. The author of the *Gesta Stephani* in his account of the events which followed the king's release in the autumn of 1141, describes the castle building of the empress and her friends in a remarkable but little-quoted passage.[1]

'She built castles over the country wherever she might to best advantage; some to hold back the king's men more effectively, others for the defence of her own people—one at Woodstock, king Henry's place of most private retirement, another at the village of Radcot, surrounded by water and marsh, a third at the city of Cirencester, next the holy church of the religious like another Dagon before the ark of the Lord, a fourth in the village of Bampton, on the tower of the church there, which had been built in ancient days of wonderful design by the amazing skill of ingenious labour: and she allowed her helpers to build other castles in different parts of England, from which there arose grievous oppression to the people, a general devastation of the realm, and the seeds of disorder on every hand.'

However wonderful may have been the design of Bampton church tower, the 'castle' which it supported can have been nothing elaborate. The only kind of castle which we can easily conceive in this extraordinary position is a wooden tower, and the complete disappearance of the other three castles named in this passage suggests that they consisted of similar erections, strengthened with such earthwork as could be thrown up most rapidly. It is significant that at Cirencester in the course of a rapid campaign, Stephen could not only burn the 'castle' but also level its earthworks with the ground.[2] Castles even of this elementary type might be an intolerable nuisance to a whole country-side. There is no need to suspect exaggeration in contemporary accounts of the horrors of the war, nor to dispute the part which unlicensed castles played in them. When independent narratives relating to

[1] *Gesta Stephani*, ed. Potter, 92.
[2] Loc. cit. 'civitatem Cirencestriae improvise devenit, castellumque, custodibus furtive dispersis, evacuatum reperiens, ignibus depascendum commisit, valloque et propugnaculis usque ad imum diruto.'

the south of England generally, to the north-east Midlands,
and to south Yorkshire tell the same story, it deserves to
be taken seriously.[1] But the castles which arose in these
years have no place in the development of fortifications in
feudal England.

In connexion with the problem of the 'adulterine
castle' it may be noted that the phrase *castellum firmauit*,
common as it is in twelfth-century histories, is really
ambiguous. It could certainly be used of the making of a
new fortification, as when the *Gesta Stephani* relates how
the earl of Chester *ante castellum Coventerii ubi se regales
receperant . . . castellum firmavit.*[2] But it could also mean to
strengthen or re-fortify an existing castle, and there is
more than one passage in the *Gesta* where the context
leaves the meaning open. The danger of assuming that the
words *castellum firmare* imply the making of a new castle
appears very clearly on a comparison of two narratives
relating to the rebellion of 1173–4, in which the private
castle once more became a public danger. The *Gesta Regis
Henrici Secundi* states that Roger de Mowbray early in
the rising *firmauit castellum apud Kinardeferiam in insula
quae vocatur Axiholm.*[3] By itself this passage certainly
suggests that Roger's castle of Kinnardferry was a new work.
But Ralf de Diceto in describing the same events is more
precise, and his *castellum ab antiquo constructum sed tunc
temporis dirutum reaedificauit*[4] shows that Roger did no
more than restore the defences of an ancient castle, the
large motte and bailey which still arise above the Trent

---

[1] The author of the *Gesta Stephani*, whose knowledge relates mainly to
southern England, is among the writers who most definitely connect the
miseries of this period with the garrisons of castles (e.g. p. 99 of Potter's
edition). The famous passage in the *Anglo-Saxon Chronicle* presumably
refers primarily to conditions around Peterborough, and similar conditions
in south Yorkshire are described very clearly in the little-known Historia
Monasterii Selebiensis, prefixed by J. T. Fowler to his edition of the
Coucher Book of Selby, Yorkshire Archaeological Society. The evidence
from Selby is very much to the point, for Henry de Lacy built a castle
there in the war.

[2] Ed. Potter, 132.

[3] Ed. Stubbs, i. 64.

[4] *Ymagines Historiarum*, ed. Stubbs, i. 379.

near Owston Ferry in Axholme. Other writers do little
to clear up ambiguities in the *Gesta Stephani*. But in view
of the real nature of Roger de Mowbray's work at Kinnardferry it becomes something more than probable that the
municipium at Trowbridge which Humphrey de Bohun
ad regi adversandum defensione inexpugnabili firmarat[1] and
the *castellum* at Wareham which the earl of Gloucester
munitissime firmarat were already in being before the wars.[2]

Later in the century, materials gradually appear from
which it is possible to recover something of the contemporary arrangements for the maintenance, and when
necessary the defence, of English castles.[3] The Pipe Rolls
yield information about the wages of knights, and of the
sergeants and miscellaneous servants who formed the staff
of a castle in being. Private charters, and in course of time
final concords, record the payments by which the average
military tenant acquitted himself of his duty of castle-
guard. When, late in the thirteenth century, the great
series of *Inquisitiones post mortem* has reached its full
development, the military organization which centred
upon the castle can be illustrated with a remarkable wealth
of detail. It must be confessed that much of this organization has an anachronistic appearance. It is, no doubt,
possible to underestimate the part played by the smaller
English castles in the wars and the preparations for war of
the thirteenth century. The ancient motte and bailey of
Stogursy in Somerset, the *caput* of the Courcy honour,

[1] *Gesta Stephani*, 61. For *municipium* as castle see below, 236, note 2.
[2] Ibid. 96.
[3] A remarkable amount of information about these arrangements is
given by the Pipe Rolls of the reign of Richard I. Owing to the disaffection
of the count of Mortain and the danger of invasion from France, the king's
representatives were compelled to keep a large number of castles in a state
of readiness for immediate attack, and some castles of which there is hardly
any other record appear as defensible positions at this time. In particular,
the Pipe Rolls show more than one baronial castle maintained with the
assistance of the central government. Lavendon Castle in Buckinghamshire,
for example, was the head of the Bidun honour, and in 1193 Henry de
Clinton, who had recently married the eldest co-heiress of this fee, received
twenty loads of wheat *ad muniendum castellum de Lavedon* (Pipe Roll
Society, n.s. iii. 93).

had been fortified in 1233 for the protection of the country.[1] It may well have been garrisoned during the Barons' War by its Montfortian lord. But its tenants in the next generation, who were bound to find for the defence of the castle 'an armed horseman with barded horse, a crossbowman and six other men on foot armed with basinets and hauberks for forty days whenever summoned in time of war at their own charges, and afterwards at their lord's charges, if he will, during war',[2] were obviously maintaining a system which had arisen long before the reign of Henry III. The interest of passages like this lies in their retrospective character, and their number is fortunately considerable.

The organization which they presuppose was more elaborate than modern writers have always realized. Its most striking feature was the service to which the name castle-guard should properly be restricted. Everything points to the conclusion that in the age of the first feudal enfeoffment a knight who received a knight's fee, to take the simplest of all cases, was bound to personal service in a castle belonging to his lord and often also in a castle belonging to the king. Long before feudal bargains were commonly expressed in writing, this service had generally been commuted into a money payment, and the scheme of garrison duty of which it had once formed part has usually disappeared without record. But the existence of such schemes of service has never been doubted, and castle-guard has always been regarded as an essential part of a knight's original duty. When, however, a feudal service is regarded from the lord's standpoint it at once becomes evident that men of less than knightly rank played a highly important part in the organization which centred around the castle. It would seem, in fact, that in a castle garrison of the twelfth century the knights must usually have been outnumbered by the men whom the Pipe Rolls of that age describe as sergeants, whose successors appear in later records as owing forty days' castle duty in the time of war,

---

[1] *Close Rolls of Henry III, 1231–4,* 546.
[2] *Calendar of Inquisitions post mortem,* iv. 341.

with their arms, and generally with a horse or two.[1] This
class has been little studied as yet, for tenure by sergeanty,
in all but its highest forms, has received less than the
attention which is its due. But its importance in feudal
society must have been considerable. It certainly included
men of substance; there were local landowners of very good
position among the sergeants who were taken when Belvoir
Castle fell in 1215.[2] In arms and equipment these sergeants can have been little inferior to the knights who fill
the centre of the feudal picture. To a considerable extent
they fell outside the process which in the twelfth century
brought tenure by knight-service more and more definitely
under the royal control. Save in the most general manner,
the king was not interested, nor did he intervene, in the
relationship between a lord and the man who held of him
by military sergeanty.[3] The Norman kings insisted that
no castle should be built without their licence, but they
were not concerned with the arrangements which their
barons might make for the garrisoning of their lawful
castles.

If early charters granting land in return for knight-
service are rare, those which create military sergeanties of
this type are even rarer. One of the earliest examples of
which a copy has been preserved was issued by the
illustrious Gilbert Foliot as bishop of Hereford, and
records the grant of certain lands for a money rent and the
service of finding a sergeant for forty days each year at the

---

[1] The best general impression of the number of these castle sergeanties
is given by the indexes to the various volumes of the *Calendars of Inquisitions post mortem*, under 'Services; Local'.

[2] *Rotuli Litterarum Patentium*, ed. Hardy, 162. Many of these 'sergeants' occur frequently in Nottinghamshire and Leicestershire charters
of this period. For some of these men see Round's notes in his *Report on
the Manuscripts of the Duke of Rutland* (Historical Manuscripts Commission), vol. iv.

[3] With regard to this subject it should be said that many sergeanties
were created for a specific military service, wholly unconnected with
garrison duty. For comparison with the garrison sergeanty quoted below
in the text, a charter is given in the Appendix, No. 43, which obliges a
tenant to find a horse and a man for his lord when the king leads an army
into Wales and the lord accompanies him.

tenant's expense in the bishop's castle of Lydbury North.[1]
Another example, which also belongs to the middle of the
twelfth century, occurs in the Missenden cartulary. It relates
to the castle of Weston Turville in central Buckinghamshire, a fine motte and bailey fortress in the grounds of the
present manor house.[2]

'Be it known to all faithful men, present and future, that I,
Geoffrey de Turville have given to John of Lee one hide of my
demesne in Weston, with all its appurtenances, as was settled before
me and my men, and with the hide I have given him the mill which
William held with all its appurtenance in land and in meadow.
All this I have granted to him in fee and inheritance, free and quit
of all service and exaction, except that John and his heirs shall keep
post for me in the castle of Weston for forty days in time of war
with a destrier and a rouncey, and for three weeks in time of peace.
Be it known also that I have done this because John has given up
to me his inheritance, namely the land of Lee which I have given
to the canons of Missenden in alms, and the aforesaid John has
quitclaimed it to the aforesaid canons and pledged his faith to acquit
it to them according to his power against all men so far as he is
concerned, and has released it and abjured it.'[3]

This charter is one of the very few early documents which

[1] Eyton, *Antiquities of Shropshire*, xi. 208. Lydbury North is now
represented by the town of Bishops Castle, on the hill above which stands
the bishop of Hereford's motte.

[2] *Report of the Royal Commission on Historical Monuments, Buckinghamshire*, i. 316–17.

[3] Harl. MS. 3688, f. 59; Appendix, No. 42. The date of this charter
cannot be fixed closely. It must be later than the foundation of Missenden
Abbey, and the foundation charter of this house (*Mon. Ang.* vi. 548) is
dated 1133. The grantor can safely be identified with Geoffrey de Turville, a tenant of Robert earl of Leicester, who was present with him at
Eling in Hampshire in 1127, when Henry I was about to cross the Channel
(Egerton MS. 3031, f. 36; cf. f. 15), figures prominently in the Pipe Roll
of 1130, and according to the *Carta* of the earl of Warwick was holding
a knight's fee of him in 1166 (*Red Book*, 325). There is a reference to
Geoffrey's former possession of the castle in the Pipe Roll of 1174 (82),
where money is allowed to the sheriff of Buckinghamshire *in custodia
castelli de Weston' quod fuit Galfridi de Turevill' antequam prosterneretur*.
The present charter evidently comes from the central years of the twelfth
century, but there is nothing to show whether it was made before or after
the accession of Henry II. On the Turville family see G. H. Fowler,
Bedfordshire Historical Record Society, vii. 204–7.

illustrate the military aspect of a small private castle in central England. It is natural to assume a sharp distinction, if not a strong antipathy between the garrison of a private castle of this period and the men of the surrounding country. Yet one member at least of the garrison of Weston Turville was evidently a man of the neighbourhood, and it may be added that the charter which recorded his enfeoffment for garrison duty was witnessed by the lord's hallimot, by two priests, one of them of English descent, by a local smith, a blood-letter, and by all the men of the village. Even in the mid-twelfth century it would seem that a private castle could be regarded as a normal feature of English country life.

There is little evidence to show the nature and organization of the castle-guard exacted from tenants by knight-service in the Norman period. Now and then, a chronicler will record some fact which illustrates the character of this service when it was still a personal duty. John of Worcester, for example, states that when Henry I granted the keepership and constabulary of Rochester Castle to the archbishop of Canterbury, he provided that the knights assigned to the custody of the castle should enter and depart in their appointed turns, and should give security to hold the castle as the archbishop might direct.[1] But passages like this are rare, and although castle-guard is often mentioned in private charters of this time, it is generally introduced in an allusive way. Most of our information about castle-guard comes from documents which are not earlier than the thirteenth century. By this time, south, at least, of Humber and east of Severn, castle-guard had long lost its first military quality and had normally been commuted for a monetary payment. Nevertheless, the castle-guard rents of the thirteenth and even later centuries are useful materials for earlier history. They continually illustrate the smallness of the wage—eight pence a day in the reign of Henry II—for which knights could once be hired, and they prove the ancient military importance of many castles which never played any part in

[1] *Chronicle of John of Worcester*, ed. Weaver, 23.

recorded history. Our information about these rents may be scattered and fragmentary, but it proves at least their high antiquity.

The essential fact in the history of castle-guard in England is the distinction between the service of this kind which a knight owed to his lord and that which the king exacted from him, through his lord, at a royal castle. Of the two, the former, though historically less interesting, is illustrated the more fully by surviving records. Rents which stand for a commutation of this duty can easily be found among the payments reserved in final concords or recorded in *Inquisitiones post mortem*. Among the private castles whose lords received such payments, Belvoir in Leicestershire and Eye in Suffolk, the original *capita* of the Albini and Malet honours, are two out of many possible examples.[1] Of the original organization into which these payments had once fitted, there is generally little that can now be learned. Richmond, the head of one of the greatest fees in England, is the private castle of whose defensive organization the most is known. No early or complete record of the system has survived, but its remains in the thirteenth century suggest that the knights enfeoffed within the honour had originally been divided into six groups, each group owing service at the castle for two consecutive months in each year.[2] Long before the first detailed records of this service were compiled, it had been replaced by a system of monetary payments according to which each knight's fee was charged with a definite sum by way of commutation, the fees lying in the northern portion of the honour, the original castlery of Richmond,[3] being assessed at the very low rate of half a mark each. Some arrangement of this kind was no doubt followed on lesser honours than that of Richmond, but its

[1] Thus in the reign of Edward I, Roger de Coleville owed two shillings and sixpence for the guard of Belvoir Castle, and John Cordeboef owed three pence for castle-guard at Eye, then held by Edmund earl of Cornwall (*Calendar of Inquisitions post mortem*, ii, No. 688; iii, No. 554).

[2] For Castle-guard at Richmond as part of the military organization of the honour see *Early Yorkshire Charters*, ed. C. T. Clay, vol. v.

[3] For this castlery see above, 194–5.

details have generally disappeared. Here, as throughout the history of castle-guard, the records which have survived reveal only the poor relics of a system which had once influenced the whole organization of feudal society.

But its decay can easily be antedated. Late in the twelfth century, for example, a dispute between Ralf fitz Simon, who held Pulford on Dee of the earl of Chester, and one of his Lincolnshire tenants was ended by a settlement which included a precise definition of the tenant's service at Pulford castle. After Hacon son of Osbert of Stain, the tenant, had done homage for his Lincolnshire inheritance, it was agreed that he should hold his land of Stain *faciendo forinsecum servicium regale predicto Radulfo et heredibus suis, ille et heredes sui, quantum pertinet ad feudum dimidii militis, et faciet servicium unius militis ad custodiam de Pulford scilicet per quadragesime dies unoquoque anno. Et incipiet facere eandem custodiam ad Clausum Pascha (sic).*[1] The careful wording of this passage, which shows that castle-guard at Pulford was still a matter of personal service, implies that in this instance its duration was fixed by a separate agreement between the tenant and his lord. It would be unsafe to draw general conclusions from the arrangements for the defence of a castle which, like Pulford, was an important post on a threatened frontier. But the fact that an estate charged at half a knight's fee to 'royal forinsec service' could be required to provide a knight's full service for the keeping of a chief lord's castle shows that the neat categories of medieval feodaries may not always correspond to the facts of military tenure.

Now and then an earlier charter made on some exceptional occasion will illustrate this system in the time of its full vitality. Early, it seems, in Stephen's reign, Earl Roger of Warwick gave his daughter in marriage to Geoffrey de Clinton, formerly King Henry's chamberlain. The charter in which the earl set out the terms of his daughter's marriage settlement shows more clearly than

---

[1] Lincolnshire Archives Office, M.M. 1/3/1. I owe my knowledge of this charter, which is preserved in a sixteenth-century copy, to Mrs. Dorothy Owen.

any other document the place of castle-guard among the payments and services due from a knight under the Norman kings.[1] Geoffrey was already the earl's tenant, and owed him the service of seventeen knights. Upon the marriage, the earl released to Geoffrey the service of ten out of the seventeen knights, expressly granting that they might thenceforward do their castle-guard at Geoffrey's castle of Brandon. He then went on to provide that if the king should take a 'common aid' from his kingdom Geoffrey should pay in respect of those ten knights no more than was due from such a number, that if the king should lead a military expedition within England the ten knights should go at the earl's cost, and that Geoffrey should receive as much as belonged to the ten knights out of any pardon, acquittance, or allowance which the earl might have from the king. Finally, he granted that whenever the earl took an aid from his own knights, Geoffrey might do the same. Some of these provisions are obscure. If the earl had defined the common aid which the king sometimes took from his kingdom, he would have thrown light on a dark region of Anglo-Norman finance. But it is evident that all the familiar features of early feudalism are present here in an ancient form, and that among them castle-guard has the first place. The chief advantage which Geoffrey gained from this settlement was a concession that ten of his knights, released from service at a castle of his lord's, might do their castle-guard at a castle of his own.

The organization for the defence of royal castles was no less ancient, and was even more elaborate. There is good evidence for the existence, in the twelfth century, of a system by which garrisons for at least the greater royal castles were provided by groups of baronies associated for this purpose. The system can be traced most clearly in the case of Windsor Castle,[2] for which a garrison was found by the combination of four baronies, one of them, that of the abbot of Abingdon, owing a service of thirty knights,

---

[1] Round, 'A Great Marriage Settlement', *Ancestor*, xi. 153–7.

[2] The figures which follow were worked out by Round in his article on Castle-guard, *Archaeological Journal*, lix. 150–1.

two owing a service of fifteen each, and one, a service of ten. The addition of three single knight's fees to this group brought the knights provided for Windsor Castle to a total of seventy-three, and commutation of this service at a rate of twenty shillings for each knight gave the king, each year, a round sum of four shillings a day, a sum for which six knights could be hired for a day's service in the reign of Henry II. It is only at Windsor that the details of the system can be traced with this precision, but the system itself was undoubtedly in operation at other, and distant, castles. At Dover Castle nine baronies, one of them being the constable's great honour of Haughley, were combined to supply a force of more than 170 knights.[1] At Rochester under Henry II a force of sixty knights was provided by five barons, including Warin de Montchesni, the lord of Swanscombe, and Enguerrand Patrick, whose surname is still preserved in the name of Patrixbourne, the *caput* of his honour.[2] In the Midlands Rockingham Castle was the centre of a small but important group of associated baronies, which included the fief of the abbot of Peterborough, and a similar group was based on Northampton, though its constituent honours cannot all be identified at the present time.[3] There is no mistaking the general prevalence of a system which can be traced in operation at Windsor and Rockingham, Northampton and Dover.

Its great antiquity is no less plain. Clerks performing a mechanical task have sometimes included men who lived at the middle of the twelfth century among the barons who owed castle-guard to John or Henry III—it is safe to assume that their names come from ancient lists which have never been brought up to date. But there is direct evidence for the existence of the system under the Norman king's. The knights of Abingdon Abbey owed their service at Windsor in the time of William I.[4] The grouping of

---

[1] See the lists given in the *Red Book of the Exchequer*, ii. 613–19 and 717–22, the later being a virtual duplicate of the former.

[2] *Archaeological Journal, ut supra*, 158–9.

[3] Ibid. 149, 150.

[4] Compare *Chronicon Monasterii de Abingdon*, ed. Stevenson, ii. 3,

baronies for castle-guard at Rockingham a generation later is proved by a writ of Henry I commanding the barons and vavassors who owed service there to come into residence at the summons of Michael of Hanslope, the keeper of the castle.[1] The same organization must lie behind the writ by which Henry I released Hervey bishop of Ely from the castle-guard due from his knights at the king's castle of Norwich so that he might have their service thenceforward in the Isle of Ely itself.[2] It is presupposed again in a less familiar writ of the same king granting to Alexander bishop of Lincoln the third part of the service of his knights that he might use it for the keeping of his castle of Newark.[3] The king does not name the royal castle at which it was understood that the remainder of the bishop's knights would do their service, but a bull of Pope Innocent II states that the knights of the bishopric had formerly done their guard at Lincoln Castle,[4] and under Edward I there were still military tenants holding of the bishop's successor who owed castle-guard to Lincoln.[5] It is, in fact, clear that this system, of which we only know the details from late and often imperfect evidence, arose in the time immediately following the Norman settlement.

It is rarely mentioned in early charters recording enfeoffments for knight-service. This is natural, for most of the charters were primarily addressed to a group of men, the *pares* of an honour, familiar already with the amount of service to a royal castle due from their body, and competent to fix the proportion of it which a new

'Huic abbatiae militum excubias apud ipsum Wildesore oppidum habendas regio imperio iussum,' with the statement on page 7 of this work that these knights did their castle-guard under Walter son of Other, the first known castellan of Windsor. This section of the *Chronicon* was composed before 1164 by a writer who was a monk of Abingdon already before 1117, and shows himself remarkably well informed about the history of the monastery in the Norman period. See F. M. Stenton, *Early History of the Abbey of Abingdon*, 4–6.

[1] Above, 20, and Appendix, No. 44.
[2] Bentham, *Antiquities of the Church of Ely*, appendix, No. xviii.
[3] *Registrum Antiquissimum of Lincoln Cathedral*, i. 35.
[4] Ibid. i. 191.
[5] *Calendar of Inquisitions post mortem*, ii, No. 371.

tenant might be expected to bear. The interest of the system is so great, and the texts which refer to it are so few, that any early charter which illustrates its working becomes important for this reason alone. There is, for example, nothing remarkable in the arrangement by which Roger de Burun assigned to the canons of Derby a rent of five shillings from his tenant Henry son of Fulcher.[1] But the charter which records the assignment opens with an address—*Benedicto regi Anglorum H. et omnibus hominibus castellarie de Notingham et omnibus hominibus suis Francis et Anglis*—which lifts it at once out of the commonplace. The interest of this extraordinary formula lies, indeed, below the surface. At first sight, the castlery of Nottingham seems no more than an unusual way of describing the honour of Peverel, the 'honour of Nottingham' of the Great Charter. But Roger de Burun was not a tenant of this honour. He was himself the lord of an honour of ten knights whose head was at 'Harestan' Castle, near Horseley in Derbyshire.[2] If he expected the king and the men of the castlery of Nottingham to be interested in the internal arrangement of his fee, it is reasonable to assume that it owed service to the king's castle of Nottingham.

It is to be hoped that more evidence of this kind will come to light, for the grouping of honours for the defence of royal castles is one of the most remarkable features of twelfth-century feudalism. Nothing illustrates more clearly the essential fact in the history of English feudal society, the original interdependence of king and baronage. In retrospect the Norman kings appear as strong rulers, whose policy tended towards autocracy, while the barons form a body of militant aristocrats, aiming at an independence which might at any time become anarchy. That the Norman kings were strong, and that their strength was the best safeguard of public order, needs no argument. Yet

---

[1] Jeayes, *Derbyshire Charters*, No. 2545. For Henry son of Fulcher see above, 52–54.

[2] See Thoroton, *Antiquities of Nottinghamshire*, 260. For the *Carta* of Roger de Burun see *Red Book of the Exchequer*, i. 342.

when their work is examined closely it is remarkable to what a great extent it depended on baronial loyalty. In local government, in the administration of justice, in the management of the king's own household, men of baronial rank co-operated with royal officers of lesser condition. Even within the sphere of military organization the king depended on baronial support. Henry I might engage Flemish knights for the defence of his kingdom against his brother. In England as in Normandy he may have sometimes treated as his own, baronial castles which for any reason came into his hand.[1] But throughout his reign, and even after the troubles which followed its close, the feudal army remained the ultimate defence of the land, and the chief royal castles continued to be garrisoned by knights who were the tenants of baronial lords.

After this survey of a knight's manifold duties, a few words may be said on one general question invited by these facts—the question whether anything that should be called feudalism had existed in England before the Norman Conquest. The question will never be finally answered, for feudalism is only a term invented for the historian's convenience, and every historian inevitably uses it in accordance with his own interpretation of the recorded course of social development. But unless the term is to lose all significance, it should at least be reserved for some definite form of social order, and the modern tendency to speak of feudalism in England under Edward the Confessor may easily lead to confusion of thought. Knighthood in pre-Conquest England had few representatives beyond the garrisons of the castles built by the Confessor's French dependants, and the English antipathy

---

[1] Robert of Torigny, Additions to William of Jumièges, *Gesta Normannorum Ducum*, ed. Marx., 310: 'Unum in ipso quidam non immerito, ut pluribus videtur, reprehendendum ducebant. Cum etiam haberet in manu sua nonnullorum baronum suorum, et etiam vicinorum aliquorum collimitantium suo ducatui munitiones, ne illi confidentes in eis aliquid contra pacem sui imperii agerent, illas velut proprias ambitu murorum et turribus nonnunquam muniebat. Qua autem intentione illud faceret, a multis nesciebatur, unde id ipsum reprehendebant.'

to these men had deep foundations. For the differences between English society in King Edward's time and that of any part of contemporary France were fundamental, and the result of centuries of contrasted development. Within each society there still survived conceptions once general throughout the whole Germanic world. The relationship between lord and man was as common in pre-Conquest England as anywhere in France. But in England this relationship was only one element in a social order based essentially on hereditary status, and in France it had become the basis of a new type of society organized specifically for war. No process of evolution could have bridged the gap between two societies thus contrasted, and indeed, when something more than due emphasis has been laid on the signs of social change in pre-Conquest England—the leases granted by great ecclesiastics to thegns or *cnihts*, the increasing dependence of free men on lords, even the appearance of a new military element in Cnut's housecarles—the essential difference between English and Norman society remains as wide as ever. It is turning a useful term into a mere abstraction to apply the adjective 'feudal' to a society which had never adopted the private fortress nor developed the art of fighting on horseback, which had no real conception of the specialization of service, and allowed innumerable landowners of position to go with their land to whatever lords they would.

VII

THE END OF NORMAN
FEUDALISM

IN any survey of English history written from the royal standpoint, the nineteen years of Stephen's reign seem to interrupt the course of an inevitable development. For nearly seventy years after the Norman Conquest the trend of that history had been towards the establishment of a centralized monarchy, which could afford to treat feudal liberties as mere exceptions to the universality of its control. It is natural to regard the work of Henry II as a continuation of that of his grandfather, and to trace in the disorder of the intervening years the expression of a fundamental antagonism between royal authority and feudal privilege, released from its former subordination by the accident of a disputed succession to the throne. There can, indeed, be no doubt as to the reality of the feudal reaction which followed the death of Henry I, nor as to the fact that the feudal aristocracy came at last to see that a strong monarchy was the only safeguard of public order. But the assumption of a permanent antagonism between royal and feudal interests is an undue simplification of a complex problem. The whole organization of English feudalism required the presence of an effective king at its head, but none of the Norman kings disputed the social consequences of the fundamental relationship between lord and tenant. Even Henry I, under whom Anglo-Norman centralization reached its height, was prepared to create new honours on a great scale, and the elaborate law book which comes from his court and represents its practice expressly allows to the feudal lord the right of hearing pleas between his men.

It would rather seem that the baronial autonomy characteristic of Stephen's later years was the result, not of any deliberate opposition to royal power, but of the

unprecedented situation created by a disputed succession
to the kingdom itself. With the weakening of the central
authority which all had once obeyed, the military side of
feudalism at once assumed a new importance. Many
features of the time which are often regarded as illustrations of baronial independence were really the baronial
response to a condition of civil war. The inconsistent
policy of individual barons, the alliances formed by great
lords among themselves, and the sporadic outbreak of
private hostilities were all natural features of a time when
no one knew who would at last be left as king in England,
and each man was driven to fight in the first place for his
own hand. They cannot fairly be regarded as the expression of feudal ideas.

The barons of this time have found few apologists. As
a class, they stood for the reversal of the attempt towards
centralization which has given Henry I his place in history,
and for the toleration of private warfare. The chief of
them were undoubtedly trying to secure for themselves
a position in which they would be able to deal with the
king of their choice on terms as nearly approaching equality
as feudal custom allowed. They reduced England to an
almost unprecedented state of misery, acquiesced in the
annexation of the northern counties by the king of Scots,
and proved incapable of maintaining the position which
their ancestors had won in Wales. There can be no doubt
that they deserve the hard measure which historians
always give them. But it may at least be suggested that
reflection upon the consequences of baronial rebellion has
led to a certain idealization of King Henry I and his
ministers. Henry of Huntingdon, who had known many
of the leading figures of his time, says candidly that in
comparison with the wretchedness of the following age,
whatever King Henry had done seemed admirable,
whether he behaved as a tyrant or as a king.[1] The interest

---

[1] *Historia Anglorum* (ed. Arnold), 256, 'Successu temporis atrocissimi,
quod postea per Normannorum rabiosas proditiones exarsit, quicquid
Henricus fecerat vel tyrannice vel regie, comparatione deteriorum visum
est peroptimum.'

of scholars has always been aroused by the achievements of the reign of Henry I, by the development of the Exchequer, and the activities of the justices who went out over the country from the king's court. But the work of Henry I and his servants can be regarded from more than one standpoint, and the merits which attract an historian were less plain to the men of King Henry's own day.

Complaints of the harshness of a king and his ministers are common enough in medieval literature. To illustrate the oppression of Henry I and his officers we have what is much rarer, a confession from one of the king's own justices. In view of the evidence which Liebermann brought together, there can be no doubt that the author of the *Leges Henrici Primi* was a justice of the king's court. He was conservative in outlook, anxious to preserve the ancient customs of the kingdom, and he found no satisfaction in reflecting upon the tendencies of his own judicial work and that of his colleagues.[1]

'Law varies through the counties as the avarice and the sinister, odious, activity of legal experts add more grievous means of injury to established legal process. There is so much perversity, and such affluence of evil that the certain truth of law and the remedy established by settled provision can rarely be found, but to the great confusion of all a new method of impleading is sought out, a new subtlety of injury is found, as if that which was before hurt little, and he is thought of most account who does most harm to most people. To those only we pretend reverence and love whom we cannot do without, and whatever does not agree with our cruelty does not exist for us. We assume the character of tyrants, and it is desire of wealth which brings this madness upon us. . . . Legal process is involved in so many and so great anxieties and deceits that men avoid these exactions, and the uncertain dice of pleas.'

This is very different from the tone of Glanville on the

---

[1] *Leges Henrici Primi*, 6, 3 a—6, 6. The interest of the passage was first pointed out by Liebermann, *Über die Leges Henrici*, 46–47, who showed how it fits in with other evidence that this curious work came from a justice of the court of Henry I. In translating this passage it is impossible to follow the author's twisted Latin word for word and at the same time make sense. But there is no doubt as to his meaning.

Grand Assize. There is obvious exaggeration here, but it is the exaggeration of a man compelled by his profession to administer a new legal system, and conscious of the temptations which it offered to himself and his fellows, and the hardship with which it bore on the common people. These innovations are evidently connected with the process by which in the reign of Henry I criminal offences in increasing number were being brought under the cognisance of the king's justices, and with the new significance of the king's writ as a means of beginning civil pleas. It is interesting to see these changes regarded by a well-informed contemporary as an oppression to the country and the cause of wrong-doing by those who were carrying them into effect, but his evidence cannot easily be set aside. It suggests, in fact, that an element of arbitrary extortion entered into the judicial reforms of Henry I which essentially threatened their permanence, and that a king of less personal force, even if he had succeeded under a clear title, would hardly have maintained the centralization of the years before 1135.

This impression is confirmed by the evidence which we possess as to the king's dealings with individual barons. The Pipe Roll of 1130 shows the king's financial and judicial system in relation to every class of his free subjects, but most clearly, perhaps, in relation to the higher baronage, and there can be no question as to the severity with which he was treating his greater tenants in chief. It was only to be expected that he should turn to his own advantage the vagueness of feudal custom in regard to the amount of baronial reliefs, and sell wardships, marriages, and escheats for as high a price as he could get. More significant, because tending more definitely to an ultimate reaction, are the sums which he was taking from his barons by way of amercement. The forest law bore hardly on the baronage. Baldwin de Redvers rendered account of five hundred marks for pleas of the forest,[1] and the earl of Warwick was charged with £72. 16s. 8d. and two destriers *pro placitis cervorum*.[2] Among amercements

[1] Pipe Roll of 1130, ed. Hunter, 153.   [2] Ibid. 106.

arising from the ordinary course of law, the £102. 16s. 8d.
laid on Simon de Beauchamp because he had been the
pledge of a man whom he did not produce in court seems
grotesquely severe.[1] Osbert of Leicester was rendering
account of two hundred marks that the king might remit
his ill will towards him and Osbert his clerk,[2] and more
than one baron was paying as much as a hundred marks
for amercements incurred in the course of recent eyres.
But for the general history of feudalism, the most interesting entries on the roll are those which suggest that the
king was beginning to intervene in the relationship between
lord and tenant. Walter de Gant is accounting for
£98. 3s. 0d. to have the wardship of the land of William
de Alost of his fee.[3] It is possible that William had been
holding land of the king as well as of Walter de Gant, and
that on this account the king claimed the right of wardship in respect of his whole estate. We may, in fact, be
reading of a case of the unpopular prerogative wardship
which King John was to abandon in Magna Carta. But
there seems no principle of feudal custom which will
explain the king's acceptance of money from a tenant of
Simon de Beauchamp, 'that Simon his lord may not make
a gift of his service without his consent'.[4] Here, at least,
the king seems to have passed beyond mere insistence on
the strict rights of the crown to direct interference in the
internal economy of an honour. We have no means of
knowing whether this was an isolated aggression on the
king's part, but even by itself it shows the direction in
which his policy was tending. If he often intervened in
this way, the barons must have regarded him as an enemy
to the essential rights of their order. In any case a study
of the Pipe Roll of 1130 leaves little room for surprise at
the events which happened when King Henry's authority
had passed into weaker hands.

That the hands were weaker there can be no question.
The insistence by Round[5] and others on the peculiar

---

[1] Pipe Roll of 1130, ed. Hunter, 103.   [2] Ibid. 82.
[3] Ibid. 111.   [4] Ibid. 62.
[5] See especially *Geoffrey de Mandeville*, 24–25.

difficulties of Stephen's position has made the question of his personal quality seem comparatively unimportant, and modern work on his reign has naturally been concentrated on its political rather than its personal aspects. But it is impossible to read even the narrative of a writer so well disposed towards the king as the author of the *Gesta Stephani* without feeling that Stephen was chiefly responsible for his own failure. He had energy and a high standard of knightly conduct, and there was nothing in him of the cruelty of his formidable predecessor. But he was obviously incapable of following out a long course of consistent action, and there is no sign that he so much as understood the meaning of policy. Even among the counts and barons of his age he seems by no means a distinguished figure. To the last, his mental attitude was that of a count of Mortain rather than that of a king, an attitude which alone explains his agreement in 1153 that his son's claim to the throne should be set aside in return for a guarantee of his honours in England and France.[1] There is much, in fact, in Stephen's conduct to make a reader agree with Walter Map's description of him[2] as *vir armorum industria preclarus, ad cetera fere ydiota*, though the *nisi quod in malum pronior* which follows seems unkind and the *preclarus* an exaggeration.

The accession of Stephen meant that a feudal magnate of no political competence was faced by a situation which would have taxed the abilities of the strongest of English medieval kings. Apart altogether from the financial exactions of Henry I, the general character of his government had invited a baronial reaction. Obscure as is the history of his reign in detail, it is at least clear that by its close the higher baronage was no longer playing the part in local administration which it had played under his father. To a great extent the government of the shires had passed from men with strong local interests to men who were essentially the king's ministers. Only a strong

[1] See Round, *Studies in Peerage and Family History*, 168–71, for the position in 1153 of Stephen's son William count of Warenne, Mortain, and Boulogne.   [2] *De Nugis Cruialium*, ed. M. R. James, 236.

ruler could have maintained the centralization of Henry I, and ancient baronial claims to local office, civil and military, were soon asserted in the confusion which followed his death. It is customary to regard the barons of Stephen's reign as moved to rebellion or to frequent changes of faith by desire for independence of the crown. But independence is a vague word, and the concessions which individual barons obtained from Stephen or the empress were highly concrete. Moreover, in many cases these concessions have a retrospective character—a baron is taking the opportunity of recovering rights or possessions which had once belonged to his ancestors. The typical baron of this period was obviously anxious to improve his financial position by grants from the royal demesne, and his military position by obtaining grants of escheated fees or of the service of knights holding directly under the king. But he also wished to recover sheriffdoms, the custody of royal castles, and offices at the king's court, once in his family. Grants of this kind occupy an important place in the charters by which the rival claimants to the throne bought the adhesion of individual lords. The charter which Geoffrey de Mandeville at the height of his power obtained from the empress begins with a 'restoration', of all the *tenementa* ever held by his father, grandfather, or himself, in lands and towers, in castles and baileys, and these 'tenements' included the custody of the Tower of London and the sheriffdoms of London and Middlesex, Essex, and Hertfordshire, at the farms by which his grandfather had held them.[1] It is possible that the Tower had never passed out of the custody of the Mandevilles since the first Geoffrey received it from the Conqueror. But there had certainly been no continuous Mandeville tenure of the sheriffdoms of London and Middlesex, Essex and Hertfordshire, and in claiming these particular offices,[2] Geoffrey de Mandeville was looking beyond the reign of Henry I to the time of the Norman settlement.

[1] Round, *Geoffrey de Mandeville*, 166–7.
[2] For other offices received by Geoffrey at this time see p. 226.

Similar hereditary claims lie behind another remarkable charter given by the empress during her ascendency. In 1141 William de Beauchamp secured from her a 'restoration' of the castle and motte of Worcester, of the sheriffdom and custody of the forests of Worcestershire at the farms by which his father had held them, of the castle and honour of Tamworth, and of the royal constableship and dispensership which Urse de Abetot had once held.[1] In demanding these grants, William de Beauchamp was setting a high rate on the value of his service to the empress, but none of them can fairly be called an encroachment on the rights of the crown. The hereditary sheriffdom of Worcestershire had survived even the centralization of Henry I, and William de Beauchamp had an unquestionable claim to it. He was heir to the lands and offices of Urse de Abetot, the first castellan of Worcester, and he was claiming against Robert Marmion the fee of Urse's brother Robert Dispensator, the first Norman lord of Tamworth. In each case, in fact, he was asking for something which had been possessed either by his father or by kinsmen of a still earlier generation. Here, as in many similar instances, the claims which a baron makes on his chosen sovereign illustrate feudal conservatism rather than feudal aggression.

It is naturally impossible to bring the very various objects followed by different barons under different conditions under any general definition. Each individual was governed by a particular set of circumstances. But there can be no doubt that throughout the reign of Stephen one main object of the greater barons was to obtain positions in which they could exercise the royal power in the shires where they had territorial influence. There was nothing revolutionary in this. Few barons of this period can have hoped for a larger delegation of royal power than had been exercised by the great baronial sheriffs of the Conqueror's time.[2] It was, no doubt, an object which often led to

---

[1] *Geoffrey de Mandeville*, 313–15.
[2] On whom see W. A. Morris, 'The Office of Sheriff in the Early Norman Period', *Eng. Hist. Rev.* xxxiii. 145–75, especially 150–4.

antagonism between different families of approximately the same standing, and these antagonisms may well have helped to keep alive a state of war in parts of the country little interested in the main struggle. But in itself, a wish to act as the king's officer in a shire or group of shires did not imply any intention of rejecting the royal authority. None of the barons of this period stands more clearly for irresponsible baronial ambition than Geoffrey de Mandeville, and the successive charters which he obtained from Stephen and the empress admirably illustrate the objects generally desired by men of his order. But they also show that until the later phases of his career even this most aggressive of all barons was prepared to accept charters which clearly implied that the ultimate control of local offices lay with the crown.[1] In the first of the two charters which he obtained from the empress[2] he received the office of chief justiciar of Essex, which carried the right of holding all pleas of the crown arising locally. But the grant was combined with a definite reservation, to the effect that although the empress would not send another justice to take precedence of him in that shire, she was free to send one of his peers there, occasionally, to hear that her pleas were held rightly. In charters which Geoffrey afterwards obtained from Stephen[3] and the empress[4] the justiciarship of London and Middlesex is added, that of Essex is extended to cover Hertfordshire, and the clause reserving the royal right of intervention is omitted. But its appearance in the first charter of the empress shows that even in his own county the position of a lord who was both sheriff and justiciar fell in itself far short of independence.

[1] None of the materials for Anglo-Norman history printed since 1892 adds anything important to the evidence about this baron which Round published in *Geoffrey de Mandeville*, or suggests any serious modification of his conclusions. But in tracing the increasing demands which Geoffrey made upon Stephen and the empress Round, naturally, did not emphasize their limitations or the retrospective character which many of them bear. It is only in the closing phase of his brief career that Geoffrey shows any real sign of aiming at independence of the crown.

[2] *Geoffrey de Mandeville*, 88–95.

[3] Ibid. 140–4.   [4] Ibid. 166–72.

Nevertheless, it was through the acquisition of such administrative offices that the barons of Stephen's time made their most material encroachments on the civil authority of the crown. However it might be safeguarded, the justiciarship of a county in the hands of Geoffrey de Mandeville, earl of Essex, or William de Roumara, earl of Lincoln,[1] must have limited very narrowly the sphere within which the king could exercise direct control. At present it is impossible to estimate the extent to which members of the higher baronage had acquired sheriffdoms and county justiciarships. The materials for such an estimate lie in the royal charters of the time, and these have not yet been collected. The result is that in any survey of the time, attention tends to be concentrated on illustrations of the enlargement of baronial influence which are more obvious, though perhaps, in reality, less significant. And among these illustrations the most remarkable is certainly the increase in the number of English earldoms from eight[2] in 1135 to twenty-two[3] in 1154.

Despite uncertainty at various important points, the history of the Anglo-Norman earldoms is not inadequately

[1] Earl William's justiciarship in Lincolnshire seems only to be known from a writ of Stephen in the *Registrum Antiquissimum* (ed. Foster, i. 60). Normally, the office was held by the bishop of Lincoln. In 1153–4 Stephen granted it to bishop Robert II as bishops Robert Bloet and Alexander had held it, commanding all faithful men of Lincoln and Lincolnshire to come on summons by the bishop's servants to hold the kings's pleas and make his judgements (ibid. i. 63–64). On the office of local justiciar see D. M. Stenton in *Cambridge Medieval History*, v. 584.

[2] Counting separately the earldoms of Northampton and Huntingdon, both of which were apparently held by the king of Scots in 1135.

[3] Chester, Surrey, Buckingham, Warwick, Leicester, Northampton, Huntingdon, and Gloucester, existing before 1135; Derby, York, Pembroke, Essex, Lincoln, Norfolk, Arundel (or Sussex), Hertford, and Worcester, created by Stephen; Cornwall, Devon, Hereford, Oxford, and Salisbury (Wiltshire), created by the empress. Of the earldoms which appear in Round's list of the creations between 1135 and 1154 (*Geoffrey de Mandeville*, 271), Somerset no longer existed at the latter date, and it is virtually certain that the Beaumont earldom of Bedford never really came into being (*Trans. of Royal Historical Society*, 4th series, xiii. 77–82). Of the earldoms mentioned above, Northampton was held in 1154 by Simon de Senliz III (Farrer, *Honors and Knights' Fees*, ii. 298), and Huntingdon

known. In all but a few cases the date at which each earldom was created has been at least approximately fixed. The successions to the different earldoms have been established, and the relationships of kinship or marriage connecting them have been worked out in detail. The attitude of the Anglo-Norman kings towards the creation of earldoms can only be gathered from their practice, and this is now reasonably clear. There seems to have been a military object in each new earldom created by William I —Cheshire, Shropshire, and Herefordshire along the Welsh border, Kent and Sussex commanding important Channel ports, and Richmond, if indeed it can be called an earldom, guarding the Yorkshire plain from the Scots.[1] The three new earldoms created by William II, Warwick, Buckingham, and Surrey, had no military significance. It was probably a personal rather than a political motive which lay behind these creations, but it is significant that each of the new earls belonged to the most ancient Norman nobility. The rarity of new creations under Henry I is one of the most remarkable features of his reign. He created an earldom of Gloucester for one, and perhaps the eldest, of his many illegitimate sons, and within a year of the death of his friend Robert count of Meulan, the latter's son, Robert, appears as earl of Leicester,[2] but the king

was in dispute between Simon and the king of Scots. Northumberland, which David king of Scots had given to his younger grandson William, can hardly be regarded as an English earldom in 1154. It is a curious fact that the holders of six of these earldoms—Chester, Warwick, Hereford, Northampton, Devon, and Lincoln—died between the beginning of 1153 and the end of 1155. They were all men of outstanding importance, and their disappearance helps to explain the rapidity with which Henry II re-established the royal power, and the dominant position held during his early years by Robert earl of Leicester.

[1] F. M. Stenton, *William the Conqueror*, 424–33.

[2] On the difficult question whether Robert count of Meulan was ever earl of Leicester see the *Complete Peerage*, vii. 525–6. The count died in 1118, and in the following year Robert his son issued a charter in favour of St. Nicaise-de-Meulan as earl of Leicester (ibid. 527). This charter has only been known hitherto from a modern copy (Haskins, *Norman Institutions*, 295), but the accuracy of the date is confirmed by the thirteenth-century text of this charter preserved in the Cartulary of St. Neots (Cott.

was plainly unwilling to increase the dignity of any other baronial house. Even Stephen, much as he needed the support of the greater baronage, was slow to bid for it by offering earldoms. So far as can be seen it was not until the beginning of his third year that he proposed the creation of his first new earldom,[1] and throughout the creations of his later reign he was careful—more careful than the empress[2]—to confine the dignity to the greatest of baronial families. In view of these facts the Norman kings seem to have been remarkably consistent in upholding the dignity of an earl. Every king of this line clearly held that earldoms should only be given to men distinguished either by some special relationship of service or kinship to the sovereign or by territorial importance, and in regard to this, their standard of an earl's qualification was high. More than seventy years passed after the Conquest before an earldom came to the houses of Ferrers, Bigot, or even Clare.

These earldoms did not all conform to the same model. An earldom under the Norman kings was essentially a personal honour, and it was for the king to decide what rights should be carried by the title. Of the earldoms created by William I, it seems certain that those of Hereford, Shropshire, and Cheshire meant the withdrawal of each shire from the ordinary administrative system of the country, that they were earldoms 'palatine', in the language of a later time.[3] Among the earldoms of Stephen's reign, that of Cornwall, created by the empress for her half-brother Reginald, probably belonged to the same type.

Faust. A. iv, f. 88). As Robert was only 15 years old in 1119 it is probable that the earldom of Leicester had previously belonged to his father, for it would be hard to find a parallel in this period to the creation of a new earldom for a youth under age.

[1] The unfortunate Beaumont earldom of Bedford. See below, 237–8.

[2] Patrick earl of Salisbury was less important, territorially, than any of Stephen's earls, and the fief of Aubrey de Vere, though large, was hardly of the first importance.

[3] On the Norman earldom of Hereford see Round, *Victoria County History of Herefordshire*, i. 270–2, and on that of Shropshire, Tait, *Victoria County History of Shropshire*, i. 288. In each county, as in Cheshire, the Norman earl was lord of the county town, and possessed the ancient royal demesne within the shire.

It survived into the reign of Henry II, and it is highly
suggestive that no accounts were rendered from this
county into the Exchequer until the death of Earl Reginald
in 1175. It is no doubt possible that, in the latter part of
Stephen's reign, a number of Earl Reginald's contemporaries exercised similar rights over the counties which
gave them titles. Some of them use language indistinguishable from that of a royal writ when granting
privileges to be enjoyed within their earldoms.[1] There
must have been periods towards the close of the war when
an earl, like Roger of Warwick or Robert of Leicester, who
was the dominant territorial magnate in his county,
carried on its civil administration in his own name.[2] But
there were few earls without a territorial rival in their
shires, and if Chester and Cornwall are set apart, the later
history of the earldoms which lasted into the reign of
Henry II suggests that if any of them had ever been
autonomous it had only been under the exceptional
conditions of a time of general war.

The chief difficulty in the history of the Norman
earldoms is, indeed, to discover any rights which were
inseparably attached to the dignity of the earl. Of the
earl's importance at the beginning of the eleventh century

[1] See the writs issued by Waleran count of Meulan as earl of Worcester
quoted by G. H. White, in *Transactions of Royal Historical Society*, 4th
series, xiii. 69, 70.

[2] A very remarkable illustration of the authority which an earl might
exercise in his county during Stephen's latter years is given by a charter of
Earl Simon of Northampton printed by Farrer in *Honors and Knights' Fees*,
ii. 297–8 (Cott. Chart. x. 14). The charter states that in the presence of
the earl and of some of his barons at Northampton, Anselm de Chokes has
restored two-thirds of his demesne tithes of Wollaston to St. Andrew's
Priory, as the monks had deraigned them before Robert bishop of Lincoln
in a full synod. A portion of Wollaston belonged to the earl's own fee
(Farrer, op. cit. 363), but the part of the village to which this charter refers
was held by Anselm de Chokes as a tenant in chief of the crown (Farrer,
op. cit. i. 20 et seqq.) and seems, indeed, to have been the *caput* of the
Chokes barony. In normal times a transaction of the kind described in the
charter would have been confirmed by the king, but Stephen can have
possessed little effective power in Northamptonshire in the period 1149–53,
to which the charter belongs, and the earl, who was Stephen's consistent
supporter, naturally acted in his stead.

there can be no question. His traditional functions of presiding in the shire court and commanding its fyrd were really the expression of a general responsibility for the maintenance of justice, the suppression of men dangerous to public order, and the execution of royal commands. It is probable enough that the merely administrative importance of his position declined during the Confessor's reign.[1] The sheriff was coming into greater power, and the development of his office was the symptom of a movement towards centralization which the Conqueror turned to unforeseen purposes.[2] Even so, the difference between the position of an earl in the Old English and the Anglo-Norman state remains remarkable. The Conqueror's earls were men of the first importance, but for personal reasons, and as the lords of castleries and the knights grouped around them, and not in any real sense as the holders of Old English offices. There are, no doubt, many points of contact between the Old English and the Anglo-Norman earldoms. Throughout the Norman period every earl was associated by his title with a county, or a sheriffdom which could be so regarded,[3] or a group of counties formed before the Conquest.[4] The ancient earldom of Northumbria

[1] Throughout the history of the Confessor's reign, the earldoms appear as provincial governments rather than as units of local administration. The importance of the earls in this period was not derived from administrative duties, but from the estates and revenues annexed to their offices, and above all from their influence over the landed thegns who had become their men. Under these conditions the geographical limits of an earldom were a matter of secondary importance—Oxfordshire, for example, could be added to the East Anglian earldom held by Gyrth, King Harold's brother —and by the date of the Conquest the earldoms had become artificial creations which disregarded both the ancient regions of which the kingdom was composed and its existing division between the three great systems of local customary law.

[2] On the positions of the earl and the sheriff before the Conquest see Morris, 'The Office of Sheriff in the Anglo-Saxon period', *Eng. Hist. Rev.* xxxi. 20–40.

[3] Pembroke, which was a land of recent conquest, appears as a sheriff-dom in the Pipe Roll of 1130 (ed. Hunter, 136–7).

[4] There can be no doubt that the Norman earldom of Derby covered the two shires of Derby and Nottingham. These shires were already associated in the Conqueror's reign, when they bore witness together that

survived under Norman earls until the reign of William
II, and the twelfth-century earldoms of Huntingdon
and Northampton represent with some attenuation
the midland province of which Waltheof had been earl
until his fall in 1074. For a long time there survived a
faint tradition that the earl of a shire had once been the
leading layman in its moot. His name will sometimes,
though rarely, stand next to that of the local bishop,
among the names of those to whom royal writs are
addressed,[1] and he expects, though he does not always
receive, the third penny of the pleas of the shire which
had fallen to his Old English predecessor.[2] With all
allowance for these facts, it is evident that under William I,
and far more definitely under his successors, the dignity of
an earl carried the mere shadow of its former power. And
early in the reign of William II, when William de Warenne
was created earl of Surrey, there appeared for the first
time in England an earl with nothing that can properly
be called a territorial interest in the shire from which he
took his title.[3]

certain profits coming from Appletree wapentake in Derbyshire were in the
sheriff's hand (D.B. i. 280), and the first earls of the Ferrers line frequently
style themselves earls of Nottingham.

[1] Until the writs of all the Anglo-Norman kings have been collected, it
is unsafe to generalize about their formulas of address, but there seems no
doubt that the earl was generally ignored even in the addresses of writs
which were obviously directed to the shire court. It seems unusual, for
instance, when Stephen addresses a writ 'Episcopo Wirecestrensi et comiti
de Warwic' et justicie et vicecomiti et baronibus et ministris de War-
wicsir' (Add. Chart. 19580; cf. *Archaeological Journal*, xx. 292). The
bishop's connexion with the shire court was much more clearly remembered, as in the address to the charter of Hugh de Gurnai quoted above,
108–9.

[2] Although the history of the third penny of the pleas of the shire is still
obscure, there seems no sufficient reason for rejecting the impression given
by the *Dialogus de Scaccario* (ed. Crump, Hughes, and Johnson, 109) that
though this third penny was normally attached to the dignity of an earl at
his creation, it was for the king to decide whether it should be given to an
individual earl for his life, or as a revenue to descend to his successors. See
Round, *Geoffrey de Mandeville*, 293–4.

[3] William de Warenne, who receives no title in Domesday Book, had
been created earl of Surrey before his death in 1089. In 1086, although he

There was certainly no tendency towards the extension of an earl's rights during the next generation. No king was less likely than Henry I to give his barons greater scope in local administration, and the Pipe Roll of 1130 could be read without learning that there was an earl of Buckingham or that the *Comes de Warenna* was really earl of Surrey. Everything suggests, in fact, that by the beginning of Stephen's reign an earldom gave to its holder little more than a title and the precedence which it implied.[1] To a lord who was a baron and nothing more in either England or France, the title meant a definite advancement in rank, and to one who was already a count in France,[2] it was a notable sign of power and influence in England. For the rest, an earl at his creation was the central figure in a solemn ceremony of investiture, and the financial profits annexed by custom to the dignity, if they could be obtained from the king,[3] would be a certain if small addition to a baronial income. Beyond this, the use which a newly created earl could make of his dignity would depend entirely on his personal circumstances. If the county of which he was made earl was the county in which he was indisputably the greatest lord, his title might help him towards the attainment of something more than baronial power. But the earldoms which gave scope to this ambition were very few. The very idea that an earl should be a great magnate in the county of his title was disregarded when Stephen made William de Albini earl of Lincoln,[4] and when the empress offered to Aubrey de

possessed one of the five great fiefs between which Sussex was then divided, he held no land in Surrey, and any subsequent acquisitions which he may have made in this county can only have been small.

[1] Private charters, naturally, do not often illustrate this aspect of the Anglo-Norman earldom, but a baron's pleasure in a new dignity certainly underlies the language with which Earl Miles of Hereford opens a charter to Lanthony Priory—'Anno ab incarnatione domini MCXLI, apud Bristoium positus, iamque consulatus honorem adeptus' (M. Gibson, *A View . . . of the Churches of Door, Home-Lacy, and Hempsted,* 146). Miles was created earl of Hereford by the empress on 25 July in this year.

[2] Such, for example, as Aubrey de Vere, who was count of Guisnes in right of his wife.   [3] See above, 231.

[4] On this temporary earldom see *Complete Peerage,* vii. 666–7. Although

Vere the choice of Oxfordshire, Berkshire, Wiltshire, or Dorset for his earldom.[1] Aubrey's lands extended into at least five counties, but none of these was among them. When all allowance has been made for the vague possibility of reviving ancient official powers under a weak monarchy, the social distinction carried by an earldom remains its one essential advantage. Neither Stephen nor the empress was really weakening the royal power when they purchased support by the grant of earldoms.

It would seem, in fact, that to all but a small minority of the barons who received this title, it can have meant little beyond a formal recognition of existing power. In nearly every case this power was based on inherited lands, often combined with local offices which gave their holder influence beyond the circle of his own tenants. But the course of events in Stephen's reign shows that many barons were invading a sphere which earlier kings had tried, with general consistency, to keep under their own control. Much of the history of this time turns on the possession of the ancient boroughs, the county towns, of England, and the castles which commanded them. Under the Conqueror and his sons, few of these towns had ever been granted away from the crown. Apart from Chester, Shrewsbury, and Hereford, the chief towns of independent earldoms, the only county towns which had been 'mediatized' between 1066 and 1130 were Gloucester, Warwick, Leicester, Colchester, and Northampton, and of these all except Chester, Warwick, Gloucester, and Leicester were in the king's hands when the Pipe Roll of 1130 was written.[2] Moreover, although in the early Norman period the castle of a county town was often in the hands of an

William de Albini held no land in Lincolnshire there can be no doubt that for a short time he was earl of this county, for two original charters survive in which he styles himself *Comes Lincolniæ*. One of them is published in the Facsimiles of Royal and other Charters in the British Museum No. 14 and the other is printed below from the original in the Public Record Office (Appendix, No. 9).   [1] Round, *Geoffrey de Mandeville*, 181.
    [2] See Tait, 'The Firma Burgi and the Commune in England', *Eng. Hist. Rev.* xlii. 334–5. Small boroughs on the royal demesne stand apart from these ancient towns, and could be granted away with less serious financial

important local baron, he normally held it as a custodian on the king's behalf, and not in his own right. It was as custodians, and not as lords, that Henry de Beaumont and William Peverel had received the castles of Warwick and Nottingham from the Conqueror,[1] and there can be no doubt that in his time Robert de Oilli and Miles Crispin respectively held the castles of Oxford and Wallingford in the same capacity.[2] In the days when an English rising was still to be expected, there was good reason for the king to entrust the castles of important towns to barons with strong local interests, and each of the Norman kings was strong enough to prevent any baron from using the custody of the castle as a means of usurping lordship over the town. But under a weak king, and still more when the royal power was in virtual abeyance, a town inevitably tended to fall under the immediate lordship of a great baron who held its castle.

At the beginning of Stephen's reign, these castellanships were for the most part hereditary. Most of them had doubtless borne this character from the Conqueror's time. Hugh de Grentemesnil, the greatest baron in Leicestershire, who had assisted in the conquest of England, received the custody of Leicester Castle from the Conqueror, and was succeeded in that position by his son

consequences to the crown. Henry I, for example, gave Reading and Thatcham to Reading Abbey at its foundation. In an intermediate class between these small boroughs and the places mentioned in the text come towns like Bath, Tamworth, and Bristol, of which Bath was given by William II to the bishop of Wells, Tamworth seems to have passed to the Marmions, and Bristol formed part of the earldom of Gloucester.

[1] See Orderic, *Historia Ecclesiastica*, ed. le Prevost, ii. 184: 'Rex itaque castrum apud Guarevicum condidit et Henrico Rogerii de Bellomonte filio ad servandum tradidit. . . . Deinde rex Snotingheham castrum construxit, et Guillelmo Peverello commendavit.' Compare, ibid. 185: 'Rex post hæc in reversione sua Lincoliæ Huntendonæ et Grontebrugæ castra locavit, et tutelam eorum fortissimis viris commendavit', and the statement on p. 186 that Humfrey de Tilleul 'Hastingas a prima die constructionis ad custodiendum susceperat'. These passages were probably derived by Orderic from William of Poitiers, and if so, are contemporary.

[2] For Miles Crispin see below, 236, note 3. Robert de Oilli is described as 'castelli urbis Oxenefordensis oppidanus' in the *Chronicon Monasterii de Abingdon*, ii. 7.

Ivo. In several ways Ivo's career curiously resembles that of one of Stephen's more aggressive barons. Early in the reign of Henry I he appears both as sheriff of Leicester-shire and as farmer of the king's dues and property and keeper of the king's castle in the county town.[1] He made war on his neighbours, and had to be suppressed at last by the king.[2] But, as a rule, Henry I seems to have allowed hereditary succession to these castellanships, and indeed to have allowed their descent through heiresses. Through-out the wars of Stephen's time, the course of events was influenced by the fact that Wallingford Castle was held for the empress by Brian fitz Count, whose wife inherited a claim to its custody.[3]

[1] 'Municeps erat et vicecomes et firmarius regis' (Ordericus Vitalis, *Historia Ecclesiastica*, iv. 169). Brian fitz Count, in the next generation, who was castellan of Wallingford (see below), was also *firmarius* of the borough (Pipe Roll of 1130, 139).

[2] The authority for the position held by Hugh and Ivo at Leicester is Ordericus Vitalis, and his language is not as precise as could be wished. In one passage (ii. 222) he states that William I committed to Hugh the 'municipatus' of Leicester, and in another, quoted above, that Ivo was 'municeps' as well as sheriff and 'firmarius'. In the latter context, *municeps* can hardly have any other meaning than castellan, for Ivo, though a great landholder in Leicester, was far from being lord of the whole town. Orderic's *municeps* and *municipatus* presumably result from the twelfth-century use of *municipium* to denote not a town but a castle, of which there are several instances in the contemporary *Gesta Stephani*. The clearest of them is the passage in which the author sets down the reasons for arresting Roger bishop of Salisbury and his kinsmen, *donec municipiis suis et quae Caesaris essent Caesari redditis, a discordanti suspicione quam eis imputabant, et rex securior et regio illius esset pacatior* (ed. Potter, 49, 50). The word *municeps* occurs in the *Gesta* with the sense 'castellan' in the passage describing the death of William, *civitatis Saresbiriæ præceptor et municeps* (ibid. 98).

[3] Although the early history of Wallingford Castle is far from clear, it seems certain that its first castellan was Miles Crispin, lord of the great fief afterwards known as the honour of Wallingford. He appears as 'Milo de Walingaford' in the *Abingdon Chronicon* (Rolls Series, ii. 12), a description which proves that he was permanently connected with the town, and suggests very strongly that he was its castellan. In Stephen's reign both the castle and honour of Wallingford were held by Brian fitz Count, and it is very suggestive that Maud, his wife, speaks of two of the manors upon the honour as land of her inheritance (*Mon. Ang.* vii. 1016), and styles herself 'Domina Waringefordie' upon her seal (ibid.). Her relationship to Miles

The baronial attitude towards the hereditary custody of royal castles is well brought out by the author of the *Gesta Stephani* in his account of the events leading up to the siege of Bedford in the last days of 1137. Stephen, who at this time was anxious to conciliate the powerful Beaumont family, wished to make Hugh de Beaumont earl of Bedford, and to give him something more than a titular connexion with the county. He therefore married Hugh to the daughter of Simon de Beauchamp, the greatest tenant in chief in Bedfordshire, and granted to him the whole 'honour' of his wife's father, to which belonged the hereditary custody of Bedford Castle. The grant was, however, opposed by a certain Miles de Beauchamp, probably, though not certainly, Simon's nephew, who was in possession of Bedford Castle, and, apparently, of the whole Beauchamp honour.[1] The king demanded that Miles should surrender Bedford Castle to Hugh de Beaumont, and the *Gesta Stephani* thus describes Miles's reception of the demand:

'While the court was being held with splendour and solemnity appropriate to Christmas,[2] the king sent messengers to Miles de

Crispin has not yet been exactly ascertained. In 1183 a jury of knights and clerks of Oxfordshire and the honour of Wallingford committed itself to the improbable statement that she was the daughter of Robert de Oilli (tenant in chief in 1086) and that Miles Crispin (Robert's contemporary) had been her first husband (Cott. Vitell. E. xv, f. 22). Chronologically, she is much more likely to have been the daughter than the wife of Miles Crispin. But despite this difficulty, there can be no doubt that her marriage to Brian fitz Count brought him both the honour and the castle of Wallingford.

[1] The difficult question of the succession to Simon de Beauchamp is discussed by C. Gore Chambers and G. H. Fowler in *Publications of the Bedfordshire Historical Record Society*, i. 4–8 (compare G. H. White in *Transactions of the Royal Historical Society*, 4th series, xiii. 78–79). The two chief authorities for these events are Orderic (ed. le Prevost, v. 103–4) and the *Gesta Stephani* in the passage which is translated here (ed. Potter, 30–31). The genealogy of the early Beauchamps of Bedford is obscure, but it is probable that behind this dispute there lay the difficult question whether a barony should descend through the daughter of its last possessor or pass to a collateral kinsman descended in the male line from a common ancestor. But this does not affect the interest of these events as illustrations of the way in which a baron regarded the hereditary charge of a royal castle.

[2] It is one of the minor complications of this story that while the *Gesta*

Beauchamp, who with the king's permission was in charge of Bedford castle as its custodian, commanding him to tender to Hugh both the castle and the service which he owed the king, adding that if he would acquiesce in this, he should receive many notable gifts, but that if he should oppose it, he himself would quickly bring disaster upon him. Miles, on receiving the king's message, replied that he would serve and obey him most willingly so long as he did not attempt to deprive him of his inheritance, and that if the king were determined to do this, and to turn against him unrelentingly, he would bear his anger as patiently as he might, but that the king should never have the castle unless he himself were brought to the last extremity.'

It is evident from this narrative that the issue which forced Miles de Beauchamp into rebellion was not the king's intended disposal of the Beauchamp honour, but his attack upon Miles de Beauchamp's position as castellan of Bedford. There is no need to accuse the king of breaking feudal understandings in demanding the surrender of the castle. In theory the custody of a royal castle must always have been revocable at the king's pleasure. Moreover, feudal custom expected great forbearance from a man towards his lord. A mesne tenant must endure injury or insult for thirty days in time of war and for a year and a day in time of peace before the lordship would be forfeited,[1] and the king could certainly require no less restraint from a tenant in chief. But the defence of Bedford Castle which followed the interchange of ominous courtesies described in the *Gesta Stephani* cannot be fairly described as an act of feudal aggression on the part of Miles de Beauchamp.

Stephani assigns the king's demand for Miles's surrender to the Christmas feast (of 1137), Orderic and other authorities state that the siege which followed Miles's refusal occurred at Christmas.

[1] *Leges Henrici Primi*, 43; 8, 9. 'Si dominus terram suam uel feodum suum auferat homini suo, unde est homo suus, uel si eum in mortali necessitate deserat supervacue, forisfacere potest dominium suum erga eum. Sustinere tamen debet homo dominum suum, si faciat ei contumeliam uel injuriam huiusmodi, in werra triginta dies, in pace unum annum et unum diem; et interim private per compares, per uicinos, per domesticos et extraneos per leges requireret eum de recto.'

The king had already experienced the events which might happen when a disaffected baron held the custody of a royal castle. In 1068, after suppressing a rebellion in the south-west, the Conqueror had chosen a site for a castle at Exeter, and left Baldwin son of Count Gilbert of Brionne, the lord of Okehampton, to complete and guard it.[1] For a long time the history of the castle is obscure, but in 1135 it seems to have been in the hands of Baldwin de Redvers, the head of a family which had recently become important through the favour of Henry I.[2] In the next year he revolted, apparently because Stephen demanded the surrender of Exeter Castle, and the *Gesta Stephani* enters in some detail into the events which followed.[3] The king was about to receive the surrender of Bampton Castle, the scene of an earlier rebellion,

'when there appeared men bearing news of great confusion in Exeter, saying that Baldwin de Redvers, a man distinguished alike by greatness and descent, was acting strangely, and as the event proved against the king's peace. For with a new insolence, accompanied by his knights, he was entering the city among the gowned citizens, requiring not only those living in the town, but all his neighbours to acknowledge his lordship, hurrying every sort of provision into the castle, which he had usurped from the royal honour, and threatening fire and sword to all who would not adapt themselves to his presumption. They therefore begged the king to help his citizens, who in these straits could look for no other help, so that with his aid they might resist Baldwin's power, and give unhindered and particular obedience to their king. On this, the king, angry at Baldwin's audacity, since it was clearer than light that he had rebelled unjustly when the king reasonably asked back from him the custody of Exeter castle which had always pertained to the crown, gave his enemies no time for ranging over the country, sending two hundred knights ahead before himself to cut them off, if possible, by a night march.'

Situations like this must have arisen in other towns when the keepers of their castles declared against the king, but

[1] Orderic (ed. le Prevost), ii. 181.
[2] For the Redvers family see the *Complete Peerage* under 'Devon', iv. 309–12.
[3] Ed. Potter, 20–21.

they are nowhere else described so clearly. No other writer shows the rebellious custodian of a royal castle in the act of making himself master of the city which lay beneath it. Above all, no other writer of the time brings out so plainly the repugnance of the king's burgesses to a baronial lord. As the present passage shows, burgesses were helpless against a baronial garrison in the castle of their town. Neither Stephen nor Henry II can have had any illusions as to the military value of the support which the towns could give to the monarchy in the event of a baronial rebellion. But burgesses must long have remembered the occasions when they had no help but in the king, and the memory must have made for their acquiescence in the rule of any king who could maintain his own rights, even if, like Henry II, he regarded them as inconsistent with the extension of burghal liberties.

Whatever his first intentions may have been, Stephen could not maintain his predecessors' opposition to the baronial control of ancient boroughs. He was in no position to resist hereditary claims supported by military power, and the civil war was still in an early stage when he 'restored' to Robert earl of Leicester the castle and borough of Hereford and the *comitatus* of Herefordshire, apart from ecclesiastical properties and the fiefs of four important barons, to hold as freely as the earl's remote kinsman by marriage, William fitz Osbern, had held in the Conqueror's time.[1] This remarkable transaction was not the creation of an earldom of Hereford. Its object was to give to the earl of Leicester whatever rights the king possessed over the county town, and, with certain exceptions, to make him lord of all the barons of Herefordshire who at the moment were holding in chief of the crown. It closely resembles the grant of 'Stafford and

[1] Stephen's charter making these grants has been printed several times; most recently by the late Professor Davis in *Essays in History presented to Reginald Lane Poole*, 173. Its date must fall between 1140 and 1145, and as G. H. White has shown (*Trans. of Royal Historical Society*, 4th series, xiii. 74) it is probably later than the first half of 1141. It is unfortunate that the circumstances of the grant are so obscure, for its terms are highly unusual and suggestive.

Staffordshire and the whole county of Stafford' which
Rannulf earl of Chester received in 1153 from Henry
duke of Normandy, and like this more famous gift, it had
no permanent effect. But it shows the direction in which
the ambition of the higher baronage was tending, and in
particular the ambition of the house of Beaumont. Robert
was already the lord of Leicester, Roger his cousin was lord
of Warwick, and his elder brother, Waleran count of Meulan,
had by this time received Worcester from Stephen.[1] In
view of these facts, it seems probable that Hugh de
Beaumont, the youngest of the three brothers of this
family, was intended to receive the borough as well as the
castle of Bedford when he became earl of the county.[2] In
any case the history of this single house is enough to show
the reality of the movement towards the mediatization of
ancient boroughs in Stephen's reign.

But of all the barons of this period, Rannulf earl of
Chester was the most ambitious in designs on the king's
boroughs and their castles.[3] A grant of the city and castle
of Lincoln comes first in the long list of concessions by
which Stephen attempted to gain the earl's support in
1140. The grant was accompanied by reservations which
prove the king's extreme unwillingness to lose control
of a castle of exceptional strength commanding one of
the largest towns in England. But by the end of 1140
the earl had taken possession of Lincoln Castle, and the
citizens, resenting the rule of a feudal master, were
beginning to appeal to the king for help. His defeat
and capture on 2 February 1141 left the earl in power at
Lincoln. In 1144 the king failed to take the castle by
siege. In 1146, when the course of the war was turning in

---

[1] On the position of the count of Meulan at Worcester and in Worcestershire see *Complete Peerage*, xii. 2, under Worcester.

[2] See above, 237–8.

[3] The discovery of a manuscript containing the lost conclusion of the
Gesta Stephani necessitates a revision of the history of Stephen's dealings
with Rannulf earl of Chester. The following account is based on Dr. A. L.
Poole's convincing reconstruction of this piece of history in the Intro-
duction to the edition of the *Gesta* by K. R. Potter (Medieval Texts, ed.
Galbraith and Mynors, 1955), pp. xv–xxix.

his favour, the king arrested the earl and made the surrender of Lincoln Castle a condition of his release. At Christmas, exhilarated by what he obviously regarded as a notable achievement, the king broke a custom which all his predecessors had observed, and caused himself to be crowned within the city. A violent attack by the earl in the following year was defeated by the citizens, supported by the king, in whose hands both city and castle remained thenceforward.

The reality of the king's success in the long contest over Lincoln is shown by the events which introduced the last phase of the war. In 1153 Henry duke of Normandy invaded England and secured the support of the earl of Chester by a series of grants far more extensive than those which the earl had obtained from Stephen in 1140. They involved the fate of three ancient county towns, but Lincoln was not among them. Henry gave to the earl by charter the castle and borough of Nottingham; Derby with its appurtenances, which, indeed, Stephen had already promised him in 1140; and Stafford, with lordship over all the smaller fiefs of Staffordshire.[1] When the duke's charter is read as a whole, these clauses seem almost insignificant among those which grant to the earl feudal rights over the fiefs of other barons, or honours which had escheated to the crown. Apart from lesser grants, the charter transfers to the earl lordship over five important Lincolnshire fiefs, and grants him the great honours of Tickhill, Lancaster, and Eye, and the lands of William Peverel of Nottingham, unless he can clear himself in the duke's court from his wickedness and treason. The duke also promises to satisfy the claims of the earl's kinsmen on lands of their inheritance, and to give a hundred *libratae* of land to six of the earl's barons out of the lands conquered from the duke's enemies. Even so, the clauses which grant lordship over boroughs remain the feature of the charter

---

[1] Cott. Chart. xvii. 2; Rymer, *Fœdera* (1816), i. 16. On the relations between earl Rannulf and the rival claimants for the throne see R. H. C. Davis, 'King Stephen and the earl of Chester revised' in *Eng. Hist. Rev.* lxxv (1960), 654–60.

most significant of baronial ambitions, and most remote from the practice of earlier kings.

Charters like these influenced the actual course of events by securing the support, or at least the neutrality, of important men at critical moments. They show the objects desired by members of the higher baronage, and at innumerable points they supplement the narrative of events preserved by contemporary chroniclers. The studies by which Round reconstructed the history of the first half of Stephen's reign were based essentially on this kind of material. But the charters which have received most attention in the past come from the chanceries of Stephen or the empress, and those of lesser persons have not yet been systematically explored. Their value does not lie so much in the events which they may incidentally record as in the illustration which they sometimes give of the way in which events were regarded by contemporaries. In particular their notes of date occasionally preserve a contemporary opinion on some significant incident which deserves to be remembered. The mere statement that a certain charter was made *in anno quo commissum est prelium inter regem Stephanum et comitem Cestrie Ranulphum* adds nothing in itself to historical knowledge, but it is made interesting by the facts that the charter in question was granted by a tenant of the earl of Chester, and that he evidently regarded the battle of Lincoln as essentially an engagement between King Stephen and his lord.[1] A more elaborate reference to contemporary history occurs in the document, not otherwise remarkable, by which Roger bishop of Chester records that he has instituted a certain chaplain into the church of Trentham *tam largitione quam presentatione venerabilis domine nostre Matilde filie regis bone memorie Henrici in plena sinodo Lichfeldie post pentecosten anno quo aplicuit prenominata domina ad castrum Arundel, de quo tam prudenter quam sapienter venit Bristol*

---

[1] This charter (printed by C. W. Foster in *Lincolnshire Notes and Queries,* xvii. 37–38) is a grant by Simon Tuschet to the nuns of Haverholme in Lincolnshire. For the Tuschet family see Farrer, *Honors and Knights' Fees,* ii. 28–32.

et evasit de obsidione regis Stephani.[1] The events of the autumn of 1139 are not so clear that we can afford to neglect this contemporary evidence, apart altogether from the fact that the bishop was nephew of Geoffrey de Clinton, King Henry's chamberlain, and well known as a supporter of the empress. It should not be pretended that many notes of date enter so much into historical detail as this. Some of them are commonplace, others are merely personal. There is little beyond a general impression of disorder to be gathered from the statement of Hugh fitz Richard, a well-known baron of the earl of Warwick, that he made an agreement with Reading Abbey *anno quo Randulfus comes Cestrie me venantem cepit.*[2] Even so, it is useful to gain such impressions, brief as they may be, and a collection of notes of date, which has never yet been attempted, would illustrate many obscure places in twelfth-century history.

It is not only through incidental passages like these that private charters reflect the conditions of what they continually describe as *tempus werre*. It would be possible to collect a considerable number of charters made for the express purpose of recompensing different religious houses for the injuries they had suffered in the troubles. Roger earl of Hereford, for example, grants a manor in his county to Reading Abbey *pro emendatione gravaminum que illata sunt hominibus et rebus predictorum monachorum per me et per meos tempore werre.*[3] At the other end of England Gilbert earl of Lincoln grants a considerable estate in Lincolnshire to Norwich Priory *pro excessu apud Linnam in diocesano (sic) Norwicensis ecclesie commisso,*[4] and by another charter gives to Pontefract Priory an important ferry over the Humber *pro sex libratis redditus per annum quas pepigeram et affidaveram sepedictis monachis persolvere*

---

[1] *Collections of the William Salt Archaeological Society*, xi. 322. This passage does not agree very closely with any of the other contemporary accounts of the empress's landing and the events which followed it.

[2] Egerton MS. 3031, f. 41 b.

[3] Ibid., f. 45 b.

[4] C. W. Foster, *History of Aisthorpe and Thorpe in the Fallows*, 106.

. . . *pro maximis dampnis que predictis ecclesie et monachis,*
culpis meis exigentibus, intuli in guerra illa que fuit inter me
et Henricum de Lascy.[1] Rannulf earl of Chester gave the
church of Repton to Lincoln Cathedral in order to make
good, by a grant of fifteen *libratae* of rent, the losses which
the cathedral had suffered through him and his men,[2]
and William earl of Lincoln, Earl Rannulf's half-brother,
states that he has given four bovates in the soke of Bolingbroke to Crowland Abbey *pro absolutione animae Willelmi*
filii mei cuius familia manum in ipsum abbatem violenter
tempore werrae miserat.[3] None of these passages gives much
new information about the course of events in the war,
though Earl Gilbert's depredations at Lynn and the
private war between him and Henry de Lacy seem to be
unrecorded elsewhere. But they illustrate, very clearly,
the widespread devastation characteristic of the time, and
the last of them shows the lengths to which the retainers
of a great lord might sometimes go.

Nevertheless, these passages give no support to the view
that a state of general war was agreeable to the baronage
as a whole. To all members of this class the anarchy meant
the devastation of estates which ought to bring in a yearly
rent or support a tenant in his service. Now and then a
baron refers in definite terms to this aspect of the war.
Simon of Chelsfield, for example, an important tenant of
Earl Gilbert of Pembroke, confirms an estate in north
Buckinghamshire to Reading Abbey free from all services
to himself as long as war lasts, but with a very plain
reservation that he is to receive his service again when
peace comes.[4] Still clearer information to the same effect
is given by a Yorkshire tenant in chief, William de Arches,
in a charter which comes from the middle of Stephen's

---

[1] *Chartulary of St. John of Pontefract,* ii. 521.
[2] *Registrum Antiquissimum,* ii. 7.
[3] F. M. Stenton, *Danelaw Charters,* 375.
[4] Egerton MS. 3031, f. 42 b: 'Ego Symon de Chelesfeld donationem
quam pater meus Arnulfus fecit ecclesie sancte Marie de Radingia . . .
scilicet tres hidas et dimidiam in Lingeberga granto et concedo et ut firmius
roboretur, sigillo meo confirmo, cum pax uenerit, saluo meo seruitio, quia
dum guerra durauerit, uolo terram quietam esse ab omni seruitio.'

reign. In granting a small but scattered estate to a man whom he calls his kinsman and knight, he provides that the latter shall only do service in respect of the land which he actually holds, but that when peace comes, and he obtains the whole estate, he shall do the quarter of a knight's service.[1] Similar evidence is given from the south of England by one of the minor actors in the general struggle, Walter de Pinkeny, King Stephen's castellan of Malmesbury. He seems to have been a faithful adherent of Stephen, he is described in the *Gesta Stephani* as *virum constantem et circa martios sudores probatissimum*,[2] and he made the following charter in favour of Lewes Priory:

'To the venerable lord the prior and the whole convent of St. Pancras, Walter de Pinkeny sends greetings and services. Know that I give and grant to God and St. Pancras and you the church of Winterbourne which my godmother Adeliza gave to God and St. Pancras and you, after the death of the clerk my kinsman, to whom I have given it. And as long as that clerk shall live he shall hold of you and give each year ten shillings while war shall last, and when God shall give peace he shall give one mark of silver. But after his death you shall have the church whole and quit.'[3]

The north of Wiltshire, to which this charter relates, was the scene of constant fighting throughout this period, and it is remarkable that Walter de Pinkeny estimates the difference between peace and war at no more than the addition of three shillings and fourpence to a rent of ten shillings. But the fortunes of any village during the Anarchy must have depended in great part on the local position of its lord, and the castellan of Malmesbury was an important person in his own county. His estimate may at least serve as a rough indication of the conditions which must have prevailed in less fortunate villages than Winterbourne Basset.

It is only on rare occasions that a charter throws light on the general state of a village to which it refers. No collection of such records will ever supersede the evidence

[1] Farrer, *Early Yorkshire Charters*, No. 534.
[2] *Gesta Stephani*, ed. Potter, 118.
[3] Ancient Deeds, A. 14257; Appendix, No. 45.

of chronicles as to the miseries caused by the war. But facts which give local substance to the generalities of chronicles are of particular value when they relate to a district which lay outside the main fields of the struggle. The following charter comes from the remote country between Banbury and Towcester, on the edge of Whittlewood forest.

'To Robert by the grace of God bishop of Lincoln and to all the sons of holy mother church Osbert de Wanci sends greeting. Know that I have given and granted to God and St. Mary and the monks of Biddlesden, in perpetual alms, a portion of my land of Astwell. . . . Part of this land was of the dowry of my wife Aaliz, namely twenty-six acres, half of which, that is thirteen acres, she has given to the monks in perpetual alms for her soul's health, while for the other thirteen acres I have given them an exchange of equal value, and I have also given them Gudlachesho . . . on which to raise dwellings, and common pasture at Astwell in wood and field. All these gifts Gilbert de Pinkeny my lord has confirmed by his charter at my request. . . . Moreover, the monks in return for this alms shall do for me and my wife after our deaths as for a monk, except that they shall not receive our bodies for burial. If, however, I shall wish to change my life before my end, they shall receive me into religion. If there shall be so great war that we cannot keep our animals in peace, they shall keep them with their own, without cost to them-selves and saving their order, that is, they shall not pledge their faith or take any oath on this account if any one wishes to take the animals away by force. If, moreover, the animals shall be taken away by theft or lost through any other mischance or shall die or be killed or seized by beasts the monks shall not make good the loss. If moreover I or my wife or son shall be captured, the monks shall send one of their brethren to help us by mediation but not with money. Once in the year, they shall lend me a plough team.'[1]

This charter, which, incidentally, has been quoted as an early example of expressed limitation to the liability of a gratuitous bailee, cannot be earlier than 1149.[2] The matter-of-fact arrangement by which Osbert de Wanci provides against the lifting of his cattle and the capture of

[1] Harl. MS. 1704, f. 21; Appendix, No. 46.
[2] T. F. T. Plucknett, *A Concise History of the Common Law*, 5th ed., 476.

himself, his wife, and his son is in its own way as suggestive of public disorder as the famous passage in which the Old English Chronicler describes King Stephen's nineteen evil years. No one stood to gain anything by this disorder except men who lived by robbery under arms, and mercenaries who were better out of the country.[1] Nevertheless it could not be ended until some measure of certainty was reached as to the succession to the throne. The negotiations which led to the recognition of Henry of Anjou as heir of England were successful because responsible persons of every class were tired of the *tempus werre*.

Henry, himself, was well fitted to take advantage of this situation. The impression which he made on contemporaries is brought out, with no more than permissible inflation, in an encomiastic poem written between his recognition as Stephen's heir in the winter of 1153 and his own coronation on 19 December 1154.[2] Through his mother he was grandson of the great King Henry who had established the supremacy of law in England. Through his father he could claim relationship with the Angevin kings of Jerusalem. He had married a brilliant wife, who had borne him a son and heir.[3] In reputation he was unrivalled among the young princes of his time. His admirer, the poet, could address him as one divinely appointed to restore peace to the land.

Nevertheless, few passages of English history are obscurer than the phase of war which preceded this recognition. To Henry of Huntingdon the turning-point in the general struggle came in the summer of 1145, when

[1] The story of Warin of Walcote, the 'honest itinerant knight' who has been brought into general history by the publication of a thirteenth-century Assize Roll recording his career (ed. D. M. Stenton, Selden Society 1940, vol. 59, pp. 167–8) is the best illustration of the war from the standpoint of a man of the former type. It is set out by D. M. Stenton, *English Society in the Early Middle Ages*, 34–35, and A. L. Poole, *From Domesday Book to Magna Carta*, 151–3.

[2] *The Letters of Osbert of Clare*, ed. E. W. Williamson (1929), 130–2.

[3] The heir was Henry's eldest son William, born in Aug. 1153, who died in 1156.

Stephen, with the help of an army from London, captured
a new castle built for the earl of Gloucester at Faringdon
in Berkshire.[1] By this success, Stephen broke communi-
cations between the adherents of the empress in the
Thames valley and the centre of her power in Gloucestershire, and opened a new period of the war in which,
indecisive as was much of the action, the advantage was
generally with the king. In 1146 he extorted Lincoln
Castle from Rannulf earl of Chester;[2] in 1147 the earl of
Gloucester died and the empress left England, apparently
for the rest of Stephen's reign.[3] On a superficial view it
would seem that Stephen's authority was restored over
the greater part of the country. An invasion in 1149 led
by Henry duke of Normandy failed to achieve any notable
result, and it was not until 1153 that Stephen and his
followers were once more reduced to the defensive. When
at some future time Stephen's writs and charters have been
collected, it should become possible to estimate the extent of his power in these final years. They seem years of
tolerable public order when they are compared with the
time of anarchy between 1139 and 1145. What we do not
yet know is the extent to which these improved conditions
were the work of the king himself. The available evidence
suggests that England in these years was divided between
a small group of great lords, each dominant within his
own country, and that the peace of the land really depended
on the maintenance of a balance of power between them.
Between the earl of Chester's outlying honours in the
northern Midlands and the Thames valley, where the war

---

[1] *Historia Anglorum*, ed. Arnold, 278: 'Tunc demum regi fortuna in
melius coepit permutari, et in sublime protelari.' The importance of this
success, which is underestimated in most modern histories of the period,
is brought out very clearly again by the author of the *Gesta Stephani*, ed.
Potter, 12: 'Hostes namque illius, tam famosum percipientes contigisse
illi triumphum magis ac magis deprimebantur; quia alii tardius et remissius
adversus eum arma sumebant, alii, sibi metuentes, pacis cum eo et con-
cordiae foedus quam citissime inibant.'

[2] See above, 241–2.

[3] For evidence that the empress came to England in 1149 see Salter,
Early Oxford Charters, No. 59 and note.

had never ended, lay a group of shires in which Robert
earl of Derby, Robert earl of Leicester, Simon earl of
Northampton, and Roger earl of Warwick maintained an
uneasy state of half-suspended hostilities. It is significant
that the documents which best illustrate the last phase
of the time of war are two treaties, each setting out the
terms of a formal agreement between two feudal magnates.
In one, which belongs to the unquiet months immediately
after the coronation of Henry II, Earl William of Gloucester and Earl Roger of Hereford renew an 'alliance of
love' by which Earl Robert and Earl Miles, their fathers,
had bound themselves to maintain each other's interests
'during the present war between the empress and King
Stephen'.[1] The war has left King Henry without a rival
to the crown, but as yet without the power to prevent
the formation of an alliance which tacitly assumes the
possibility of private war. The other treaty, made between
the earls of Chester and Leicester, is more interesting,
for it reveals something of the new feudal order which was
arising before Henry became king in reaction against the
anarchy of previous years.

'This is the agreement between Earl Rannulf of Chester and
Robert earl of Leicester, and the final peace and concord which was
granted and arranged by them before Robert II, bishop of Lincoln[2]
and their own men; on behalf of the earl of Chester, Richard de
Lovetot, William son of Nigel, and Rannulf the sheriff, on behalf
of the earl of Leicester, Ernald de Bosco, Geoffrey Abbas, and
Reginald de Bordineio;[3] namely that Earl Rannulf has given and

---

[1] The agreement between Earl William and Earl Roger is summarized
from the original document in the appendix to the *35th Report of the Deputy
Keeper of the Public Records*, 2. The agreement between Earl Robert and
Earl Miles, which it renews, was printed by Round from a seventeenth-
century copy in *Geoffrey de Mandeville*, 379–80. Round suggested that this
copy might be imperfect. The facsimile of the original document in *Sir
Christopher Hatton's Book of Seals*, No. 212, proves its completeness and
authenticity. It deserves respect as an efficient record of an elaborate piece
of feudal negotiation.

[2] Robert de Chesni, brother of William de Chesni, castellan of Oxford,
and uncle of Gilbert Foliot, bishop of Hereford.

[3] For these men see below, 253–4, n.

granted to Robert earl of Leicester the castle of Mountsorrel, to hold to him and his heirs of him and his heirs, hereditarily and as the charter of Earl Rannulf bears witness,[1] so that the earl of Leicester ought to receive Earl Rannulf and his following in the borough and baileys of Mountsorrel, as in his fee, to make war on whomsoever he wishes, and so that the earl of Leicester may not attack[2] Earl Rannulf therefrom for anything, and if it shall be necessary for Earl Rannulf, the earl of Leicester will receive him personally in the demesne castle of Mountsorrel, and so that the earl of Leicester will keep faith with Earl Rannulf saving the faith due to his liege lord. And if it shall be necessary for the earl of Leicester to go upon[3] the earl of Chester with his liege lord, he may not bring with him more than twenty knights,[4] and if the earl of Leicester or those twenty knights shall take anything of the goods of the earl of Chester, he will return the whole. Neither the earl of Leicester's liege lord nor any other may attack the earl of Chester or his men from the earl of Leicester's castles or his land. And the earl of Leicester may not for any cause or chance lay snares for the person

[1] This is the charter, already quoted in another connexion (p. 104), which is printed below, Appendix, No. 47.

[2] The text reads *non potest inde forisfacere comiti Rannulfo pro aliquo.* Throughout the treaty *forisfacere* means to do injury, and obviously, from the context, violent injury, to someone. In the present passage, for example, the treaty is providing that the earl of Leicester may not use Mountsorrel as a basis for an attack on the earl of Chester. Although in the Anglo-Norman law books *forisfacere* sometimes means to forfeit—the usual later meaning of the word—it more often means to do injury to anyone, and this sense is particularly evident in the *Leges Eadwardi Confessoris,* which are nearly contemporary with the present treaty. (For the references see Liebermann, *Gesetze,* ii. i. 76.) The present treaty, throughout, is concerned with the details of a military situation, and the repeated *forisfacere* clearly means 'to attack'.

[3] 'Si oportuerit comitem Leecestrie ire super comitem Cestrie.' The phrase is interesting as an anticipation of the famous *nec super eum ibimus* of Magna Carta, and would prove, if proof were needed, that the Charter is referring to a violent attack on an individual.

[4] The intention of this clause is identical with that of the provisions in the treaty between Henry I and Robert count of Flanders: 'Si rex Philippus in Angliam venerit, et Robertum comitem secum adduxerit, comes Robertus tam parvam fortitudinem hominum secum adducet, quam minorem poterit, ita tamen ne inde feodum suum erga regem Franciae forisfaciat. ... Si ... rex Philippus super regem Henricum in Normannia intraverit, comes Robertus ad Philippum ibit cum decem militibus tantum' (Rymer, *Fœdera,* 1816, i. i. 7).

of the earl of Chester unless he has defied him fifteen days before. And the earl of Leicester ought to help the earl of Chester against all men except the earl of Leicester's liege lord and Earl Simon. He may help Earl Simon in this way—if Earl Rannulf attacks Earl Simon and refuses to make amends at the request of the earl of Leicester, then the earl of Leicester may help him, but if Earl Simon attacks the earl of Chester and refuses to make amends at the request of the earl of Leicester then he may not help him. And the earl of Leicester ought to guard the lands and goods of the earl of Chester which are in the power of the earl of Leicester without ill will. And the earl of Leicester has promised Earl Rannulf that he will destroy the castle of Ravenstone unless Earl Rannulf shall allow that it may remain, and so that if any one wishes to hold that castle against the earl of Leicester, Earl Rannulf will help him to destroy that castle without guile. And if Earl Rannulf makes a claim upon William de Alneto, the earl of Leicester will have him to right in his court so long as William shall remain the earl of Leicester's man and hold land of him, so that if William or his men shall have withdrawn from the earl of Leicester's fealty on account of the destruction of his castle or because he refuses to do right in the earl of Leicester's court, neither William nor his men shall be received into the power of the earl of Chester to work ill against the earl of Leicester. In this agreement the castle of Whitwick remains to the earl of Leicester fortified with his other castles.

'And on the other hand Earl Rannulf will keep faith with the earl of Leicester saving the faith of his liege lord, and if it shall be necessary for the earl of Chester to go upon the earl of Leicester with his liege lord he may not bring with him more than twenty knights. And if the earl of Chester or those twenty knights shall take anything of the goods of the earl of Leicester he will return the whole, and neither the earl of Chester's liege lord nor any other may attack the earl of Leicester or his men from the earl of Chester's castles or his land. And the earl of Chester may not for any cause or chance lay snares for the person of the earl of Leicester unless he has defied him fifteen days before. And the earl of Chester ought to help the earl of Leicester against all men except the earl of Chester's liege lord and Earl Robert de Ferrers. He may help Earl Robert in this way—if the earl of Leicester attacks Earl Ferrers and refuses to make amends at the request of the earl of Chester, then the earl of Chester may help him, but if Earl Robert de Ferrers attacks the earl of Leicester and refuses to make amends at the request of the earl of Chester then the earl of Chester shall not help him. And the earl of Chester ought to guard the lands and goods of the earl of Leicester which are in the power of the earl of Chester without ill will. And the earl of Chester has promised the earl of Leicester that if any one wishes to hold the castle of Ravenstone against the earl of Leicester, Earl Rannulf will aid him to destroy that castle, without guile. Neither the earl of Chester nor the earl of Leicester ought to build any new castle between Hinckley and Coventry, nor between Hinckley and Hartshill, nor between Coventry and Donington, nor between Donington and Leicester, nor at Gotham nor at Kinoulton nor nearer,[1] nor between Kinoulton and Belvoir, nor between Belvoir and Oakham, nor between Oakham and Rockingham nor nearer, except with the common consent of both. And if any one shall build a castle in the aforesaid places or within the aforesaid limits, each shall aid the other without ill will until the castle shall be destroyed.

'And each earl, namely Chester and Leicester, has pledged his faith in the hand of Robert II bishop of Lincoln to hold this agreement as is contained in this charter, and they have set the bishop as their security for this agreement, on his Christianity,[2] so that if any one departs from this agreement and refuses to make amends within fifteen days after he has been requested to do so, without ill will, then the bishop of Lincoln and the bishop of Chester shall do justice upon him as for broken faith. And the bishop of Lincoln and the bishop of Chester shall each give up the two pledges whom they have received as security for the observance of these agreements, to him namely who shall keep these aforesaid agreements.'[3]

[1] *Nec propius.* The position of these places, which lie around Leicester in something more than a semicircle from Coventry in the south-west, through Gotham and Kinoulton in the north to Rockingham in the south-east, suggests that Leicester was the centre from which they were regarded.

[2] 'Posuerunt eundem episcopum obsidem huius conventionis super Christianitatem suam.' The wording of the treaty here implies that the bishop's Christianity is the pledge that he will act as the earls have requested. The phrase is remarkable, but the whole circumstances of the treaty were exceptional.

[3] The date of this agreement cannot be fixed closely. It must have been made some considerable time after the consecration of Robert de Chesni as bishop of Lincoln on 19 Dec. 1148 and before the death of Rannulf earl of Chester on 16 Dec. 1153. The names of the earls' men do not narrow these limits. Rannulf the sheriff may probably be identified with the Rannulf *vicecomes* who attests a Nottinghamshire charter of Earl Rannulf's printed below (Appendix, No. 23). Richard de Lovetot was not a tenant of the honour of Chester, but he held extensively of the honour of Tickhill, and his appearance as one of the earl of Chester's men is

In *Geoffrey de Mandeville* Round, who was fully aware of the interest of this treaty, suggested that behind it lay 'the intervention, if not the arbitration, of the church'.[1] The bishop of Lincoln and his less prominent associate the bishop of Chester may well have taken part, and perhaps an important part, in bringing the earls together. But against the view that the treaty was in any sense their work may be set the language of the document, which was certainly not written by any clerk of bishop Robert of Lincoln,[2] the nature of its provisions, and the strictly feudal attitude taken by its writer. From first to last the treaty is obviously expressing the mental outlook of a man who thinks, as it were instinctively, in terms of feudal conceptions, and there is no trace at any point of the influence of an external ecclesiastical mediator. The bishops of Lincoln and Chester are essential to the effectiveness of the treaty, but this is only because the earls have agreed to submit to their judgement if either breaks faith and have set the bishop of Lincoln as their joint security for the observance of their *conventio*. And under the conditions that existed between 1149 and 1153, if feudal magnates of this rank sought any external guarantee for the permanence of their treaties they could find no other than that of the church.

It would be hard to find another English document which illustrates so clearly the tendencies of a feudal society emancipated from royal control. Throughout the document, the earls of Chester and Leicester speak like men to whom the rules and courtesies of feudal society are the highest law. Each may make war upon the other, but the aggressor must first make his formal defiance fifteen days before hostilities begin. The earls admit, indeed, the existence of an authority superior to themselves, but it is evidence that the latter honour was in the earl's hands when this agreement was made. The three men who supported the earl of Leicester are all known as witnesses to his charters, and Ernald de Bosco was his steward.

[1] Op. cit. 380.

[2] There could not be any greater contrast than that between the laconic, repetitive phraseology of this document and the elaborate style of Bishop Robert's episcopal *Acta*.

the authority, not of a king, but of a liege lord, and they proceed to define by mutual agreement the conditions under which they will serve him one against the other. No other document recognizes, like this, the right of a great baron to make war at his own pleasure, or shows so plainly the military aspect of the private castles of central England. Of less obvious, but perhaps of equal, interest is the clause which implies that a tenant who feels himself aggrieved by his lord may well refuse to stand to right in his court and withdraw his fealty altogether from him. Nothing did more to protract the wars of Stephen's time than the frequent changes of fealty made by men like Geoffrey de Mandeville or the earl of Chester himself. The present treaty shows that King Stephen and the empress were not the only persons who felt the instability of feudal relationships.

It is natural that when this document is quoted at all, it should generally be used as an illustration of feudal anarchy. Its first editor, Augustine Vincent, in 1622, printed it because it 'doth liuely expresse the calamity of this state, under the exorbitant powers of the Nobility then, whereby we may see, and thanke God for the felicity we enjoy under a happy Monarch, in respect of our Ancestors under so many Tyrants'.[1] In reality the treaty represents an approach towards the restoration of order by the only means effective in a land where the royal power had fallen into temporary abeyance. In form it is a mere agreement between two great lords, a definition of their spheres of local influence and of the conditions under which either might make war upon the other. But the conditions of the time were such that the safety of the common free man had come to depend on the maintenance of alliances like this, or, to speak more generally, on the willingness of the greater magnates to limit their own independence in order that anarchy might be avoided. It was only by the co-operation of men like the earls of Chester and Leicester that lesser barons could be kept

---

[1] *A Discoverie of Errours in the first Edition of the Catalogue of Nobility, Published by Raphe Brooke, Yorke Herald,* 1619, 301–3.

from castle-building, that existing castles, built without proper authorization, could be destroyed, and that some limit could be set to the devastation consequent on private warfare. The weakness of such alliances lay in the fact that they presupposed the existence of a state of war in the country. It was something that two men of the highest rank should bind themselves to give formal warning of intended hostilities, to return the plunder which either might take from the other, to combine against the more aggressive of their own men, and to build no new castles in the debatable land between the regions where each was supreme. But no alliance of individual lords could promise a general restoration of public order, and the very elaboration of the treaty between the earls of Chester and Leicester emphasizes the fact that they and their friends were involved in a state of war from which they could only escape by submission to a king reigning by hereditary, and therefore uncontested, right. The re-establishment of an effective feudal monarchy was inevitable when the earls of Chester and Leicester made their treaty, and the earl of Leicester himself was destined to become its chief minister.

Its immediate task was the restoration of order, and in this its success was rapid and complete.[1] But if this had been all, if Henry II had done no more than restore the conditions which had prevailed in 1135, though he would have done a great service to his contemporaries, he would have added little to the ultimate strength of the monarchy which he inherited. Henry I had carried the centralization

---

[1] That the process had begun even before Stephen's death is shown by the coins of the so-called 'Awbridge type' which were circulating when Henry became king. They are of good weight and metal, and specimens from different mints resemble one another to a degree which suggests that the dies had been distributed over the country from London ('Stephen Type VII' by F. Elmore Jones, *British Numismatic Journal*, xxviii. 537–54). They all bear a distinctive representation of an old man's bearded face, which gives the impression of a genuine attempt at portraiture. Taken as a whole, they show that in at least one department of the national economy a centralized administration had been restored before Henry's accession.

of feudal authority to a point at which it was threatened by the results of its own thoroughness. Henry II was brilliantly successful in reconstructing the broken system of his grandfather's day, and he secured its permanence by turning it to purposes which lay beyond the imagination of the elder king. The administration of Henry II might be harsh, and its agents preoccupied with the maintenance of royal rights. But beneath the severity of his rule there are signs of a constructive intelligence such as no one but the Conqueror had as yet applied to the government of England. Recent events had shown the fundamental insecurity of a government which, like that of Henry I, had rested on the enforced obedience of feudal magnates. By providing legal remedies which no one but the king could make effective, and thus inducing all free men of whatever condition to seek his court, Henry II provided a new basis for the royal power. And because he avoided any direct attack on feudal institutions, more than one great lord of an earlier generation worked with him towards the new monarchy of which he was the founder.

APPENDIX

In the texts which follow, all abbreviations have been extended, unless the exact form meant by the writer is doubtful. No attempt has been made to follow the manuscripts in regard to capital letters. In documents derived from cartulary copies, *et* is printed, whatever symbol for this word may have been used in the manuscripts, but the symbol of the manuscript is always reproduced in the case of original texts. The approximate date of each document is given within brackets. The reasons for the dates assigned to a charter are given, when necessary, in notes, either below, or when the charter is quoted earlier in the book. The places mentioned in the documents are identified in footnotes unless the identifications have already been given.

Duchy of Lancaster, Ancient Correspondence 1
(See page 21.)

1. R' comes Cestrie Ricardo de Veim ceterisque uauassoribus suis de Biseleia salutem   Precipio uobis quod amodo intendatis seruicium uestrum Miloni constabulario . ita benigne sicut umquam melius fecistis. Valete. (1129–41.)

Strip with fragment of equestrian seal in white wax, and tie.
No early endorsement.

Cott. Chart. x. 7
(See pages 21–22 and note.)

2. Hugo comes Cestrie constabuloni 7 dapifero suo justic' vicecom' baronibus ministris 7 balliuis 7 omnibus hominibus suis Francis 7 Angl*is* tam futuris quam presentibus salutem Sciatis me reddidisse Umfrido de Buhun 7 heredibus suis tenendum de me 7 de meis heredibus feodum de Biseleia ut suam hereditatem . per seruicium trium militum de quinque qui recognoscuntur . 7 si contigerit quod plures milites quam quinque inueniantur in feodo ⁊ uel per dis-*rati*ocinatione*m* uel per recognitionem ⁊ ego Hugo 7 heredes mei habebimus seruicii dimidium de incremento . 7 Umfridus 7 heredes sui per hoc teneant feodum de me 7 de meis heredibus . sine feodo Philippi de Belmis quod Hugo de Laci in capite tenet de me. Testibus istis Ricardo filio comitis Gloecestrie Johanne Consta-*bulone* Cestrie   Bertram de Verdun   Rogero Malfillastre Radulfo Vicecomite de Abricis   Herueio de Missi ex parte comitis 7 Galfrido de Costentin 7 Roberto filio Walteri . 7 ex parte Umfridi de Buhun . Engelger de Buhun   Waltero filio Roberti Ricardo de Vehim   Ricardo de Abenesse   Waltero de Asseleia Willelmo de Mineres   Oliuero de Mara   Ricardo Bigot Umfrido de Sancto Vigor   Roberto de Vernun. (*c.* 1170.)

Equestrian seal. No early endorsement.

P.R.O. Rentals and Surveys $\frac{20}{8}$
(See page 16.)

3. Willelmus de Turrevilla omnibus hominibus suis tam Francis quam Anglis salutem. Sciant tam presentes quam futuri quod ego Willelmus dedi concessi et carta sigillo meo signata confirmaui Willelmo piscatori et heredibus suis tres virgatas terre in Toppelawe et duas acras in Wolerse et assartum quod Turgarius tenuit et piscariam suam cum omnibus suis pertinentiis tenendas de me et heredibus meis libere et quiete in bosco et plano in viis in aquis in semitis et pascuis pro tercia parte feodi lorice pro omni seruitio quod ad me pertinet. His testibus . Hamone Passelowe . Baldewino de Hallyng' . Hugone de Penna . Gundewino de Penna . Hugone filio Radulfi . Nicholao de Tapp' . Willelmo filio Alexandri . Jordano de Ho . Waltero de Burtund'. (Henry II.)

Sloane Roll, xxxi. 4, m. 5
(See pages 35–36.)

4. H. rex Anglorum episcopo Lincol*n*iensi. et comiti Dauid' et comiti de Legrec*estria* et comiti Ranulfo de Cestria et omnibus baronibus et dominis de quibus Galfridus Ridel terras tenebat et omnibus vicecomitibus in quorum ministeriis eas tenebat salutem. Sciatis me dedisse Ricardo Basset filiam Galfridi Ridel in uxorem . et custodiam terre predicti Galfridi Ridel . donec Robertus Ridel possit esse miles . et ducat in uxorem neptem Radulfi Basset . scilicet . filiam cuiusdam filie sue de muliere. Et tunc habeat predictus Ricardus xx. libratas terre cum uxore sua in maritagio de feodo meo in dominio . et iiii milites feodatos . et si Robertus morietur sine herede de muliere concedo Ricardo Basset et heredi suo quem habuerit de filia predicti Galfridi totam terram Galfridi Ridel de quocumque tenuisset . et si filie Galfridi Ridel in vita Roberti fratris sui uel in Ricardi Basset custodia maritate non fuerint *?* Ricardus Basset eas consulet consilio meo et consideracione mea . et hec donacio et conuencio facte sunt requisicione et consilio comitis Ran*nulfi* de Cestria . et Willelmi fratris sui et Nigelli de Alban*ni* et aliorum parentum suorum . et Geue matris sue et Gal*fridi* cancellarii comitis Ran*nulfi* de Cestria et Simonis decani Lincol*niensis* et Willelmi filii Rannulfi . et Thome de Sancto Johanne . et G. de Clinton' . et Pagani filii Johannis et Willelmi de Auben*ni* . et Wnfridi de Bowhun . et Roberti Musard . et Roberti Basset . et Osmundi Basset et Turstini Basset . et Willelmi constabularii comitis Rannulfi de Cestria et Radulfi filii Normanni . et Hugonis Maubaunc apud Wodestoke. (1120–3.)

Cott. Claud. D. xiii, f. 49

(See pages 38–41.)

5. Rogerus de Valoniis omnibus amicis et hominibus suis Francis et Anglis salutem. Pluribus et multis notum est et diuulgatum Walterum de Valoniis cognatum meum antequam monachus fieret Berneyam cum terra de Thursford' et cum omnibus que in ea sunt et ad eam pertinent et in bosco et extra boscum pro mea et sua omniumque nostrorum salute tam uiuorum quam mortuorum ecclesie beate Marie de Binham ad opus monachorum qui ibi deo seruiunt aut seruient inperpetuum remansura . assensu et presencia Rohaisie uxoris sue coram abbate sancti Albani et coram clericis et militibus sollempniter dedisse. Scimus etiam Agnetem filiam suam eandem terram per cultellum unum cum eodem Waltero patre suo coram omnibus astantibus super altare posuisse que scilicet Agnes heres erat Walteri de predicta Berneya iuxta statutum decretum quod ubi filius non habetur . terram patris filie per colos parciuntur . nec potest maior natu iuniori medietatem hereditatis nisi vi et iniuria auferre. Hanc igitur donacionem ego ipse Rogerus de Valoniis amore dei coactus et beate et gloriose uirginis Marie matris domini nostri Jhesu Christi . et concessi faciendam ipsius Walteri requisicione et precibus . et concedo factam atque confirmo . per seruicium tamen tercie partis militis . videlicet pro anima patris mei qui primum Berneyam ecclesie de Binham donauit Waltero precipiens hoc ipsum ita fieri . et pro anima matris mee . et pro mea propria . uxorisque mee Agnetis . et filiorum meorum salute . qui mihi in hac eadem re consencientes sunt et hoc ipsum concedunt et pro communi omnium nostrorum saluatione tam uiuorum quam mortuorum . multorum eciam sapiencium admonicione uirorum atque laudacione . maxime autem domni Theobaldi Cantuariensis archiepiscopi et tocius Anglie primatis exortacione precibus atque consilio qui mihi racionabilibus et uerissimis assercionarum ostendit iustissimum esse . ut vir nobilis et liberalis qui feodum habet sex militum . non solum terram tercie partis militis . sed eciam tocius integri uel eo amplius pro sua suorumque salute deo et sante ecclesie largiatur . addens eciam quod si heres eius elemosinam que quasi pons inter ipsum patrem et paradysum interponitur per quem pater transire ualeat auferre conatur utique et a regno celorum idem heres quantum in ipso est patrem eius exheredat . unde nec reliquam heres hereditatem iure optinebit . qui sese filium non esse testatur ubi patrem suum occidit. Hec archiepiscopus diligenti racione nobis asseruit . quapropter iure perpetuo stabilis maneat donacio Walteri predicta de Berneya cum omnibus pertinenciis suis in ecclesia beate Marie de Binham . ita libere et bene et honorifice . sicut idem Walterus eam melius tenuit tempore patris mei siue tempore meo. Quicunque ergo eandem predictam elemosinam ecclesie de Binham auferre uoluerit . cum Datan et Abiron et cum Iuda proditore sit pars eius in profunditate inferni. Qui uero eam eidem ecclesie confirmauerit adiuuerit et manutenuerit . sit anima eius in sorte electorum . et uita perfruatur eterna. Amen. Hii sunt testes . Agnes de Valoniis . Fulco de Munpunzun . Galfridus sacerdos de Herefordingberia . Radulfus filius Roberti . Radulfus filius Turgisi . Gilbertus filius Willelmi de Roinges . Godefridus capellanus . Robertus de Valoniis . Winemarus . Gaufridus de Mannauilla . Simon fiilus Willelmi . Robertus filius Radulfi. (*c.* 1145.)[1]

Lansdowne MS. 207 E, p. 201

(See pages 48–50.)

6. Notum sit etc hanc esse pactionem inter Rogerum de Beningword et Petrum de Gausa quod ipsi concordes facti sunt de calumpnia terre Geruasii de Halton apud Bulingbroke in presentia Willelmi comitis et de alia hereditate quae fuit Hodonis de Beningword nominatim de Wiuelestorp, et de Houton, et de Sarneburne, scilicet quod Geruasius de Halton tenebit terram suam de Halton cum omnibus pertinentiis suis ejusdem terre in omni vita sua de Rogero de Beningword medietatem, et Petro de Gausa aliam medietatem; Et hic Petrus de Gausa tenet et tenebit suam medietatem de Rogero de Beningword in feudo et hereditate ille et heredes sui de Rogero et heredibus suis, et hic Rogerus tenebit has predictas terras cum omnibus pertinentiis in feudo et hereditate de Willelmo comite in capud et de heredibus suis, sicut ille quem Petrus de Gausa et Geruasius de Halton concesserunt esse justum heredem de eisdem terris. Hac eadem pactione que hic dinoscitur de terris Geruasii et de pertinentiis earum scilicet de terra de Halton, et de Wiuelestorp,

---

[1] There is no very definite indication of date in the charter, but the title archbishop of Canterbury and primate of all England given to Archbishop Theobald suggests that he was not yet legate.

et de Houton, et de Siarneburne (*sic*), adquirendis hic Rogerus et hic Petrus adquirent communi potentia sua et pecunia communi. Et hic Petrus tenebit medietatem de Rogero in feudo et hereditate; et de his et de aliis terris tenebit Rogerus medietatem in dominicum suum, et ille qui plus pecunie ad eas adquirendas posuerit majorem partem terre habebit donec reddatur ei pecunia sua saluis tenuris quas hic Rogerus et hic Petrus tenuerunt in capud de comite Willelmo in die qua hanc concordiam fecerunt sic ad tenend' illi et her' sui (*sic*). Hanc pactionem sicut dinoscitur affidauerunt ad inuicem tenend' sine malo ingenio hic Rogerus et hic Petrus coram Willelmo comite . et hiis testibus . Willelmo comite . Philippo de Chime . Gilberto de Nevill' . Willelmo filio Hacun . Roberto de Barcword . Rogero de Teillol . Gilberto de Bolonia . Herberto filio Alardi . Symone de Halton . Baldwino de Bifford . Waltero de Kylingholme . Willelmo Britone Anfrido de Chandun (*sic*) Roberto filio Berengarii et multis aliis. Post supradictam conuentionem factam coram comite Willelmo in die quo Rogerus Mareschaldus saisiuit Rogerum de Beningword de seruitio Geruasii de Halton, renouata fuit couentio (*sic*) ibi et recognita inter Rogerum de Beningword et Petrum de Gausa. Inprimis conuenit inter eos quod Geruasius de Halton tota vita sua totum feudum suum tenebit et quiete sicut vnquam liberius et melius tenuit. Post mortem vero Geruasii conuenit inter prefatum Rogerum et Petrum quod totam terram de Halton dimidiam partientur, ita quod medietatem illius terre Petrus de Rogero tenebit. Vnde et in eodem loco ubi haec conuentio facta est fecit Petrus Rogero homagium suum de illa medietate. Et Rogerus postquam saisitus fuit de seruitio Geruasii, et postquam Petrus ei fecit homagium suum, statim coram omnibus saisiauit eum de predicta medietate de Rogero tenenda et de heredibus Rogerii ipse et heredes sui. Preterea conuenit inter eos etiam quod omnes conquestus suos de feudo Hodonis de Beningword medium parcientur et tenebit Petrus ipse et heredes sui de Rogero et de heredibus eius totam medietatem conquestuum suorum de feudo Hodonis saluis tenuris suis quas tenent et tenuerunt eo die in capite de Willelmo de Romara comite de Linc'. Ipsam predictam conuencionem sacramenti fidei suae assecurauit Rogerus se tenere et omnes heredes suos, et Petrus quoque assecurauit sacramento fidei suae eandem conuentionem se et omnes heredes suos tenere, et post istos ex parte Rogeri de Beningword interposita fide sua assecurauit Matheus frater predicti Rogeri istam conuencionem tenere. Et ex parte Petri de Gausa assecurauit Garcierus de Campania interposita fide sua istam conuencionem tenere. Hiis testibus Gerlone

abbate de Neuhous . Radulfo de Halton . Thoma sacrista de
Thornton . Symone capellano de Halton . Gilberto de Bolonia .
Rogero de Teillol . Gilberto filio Geruasii . Radulfo filio Ricardi .
Waltero filio Bonde . Delisone de Cotes . Waltero filio Regenaldi .
Baldwino de Gifford (*sic*) . Willelmo Britone . Eustachio Pichot .
Radulfo de Croxby . et Philippo fratre eius . Ricardo de Wicheton
et Henrico fratre suo . Vmfrido de Neuhous . Radulfo filio Petri de
Thoresway . et Alano fratre eius . Goce filio Hacun' . Warino filio
Hornald'. Willelmo nepote Geruasii . Alano homine Walteri .
Ricardo de Scures . Roberto Surrays . Roberto nepote ejus . et
multis aliis. (*c.* 1150.)

Cott. Titus C. ix, f. 143 b[1]

(See pages 51–53.)

7. Hec est compositio finalis concordie inter Henricum filium
Fulcheri et Sewallum fratrem suum . scilicet quod dictus Henricus
hereditauit dictum Sewallum de baroniis Fulcheri et Henrici fratris
sui . et inde . scilicet . de istis baroniis duabus Henricus primogenitus
fecit illum dominum et antenatum. Et pro ista donacione et adquietacione Sewallus dedit Henrico in curia domini comitis Willelmi
dimidiam marcam argenti. Et preterea Sewallus dedit Henrico et
heredibus suis homagium Swani de Mapelton' et seruicium de
Yuinbroc et seruicium de Ybul saluo recto Simonis filii Jordani
et seruicium de Acouere saluo iure heredum Radulfi filii Orm . et
seruicium totius dowarii quod Jordanus frater suus dedit uxori
sue . scilicet . dimidium Yolegreue et Gratton' cum pertinenciis
suis et Weston'[2] et unum molendinum in Derbeia . et unam
marcam argenti in Bryctichesfeld'[3] et Irton' et Acouere et ecclesiam
de Ednesouere et ecclesiam de Schirleg'[4] et quicquid iuris pater
eorum habuit in ecclesia de Yolegreue. Et si domina predicta mutet
uitam suam ante mortem . [5] Henricus et heredes sui habebunt totum
dowarium suum predictum in dominio suo. Et pro isto fine et doni
concessione : Henricus dedit Sewallo quinque marcas argenti . et
per istam compositionem et conuencionem Henricus et heredes sui
abiurauerunt[6] Sewallo et heredibus suis si ipse heredem habuerit de

---

[1] Compared with the copy printed by Mr. Evelyn Shirley in *Stemmata
Shirleiana,* 347. Unimportant variations are not noticed.

[2] *Stemmata Shirleiana* reads *Dalberry et Neston.* Presumably the first
of these names stands for Dalbury in Derbyshire.

[3] S.S. *Brittilichifield.*   [4] S.S. *Chirley.*

[5] S.S. inserts *Henrici* after *mortem.*   [6] S.S. *adjuraverunt.*

sponsa sua . et si ipse Sewallus heredem de sponsa sua non habuerit : tota hereditas remanebit Henrico et heredibus suis. Et pro isto dono et isto fine Fulcherus filius Henrici deuenit homo Sewalli. Et nec Sewallus nec Henricus poterit vendere nec inuadiare quicquam hereditatis illorum nisi unus alteri pro minore precio quam alius inde dare uoluerit. Et dotem quam Sewallus dederat[1] uxori sue Matildi Rudel : Henricus et heredes sui tenendam eidem concesserunt . sicut carta comitis Willelmi confirmat[2] et testatur. Et si aliquis eorum huic composicioni non steterit et eam non tenuerit . et per comitem et per amicos hoc corrigere noluerit prece et peticione utriusque : comes seysiet[3] feodum illius qui inde exierit donec iniuria emendetur. Huius actionis et conuencionis comes Willelmus est iusticia et testis . et hii sunt testes Robertus frater comitis et Willelmus Pantulf.[4] (1161–6.)[5]

Sloane MS. 986, f. 21

(See page 57, note 3.)

8. . H . rex Anglie (*sic*) dux Norm' et Aquiet' et comes Andeg' . archiepiscopis episcopis abbatibus comitibus baronibus justic' vicecomitibus ministris et omnibus fidelibus suis totius Anglie et Normannie salutem. Sciatis me concessisse Roberto Foliot totam terram et honorem[6] qui fuit Widonis de Raimecurt cum Margeria filia Ricardi de Raimecurt que inde heres est. Quare volo et precipio quod ipse et heredes sui terram et honorem illum teneant de me et heredibus meis in feodo et hereditarie ita libere at quiete et honorifice sicut predictus Wido de Raimecurt melius uel liberius quiecius et honorificentius umquam tenuit et Ricardus filius suus post eum cum soca et saca et tol et teham et infangeneteof et cum omnibus libertatibus et liberis consuetudinibus que honori predicto pertinent in bosco et plano in pratis et pascuis in aquis et molendinis in ciuitatibus et extra et in omnibus locis. Testibus Thoma cancellario et aliis. (1154–63.)

---

[1] S.S. *dederit*.
[2] S.S. *confirmavit*.
[3] S.S. *capiet* (?).
[4] S.S. *Pantufe*.
[5] The places mentioned here are Mapleton, Ivonbrook, Ible, Youlgrave, Gratton, Derby, Brushfield, Little Ireton, Edensor, and Shirley in Derbyshire, and Okeover in Staffordshire. Weston has not been identified.

[6] The honour in question was the Domesday fief of Guy de Reinbuedcurt, which extended into the counties of Northampton, Leicester, Lincoln, Oxford, and Cambridge. Its head was at Chipping Warden in Northamptonshire.

Ancient Deeds, A. 14208

(See pages 89 and 233–4.)

9. Willelmus Comes Lin*colnie* omnibus baronibus suis . 7 hominibus . Francis . 7 Anglis . clericis . 7 laicis . de honore de Arundell' .
salutem. Sciatis me concessisse . 7 carta confirmasse . monachis de
Sancto Pancracio . de Leusa . in elemosinam terram de Netimbre,
quam Alanus de Dunestanuilla . eis pro anima uxoris sue . dedit 7
concessit . Quapropter uolo . 7 firmiter precipio . quatinus predictam terram illam de Netimbre . cum omnibus eidem terre
pertinentibus teneant, solam . 7 quietam . 7 libere . 7 honorifice.
T. Hugone priore de Neuham . 7 Rogero capellano . 7 Hermanno
capellano . 7 Aluredo capellano . 7 Radulfo filio Sauari . 7 Gaufrido
de Tresg' . 7 Amau*rico* de Bella Fago . 7 Willelmo de Dunestanuilla . 7 Waltero fratre suo . 7 Petro dapifero Alani . 7 Harold'
sacerdote . de Burcham . 7 Roberto fratre suo . 7 Helia nepote
Radulfi filii . Sauari. (1139–41.)

Strip for seal.
Endorsed: 1. Willelmi comitis Linc' De Neti*m*bre (late twelfth century).
de terra quam tenuit Alanus de Donestanuila (fourteenth century).
2. De rapo de Arundel (fourteenth century).

Harl. 639, f. 59 b

(See page 68 for this and the next three charters.)

10. Stephanus comes Moritonie omnibus justificatoribus et
omnibus baronibus suis Francis et Anglis salutem. Sciatis quod ego
concedo deo et sancto Petro Eye et seruientibus ejusdem loci tenere
in elemosina hoc quod Adelelmus dedit eis in elemosina, scilicet
ecclesiam de Pleiford[1] et terram, et ea omnia que pertinent ad
eandem ecclesiam. Et villanum scilicet Alfricum de Fen illum et
omnia sua sicut tenebat in die qua Adelinus (*sic*) fuit viuus et
mortuus. Test' . Roberto capellano . Andrea de Baldemento
Jordano de Salcheuilla . Roberto fratre ejus . G. Blundo. (1107–25.)[2]

Add. MS. 8177, p. 134 b

11. Stephanus comes Moriton . Justic' suis . et omnibus baronibus
suis Francis et Anglis tocius Anglie salutem. Sciatis quod ego volo
et firmiter precipio quod Hubertus prior ecclesie sancti Petri Eye
et monachi eidem ecclesie servientis (*sic*) teneant et habeant omnia

[1] Playford, Suffolk.
[2] Before Stephen became count of Boulogne on the death of his wife's
father Count Eustace.

sua, scilicet terras et decimas et ecclesias ita bene et honorifice sicuti unquam melius et honorabilius tenuerunt tempore Roberti Malet et ipsa die qua ego terram Rodberti Malet a rege suscepi et ipsa die qua ego mare nouissime transiui et nominatim omnia illa teneant que tenent de feodo Herefridi in pace donec veniam in Angliam et audiam qua rac*i*one habent nec pro ullo breue siue homine placitent me absente, quia nolo ut inde placitum sit nisi in presentia mea quia de elemosina mea. T.' Ricardo camerario et Malgero capellano. (1107–25.)

Add. MS. 8177, p. 134 b

12. Stephanus comes Bolonie et Morit' R. filio Walteri salutem Precipio ut prior et monachi sancti Petri de Eya ita bene et honorifice suas terras et homines et res teneant sicut faciebant quum (*sic*) novissime mare transiui. Testibus . Ricardo clerico. (1125–35.)

Add. MS. 8177, p. 134

13. Stephanus comes Morit' et Bolon', Malgero capellano et G. Blundo, et justic' suis Anglie . salutem . Precipio firmiter vobis quod resaizatis priorem H. Eye, et monachos, de ecclesia de Ber-gebi,[1] et de decimis et rebus ad ecclesiam pertinentibus, sicuti erat in die qua nouissime mare transiui, et teneant in pace et bene et honorifice sicut tunc tenebant. Et si aliquid inde postea captum est . cito eis reddatur. Testibus Roberto dapifero et Ricardo clerico. (1125–35.)

Add. MS. 15314, f. 109

(See page 68.)

14. G. comes Mellenti omnibus justiciis et ministris suis de Esturmen*stre* tam presentibus quam futuris salutem Mando uobis et firmiter precipio quatinus singulis annis canonicis sancti Dionisii de Suthamtona viginti solidos in prepositura mea de Esturmen*stre* detis . in festo sancti Johannis baptiste uidelicet decem solidos et in festo sancti Michaelis decem solidos. Hanc autem donationem in perpetuum firmiter teneri precipio. Robertus filius Rogeri de Suthamtona inde me multum precatus fuit qui predictos denarios canonicis predictis dederat. Testibus Comitissa Roberto filio suo (*sic*) etc. (Before 1166.)[2]

---

[1] Barrowby, Lincolnshire.

[2] This writ cannot be dated at all closely. The grant which it records was confirmed by Henry II (same reference) in a charter which itself cannot be dated. All that can be said is that the grant is more likely to belong to the reign of Henry II than to that of Stephen.

Stowe MS. 925, f. 122

(See page 70.)

15. Willelmus comes Glouc' senescallo suo et omnibus ministris suis et amicis et fidelibus suis salutem. Sciatis me dedisse et concessisse et hac carta mea confirmasse Waltero citharedo meo pro homagio et seruicio suo terram que fuit Chinemeri bouarii iuxta terram Gilberti de Ruggeweie in vico ubi faciunt heras Tenendam libere et quiete sibi et heredibus suis de me et heredibus meis pro uno disco pleno fabis reddendo annuatim pro omni seruicio in die sancti Johannis ad scaccarium meum apud Bristoll'. Hiis testibus H. comitissa. H. de Valoignis Ricardo de Kardyf. Simone de Kardif. Toma de Clare. Reginaldo filio Simonis. Widone de Roche. Gilberto de Amari. Gilberto Croc Gilberto de Sancto Mauro. Gilberto capellano. Roberto filio Gregorii. Orewon' filio Gregorii. et multis aliis. (Before 1183.)

Cott. Appendix xxi, f. 65

(See page 71.)

16. The first of two long charters of confirmation issued by Archbishop Theobald of Canterbury for Stoke by Clare Priory (*Mon. Ang.* viii, 1659–60) ends with a list of witnesses, of which only the first part is printed in the *Monasticon*. The original hand of the Stoke cartulary gives the names:—Rogerus archidiaconus Cantuariensis ecclesie. Thomas clericus de Lond'. magister Iohannes Saleb'. Iohannes de Cantuar'. Philippus de Sal'. magister Guido de Pressenni. magister Iohannes de Tylberia. magister Rogerus Species. et multi alii.

At the foot of the page a fourteenth-century hand adds:

Osebertus clericus crucifer Willelmus Gilbertus Rogerus Lechardus nepotes domini archiepiscopi Thomas clericus Ebroisensis magister eorum Elinandus cancellarius Ricardus de Clare de Gloucestre monachi et capellani archiepiscopi Robertus pincerna Ricardus dispensarius Gilbertus camerarius Odo senescallus Willelmus magister cocus Laurencius ostiarius Willelmus filius Pagani portarius Baylehache marescallus et multi alii. (The whole charter is now printed by A. Saltman, *Theobald Archbishop of Canterbury* (1956), 477–82.

Feet of Fines, Box, 171, File 13, No. 244

(See pages 71–73.)

17. Hec est finalis concordia facta in curia domini Regis apud Westm' a die purificacionis beate Marie in unum mensem anno

regni regis Johannis .xvi.ᵐᵒ coram P. Winton' episcopo . Simone
de Pat' . Jacobo de Poterna Rogero Huscarl' Henrico de Ponte
Aldemer' Justic' et aliis fidelibus domini Regis tunc ibi presentibus
inter Willelmum abbatem Westmonasterii querentem . et Iuonem
de Den deforciantem . de .i. hospicio eidem abbati et suis semel in
anno per consuetudinem faciendo . cum aliis consuetudinibus et
seruiciis que idem Iuo debet de manerio de Den . quod ipse tenet
de abbacia Westmonasterii . unde predictus abbas questus fuit quod
per detencionem illius hospicii fuit domus sua dampnis et expensis
ualde grauata. Et unde placitum fuit inter eos in eadem curia.
Scilicet quod predictus Iuo recongnouit et concessit se debere
predictum hospicium per annum hoc modo . scilicet cum placuerit
eidem abbati suum hospicium habere apud Den . idem Iuo debet
premuniri per summonicionem quindene ei factam per breue
eiusdem abbatis . et die quo abbas illuc ueniet ⸫ preibunt septem
seruientes abbatis quibus tradentur septem officia domus . scilicet
senescallo ⸫ abbatis officium aule . camerlano ⸫ custodia camere .
panetario ⸫ custodia dispense et panis . pincerne ⸫ custodia butte-
lerie . et potuz ⸫ hostiario custodia hostii . coco ⸫ custodia coquine .
marescallo ⸫ custodia marescalcie. Et idem Iuo et sui honorifice
suscipient ipsum abbatem et suos cum eo venientes . et de proprio
ipsius Iuonis necessaria sufficientia eis inuenient . in cibis et potibus
et aliis necessariis ad honorificum hospicium pertinentibus primo
die aduentus abbatis. Et in crastino quousque ipse et sui prandium
suum honorificum habuerunt . ita quidem quod post prandium
illius diei non poterunt abbas vel sui per consuetudinem plusquam
semel exigere vel habere potum . nec aliquid aliud de proprio
Iuonis nisi illud emere voluerunt. Set si placuerit abbati morari
per totam noctem ad domum ipsius Iuonis ⸫ omnia que habebit
rationabiliter emet . et facta inde computacione et tallia inter
seruientes abbatis et ipsum Iuonem et seruientes suos . id quod
idem abbas et sui de proprio Iuonis habuerunt ⸫ computabitur et
allocabitur Iuoni in firma sua quam reddere debebit ad proximum
terminum. Idem vero Iuo inueniet duos cereos ardentes coram
abbate prima nocte aduentus sui quorum uterque erit de una libra
cere . et id quod inde remanebit incombustum ⸫ habebit camerlanus
abbatis . cuilibet vero predictorum septem seruientum abbatis .
dabit idem Iuo duodecim denarios. Et propter dampna et expensas
quas abbacia Westmonasterii habuit per detencionem hospicii
predicti quod idem Iuo facere contradixit ⸫ idem Iuo acreuit firmam
suam de quadraginta solidis . ita quod idem Iuo et heredes sui
inperpetuum tenebunt predictum manerium de Den cum omnibus

pertinenciis suis . excepta aduocacione et donacione ecclesie que eidem abbati et successoribus suis remanet . de predicto abbate et successoribus suis faciendo predictum hospicium prefato modo . et reddendo decem et octo libras esterlingorum per annum . in abbacia Westm' de predicto manerio . unde reddere non consueuit per annum . nisi sexdecim libras . scilicet infra octabas pasche quatuor libras et decem solidos . et infra octabas sancti Johannis baptiste quatuor libras et decem solidos . et infra octabas sancti Michaelis quatuor libras et decem solidos . et infra octabas natalis domini quatuor libras et decem solidos . pro omni seruicio.

Cott. MS. Appendix xxi, f. 114 b
(See pages 75–76.)

18. Ric' . G . fil' Peccati[1] (*sic*) salutem Precipio tibi quatinus resaisias monachos meos de Stoke de decima de Gestingatorp sicut Ger' filius Rengeri eos saisiuit precepto dapiferi mei et sicut erant saisiti die qua reddiderunt terram que fuit . Roberti fratris tui . et postea si quid aduersus eos clamaueris . uel aliquis alius *:* sint ad rectum ubi iustum fuerint . 7 si tu non facis . Adam dapifer meus faciat cito *:* ut non audiam clamorem penuria (*sic*) recti. (*c.* 1130.)

Cott. MS. Appendix xxi, f. 21 b
(See pages 76–77.)

19. Rogerus de Clar' comes Hertford' omnibus baronibus et fidelibus hominibus salutem. Mando uobis atque precipio sicut salutem et honorem meum diligitis . quatinus uice mea dum remotus fuero manuteneatis monachos meos de Stok' et homines et omnia negocia sua prout illi uobis exposuerint . et auxilio uestro indiguerint . et uobis insuper precipio qui eisdem monachis debitores estis . siue in decimacionibus siue in redditibus *:* quatinus eis sua sine intermissione ad eorum uoluntatem plene persoluatis. Et si aliquis uestrum redditus aut decimas suas detinere aut differre uoluerit *:* tunc precipio Reginaldo dapifero meo ut predictis monachis meis plenam et sufficientem iusticiam teneat *:* quemadmodum et mihi de propriis redditibus meis . Valete. (1153–73.)

---

[1] It does not seem possible to restore the exact form of this address, for the history of the family of Peche (*Peccatum*) is obscure before the reign of Henry II. As the family name *Peccatum* appears here in the genitive, the original address probably had the form Ric*ardus* G*illeberti* filius N filio N Peccati salutem, but the lost initials cannot at present be supplied.

Cott. Vesp. F. xv, f. 33
(See pages 78–79.)

20. Willelmus comes de Warenna Osmundo dispensario salutem Mando tibi et precipio ut ressaisias cito monachos Sancti Pancratii de .x. solidatis terre quas Hugo de Grinnosa ville donauit deo et sancto Pancratio pro anima sua Et hoc donum concedo et confirmo eis pro anima patris et matris mee de illis .x. solidatis terre dico que est in Cotistona. Teste Willelmo de Truble villa. (*c.* 1125–30.)

Cott. MS. Appendix xxi, f. 27
(See page 82.)

21. Ricardus de Clar' comes Hertford' dilectis hominibus suis Radulfo de Chaure . et Willelmo filio Godefridi . Willelmo Lencroe . Geruasio de Samford . Godefrido de Heham et Dauid de Samford salutem. Dictum est mihi quod uobis preceptum est ex parte iusticiar' regis iurare quod uidistis Stephanum Dammartini saisiatum de terra de Pitelege[1] sicut de feudo 7 hereditate et hic curo q*uonia*m nolo uos incurrere iram 7 maledictionem dei sicut de periurio mando uobis omnibus quod ille Stephanus dum habuit senescalciam et magisterium de tota terra comitis Gilberti ⸴ iniuste et contra racionem occupauit terram de Piteleh' que fuit Willelmi prepositi de Berdefelda et heredum suorum ita etiam quod crudeliter et iniuste occidere fecit unum ex filiis predicti Willelmi quia sciuit et intellexit eum propinquiorem esse ad hereditatem patris sui de eadem terra possidenda et quia huius rei ueritas ita se habet quemadmodum mihi ab antiquioribus hominibus meis certificatum est precipio uobis sicut hominibus meis fidelibus ne de feudo uel hereditate ipsius Stephani iuretis cum ipse neutram in eadem terra habuerit ⸴ neque feudum neque hereditatem set solam ut premonstratum est occupacionem iniustam et uiolentam.[2]

Cott. MS. Appendix xxi, f. 28
(See pages 92–93.)

22. Ricardus de Clara comes Hertfordie . dilectis amicis suis magistro Steinigin (*sic*) et Willelmo Norwicensis ecclesie archidiaconis . salutem. Discretionis uestre auctoritati notifico . q*uonia*m ex fideli et certo baronum meorum testimonio firmiter instructus

---

[1] Now represented by Pitley farm, in Great Bardfield, Essex.

[2] There seems no means at present of fixing the date of this letter, but it was probably written not long after Earl Richard's succession in 1173.

per presentem litterarum mearum significacionem uos certifico . et
omni ambiguitate prorsus remota testificor quod decimaciones
Rogerii de Ginnei que de meo feudo sunt . videlicet de Witewella
et de Haweringelande . cum ecclesia beati Clementis martiris de
Norwiz et omnibus eidem pertinentibus sunt et esse debent beati
Johannis baptiste de Stok' . et monachorum eiusdem loci . et hoc
ex tempore antiquo ʔ quando primus Gilbertus filius Ricardi . post
diuinccionem[1] Anglie monachos Becci in ecclesia beati Johannis
adductos . redditibus et decimationibus et ecclesiasticis beneficiis
promoueri constituit. Cuius itaque deuocionem et elemosinam
omnes barones sui laudantes et magnificantes . per idem tempus in
presentia domini sui . nobilissimo autem Hereberto episcopo
Norwicensi concedente et confirmante tam Rogerus de Ginnai .
auus istius Rogerii . quam ceteri omnes barones decimationes suas
pro animarum suarum salute predicti eiusdem loci monachis in
perpetuam confirmauerunt elemosinam. Inde est igitur amici mei
carissimi quod in fide et rectitudine uestra merito confisus ʔ uestram
imploro subvencionem quatinus de monachis meis iuuandis et sicut
officio uestro expedit ubique promouendum ʔ curam habeatis pro
Christo et ut me uobis et uestris de cetero per omnia obnoxium
obtineatis. Valete. (*c.* 1175.)

Duchy of Lancaster Misc. Books ii, f. 71

(See page 104.)

23. Ranulphus comes Cestrie constab' dapiferis vicecomitibus
ministris et ballivis et omnibus hominibus suis Francis et Anglis
salutem. Scitote me dedisse Henrico de Laceio in feodo et hereditate Ludeham et Brigeford' cum omnibus pertinenciis suis sibi et
heredibus suis ad tenend*um* de me et de heredibus meis pro seruicio
suo imperpetuum. Quare volo et firmiter precipio quod ipse
Henricus et heredes sui de me et de heredibus meis ita bene et
honorifice teneant sicut teneo meam hereditatem propriam in villa
et extra in foro et mercato in boscis et planis in pratis et pascuis in
stagnis et molendinis in aquis et piscariis in viis et semitis cum soca
et saca et tol et theom et infangetheof et cum omnibus aliis libertatibus et consuetudinibus. Testibus . comite Willelmo Linco*lnie*
et Bald*ewino* filio Gisleberti et Willelmo Coleuil*le* et Turstano
Banastre . et Rannulfo vicecomite . et Hugone osturcario et
Willelmo filio Haconis et Ricardo pincerna et Willelmo Maleb*isse*

---

[1] The clerk first wrote disuincc*ion*em, and then marked the *s* for deletion.
Apparently he wished to leave the word as *diuinccionem*. Fortunately its
meaning is made clear by the context.

et Willelmo capellano et Blund*ello* marescallo apud Lincoln*iam*. (1149–53.)

Add. MS. 35296, f. 411
(See page 105.)

24. Ranulphus comes Cestrie constabular' dapifer' baronibus castellan' iustic' vice*comitibus* ministris et balliuis et omnibus hominibus suis Francis et Anglis salutem. Scitote me reddidisse Wimundo filio Herberti coci totam terram que fuit patris sui[1] et suum misterium in coquina mea ut ibi sit cocus cum aliis sicut ius suum et hereditatem suam. Eapropter uolo et precipio quod ipse[2] Wimundus et heredes sui de me et heredibus meis predictam tenuram suam et rectum suum habeant integriter in coquina et extra de Minting' parua in bosco et plano in pratis et pasturis et omnibus aliis locis ita bene et libere sicut umquam pater suus melius habuit cum socc' et sacc' et tol et them et infangenthef et cum omnibus aliis consuetudinibus et libertatibus omnibus. Testibus Normanno Verd*on* Gilberto Neuil' Ricardo Pincerna Hugone Osturcario Rogero Bele ha*m*p (*sic*)[3] Roberto Folamenu*n* Hugone Pistore Radulfo Justic' Willelmo capellano apud Lincolniam. (*c.* 1150.)

Cott. Vesp. E. xx, f. 120
(See page 106.)

25. Gilbertus de Gaunt omnibus hominibus suis Francis et Anglis salutem. Sciatis me reddidisse et concessisse Seyero de Arceles . hereditatem suam scilicet Lucebyam . cum omnibus tenuris que ad eam pertinent. Quare uolo et precipio quod ipse Seyrerus (*sic*) . bene et in pace . et libere et quiete et honorifice terram predictam teneat ipse et heredes sui post eum de me et de heredibus meis cum omnibus libertatibus . et cum omnibus tenuris que ad eandem terram pertinent in bosco et plano et prato . et in pastur*is* in viis . et semitis . in aquis et molendinis et stagnis . cum soca et saca et tol et tem . infangenethef . per seruicium unius militis . Test' . etc'. (*c.* 1142.)[4]

---

[1] Interlined.　　　　　　　　　　　　　　[2] MS. *ipsa*.

[3] Presumably for Belchamp. A family of Beauchamp held of the earls of Chester, though this member of it does not seem to be known.

[4] Walter de Gant, Gilbert's father, died in 1139, and Seier de Arceles must have been in possession of his inheritance some time before his departure on the crusade of 1147.

Southwell Cathedral, Thurgarton Cartulary, f. 131

(See page 107.)

26. Walterus Deyncurt omnibus etc. Sciatis me reddidisse Eliseo de Fanecurt totam terram quam pater eius Gerard de Fanecurt de me tenuit . scilicet . feodum unius militis in Hickeling' et Kinalton' et in Brunnebia feodum unius militis . et in Scaup*ewic* iiii quadrigatas terre et in Graneby unam quadrigatam terre pro dimidio feodo militis pro cambicione terre quam habuit in Timberlund' sibi et heredibus suis ad tenendum de me et heredibus meis et sicut unquam melius ac liberius pater eius de me tenuit in bosco in plano in agris in pratis in aquis in molendinis in uiis in semitis in omnibus locis cum omnibus liberis consuetudinibus cum soche et sache et tol et tem' et infangenfh'e (*sic*) Teste Roberto etc. (*c.* 1155.)

Egerton MS. 2827, f. 116

(See page 111.)

27. Ricardus de Rollos omnibus hominibus suis Gallicis et Anglicis presentibus et futuris salutem. O uos omnes qui audieritis hoc et uideritis sciant (*sic*) quod concedo huic Erraldo nepoti meo quadrigatam terre de Scylebey (*sic*)[1] quam dedi Harsculfo rufo propter suum seruicium que fuit Godrici de Schylebei cum tota pertinencia sicut Harsculfus tenuit. Et concedo ut teneat illam de Roberto filio Harsculfi eius et suorum heredum (*sic*) saluo meo seruicio . o soc et sac . o tol e tem . infangenthef . cum tota francheisa in uilla et extra uillam . in aqua in prato in stagno in molendino et in omni pastura. Testimonibus (*sic*) Wygan Gaufrido de Montabol Roberto de Gonfreyuile . Ricardo de Cur' . Ricardo de Sararonton' et Osberto le fiz Fulco etc. (Mid-twelfth century.)

Ancient Deeds, C. 5895

(See pages 108–9.)

28. Episcopo Lincolnie . probisque hominibus de Buching*ham* tam clericis quam laicis . Francis 7 Anglicis . Hugo de Gurnái . 7 Milesent uxor eius . salutem . Sciatis quod concedimus Roberto de Turri homini meo pro seruitio suo .xx.^{ti} solidatas terre ad se hospitandum ad Bledeslewes . scilicet terram que fuit Hemming' . et terram que fuit Ailmero (*sic*) de Northgrauia . et terra (*sic*) que fuit Ailwino de Northgrauia et cum hac terra concedimus predicto Roberto de firma mea de Bledeslewes .iiii.^{or} libras de nummis . 7 hoc quatuor terminis . scilicet ad festum sancti Michaelis .xx.

---

[1] Skeeby in Easby, Yorkshire, North Riding.

solidos . et ad purificationem sancte Marie .xx. solidos . et ad
Pentecosten .xx. solidos . et ad uincula sancti Petri .xx. solidos .
quousque demus ei .iiii.ᵒʳ libratas terre. Et hec concedimus ei 7
heredibus suis tenendum de me 7 heredibus meis hereditarie . cum .
sacha . 7 socha . 7 tol 7 tema . 7 infangennethief. Concedimus etiam
prefato Roberto 7 heredibus suis tales custumas 7 libertates quales
ego ipse in predicta uilla habeo . scilicet . in nemoribus . in planis . in
pasturis . in pasnagiis . libere 7 quiete ex me 7 heredibus meis . per
.i. spreuarium sorium . aut per .ii.ᵒˢ solidos . mihi dantem . His
testibus . Radulfo capellano . 7 Johanne de Hosdeng' . 7 Willelmo
de Merló . 7 Oliuero de Age . Ansfrei dapifero . Hodo de Brumu-
stier . Hugone de Castello . Radulfo de Riueria . Hugone de Bur-
gennun . Willelmo de Moreingni . Hugone Brun . Warniero
camerario . Ricardo archario. (*c.* 1160.)

Slit for seal tag. No endorsement.

Cartae Antiquae, P. 36
(See pages 106, 155–6.)

29. Willelmus Reuer'¹ de Dour'² . Hamundo . P' . fratri³ suo . et
Willelmo .P'. nepoti⁴ suo ac omnibus fidelibus suis hominibus
Francis⁵ . et Anglis⁶ . nec non et amicis tam futuris quam presentibus salutem. Sciatis me donasse Turstin'⁷ dapifero meo et heredibus
suis Geddingam⁸ et Daiwellam⁹ pro seruitio suo de me et heredibus
meis tenendas in feodo et hereditate . et sacha et socha et tol et
theam et infangenethef¹⁰ . in nemoribus . et planis . in villa et vico .
et campis et pratis . in aquis et omnibus locis pro seruitio¹¹ dimidii
equitis. T.¹² Waltero de la Haia . et Waltero de Marisco¹³ . et
Hugone de Girund' . et Pagano de Suruia . Ærnulfo¹⁴ sacerdote de
Ketelstan¹⁵ . Waltero filio Traulf'¹⁶ . Roberto capellano . Rogero
filio Wimundi¹⁷ . Roberto filio Walteri . Reginaldo Lagud.¹⁸
(1121–2).

The variant readings given below are derived from the independent copy
of this charter in Curia Regis Roll, 88, m. 12 (printed vol. xii, 209–10).

¹ C.R.R. *Peuerel.*
² C.R.R. *Douera.*
³ C.R.R. *prefatri.*
⁴ C.R.R. *prenepoti.*
⁵ C.R.R. *Francigenis.*
⁶ C.R.R. *Angligenis.*
⁷ C.R.R. *Thurstano.*
⁸ C.R.R. *Geddinga.*
⁹ C.R.R. *Daiwella.*
¹⁰ C.R.R. *in soca in saco in tol et tem et infangenepuf.*
¹¹ C.R.R. *per seruitia.*
¹² C.R.R. *Teste.*
¹³ C.R.R. *des Mareis.*
¹⁴ C.R.R. *Arnulfo.*
¹⁵ C.R.R. *Chetelstan.*
¹⁶ C.R.R. *Tyolf.*
¹⁷ C.R.R. *Wim'.*
¹⁸ Supplied from C.R.R.

Harl. Chart. 54, G. 46

(See page 157.)

30. Willelmus Peuerel de Duure omnibus hominibus suis et amicis Francis et Anglicis salutem. Sciant tam presentes quam futuri quod ego Willelmus Peuerel dedi Hamoni Pichard pro seruitio et humagio suo dominium ecclesie de Morduna . et curiam meam et molendinum . et prata mea . et totam demeniam (*sic*) meam que est in manu mea in Morduna . et homines meos . et Moram . et homines de Mora . et terram et prata cum omnibus pertinentiis suis que pertinent ad Moram in pratis et in pascuis . et unam uirgatam terre de Ob*er*nestun quam Hetwi tenet cum omnibus pertinentiis suis. Hanc predictam terram do Hamoni Pichart et heredibus suis tenendam de me et heredibus meis pro seruitio dimidii militis . libere et quiete et honorifice et in omni libertate sicut ego unquam liberius eam tenui . uel antecessores mei . et hoc presenti ista mea carta confirmaui . His testibus . Matildis (*sic*) de Ver . Matild' de Duure . Puella Ascelina . Alano dapifero . Baldewino de Sancto Georgio . Willelmo filio eius . Eustachio des bans . Galfrido des bans . Willelmo de Musca . Euerardo de Beche . Rotberto de Beche . Herueo le Bretun . Anselmo de Wichentun . Willelmo filio Dó . Ricardo filio eius . Reginaldo de Grettun . Kerardo pincerna . Michaele capellano. (*c.* 1140.)

Fragment of equestrian seal on two tapes.
Endorsed: Willelmus Peu*er*lel [contemporary].

Add. Chart. 6038

(See pages 160–1.)

31. Hugo de Baius . clericis . laicis[1] . Francis Anglis . omnibusque suis bonis hominibus . salutem. Notum sit nobis me dedisse . & concessisse in feudo & hereditate . Roberto Rabacio & suis heredibus dimidium feudum unius militis . scilicet in Medewella & in Chailesmers quod Ricardus filius Bernardi pater eius & idem Robertus Rabacius tenuerunt de patre meo Rannulfo . faciendo idem servicium quod ipse 7[2] pater eius patri[3] meo Rannulfo facere solebat . & uolo ut illam terram teneat quam melius atque liberius ipse 7 pater eius de patre[4] meo Rannulfo tenuerunt . quoadusque perfecerim ei plenarie feudum[5] cuiusdam militis. Sciatis etiam pro concessu 7 recognicione predicte terre se facturum mihi unam percam in muro castelli Welleburnie. Teste. Colegrimo sacerdote .

[1] Corrected from *laiecis*.
[2] Interlined.
[3] Originally *de patre*.
[4] Originally *patri*.
[5] Corrected from *feiuidium* by a point under three unnecessary minims.

Berewaldo sacerdote . Azone de Santo Luca . Superio de Baius . Martino fratre eius . Roberto de Chaeres . Herberto de Sancto Lot . Gozone . Rogero de Punchardun . Wigoto de Brancewella . Willelmo Gilinello . Anfrido . Roberto de Baius . Willelmo de Sarta . Rogero Pharaone . Osberto de Chaam . 7 aliis multis. (*c.* 1158.)

Equestrian seal, on tag. No early endorsement.

Harl. Chart. 49. F. 53

(See pages 158–9.) •

32. Ingeram de Dumard omnibus hominibus suis Gallicis . 7 Anglicis . 7 omnibus hominibus tam futuris quam presentibus . 7 omnibus illis hanc meam kartam audientibus salutem. Sciatis quod ego Ingeram de Dumard dedi . 7 concessi Roberto Duredent nepoti meo propter seruitium suum 7 propter homagium suum ⁊ masuagium in Faxtona quod fuit Walteri de Baillol auunculi mei . 7 quartam partem de Faxtona . 7 quarterium de Malesleia . 7 in Waldegrauia quarterium ⁊ 7 in Multona quarterium ⁊ de feudo quod ibi habeo . 7 in bosco . 7 in plano . in pratis . in pastura . in aquis . in viis . in semitis . 7 in omnibus rebus; excepta ecclesia . sibi 7 heredibus suis tenendam de me . 7 de heredibus meis libere .7 quiete . 7 hereditarie . pro omni seruitio . per seruitium unius militis faciendo . 7 per hanc cartam meam confirmaui . Testibus his . Hugone de Normanvill' . Roberto de Chippenuill' . Jordano de Otheseluia . Ivone fratre . suo . Toma . de Piriton' . Roberto clerico . Jordano de Horburia . Waltero de Baill' Simone de Hornai . Rogero Ladde . Roberto de Alteis . Rogero de Berketot . Ricardo Ladde. (*c.* 1175.)

Equestrian seal. No endorsement.

By a charter of *c.* 1150 facsimiled in *Sir Christopher Hatton's Book of Seals*, no. 302, Bernard de Balliol granted Faxton and its appurtenances to Gerold de Dumart in exchange for the land which he, like his father, ought to hold of Bernard beyond the sea for the service of four knights. Gerold was succeeded by Ingeram before 1167, and the latter was dead by 1185 (Round, *Rotuli de Dominabus*, 23).

Royal MS. 11 B. ix, f. 43

(See pages 173–4.)

33. Sciant omnes tam presentes quam futuri quod ego Willelmus filius Ricardi dedi et concessi monachis ecclesie sancti Andree de Norhantona seruicium illius terre quam Walterannus (*sic*) de me tenuit in Sulgraue . scilicet xxx. acras de inlanda . unoquoque anno

seminandas . et preter hoc . v. uirgatas terre tenendas de me et de
heredibus meis per idem seruicium quod Walterannus[1] mihi inde
solebat facere . scilicet per octo solidos per annum de redditu . et
.v. denarios de waita et per alia seruicia que liberi homines mei
mihi faciunt . scilicet si opus fuerit . iuuabunt redimere corpus
meum et facere militem primogenitum filium meum . et ad mari-
tandam primogenitam filiam meam . et si liberi homines mei
commune auxilium mihi dederint dabunt mihi secundum suam
tenuram. Preterea concessi eis quod non summonebo eos ad placita
mea . nisi pro defectu seruicii mei . et inde ponam eis diem apud
Colewrd' uel apud Sulgrauam. Preterea ego et heredes mei ad-
quietabimus monachos per omnia de warda de Windesor' pro qua
eis aliquando controuersiam moui . eo quod eam nunquam fecerant .
et pro hac adquietacione Henricus prior sancti Andree quadraginta
solidos mihi et Roberto filio meo et heredi duos bizancios dedit
Monachi uero assecurauerunt me quod portabunt mihi fidem de
feudo meo . et quod non querent artem uel ingenium unde ego
aut heres meus a feudo nostro elongemur. Hoc affidauit ex parte
eorum . Henricus filius Ernewi et Hugo filius Ermeburg' . et ex
parte mea affidauit eis Hugo de Colewrth' hanc conuencionem
tenendam sine malo ingenio. Hec concordia facta fuit tempore quo
Radulfus Morin fuit uicecomes uidente comitatu de Norhamtonsire
Hiis testibus Radulfo Morin Willelmo de Plumptona Ricardo
fratre eius . Philippo de Dauentre . Symone Basset Ricardo de
Fardingestona Henrico de Cogenho . Willelmo de Wigeton'
Radulfo de Andeli Rogero de Bucleuilla Bartholomeo de Sulle-
graue . Philippo clerico . Galfrido Bareard . Roberto filio Dauid .
Roberto filio Hugonis de Chotes Bartholomeo filio Jordani Ran-
dulfo fratre Helie . Waltero Laurencio . et multis aliis. (1183–4.)[2]

Lansdowne MS. 207 E, p. 201[3]
(See page 162.)

34. B. de Sancto Walarico omnibus suis hominibus Francis 7
Anglicis presentibus 7 futuris salutem. Sciatis me concessisse
7 presenti carta confirmasse Bernardo filio Milonis de Harenis 7
heredibus suis duas hidas terre 7 dimidiam in Mixebire[4] tenendas

---

[1] The *t* marked for deletion.
[2] A copy with unimportant variants occurs in the late register of St.
Andrew's Priory, Cott. Vesp. E. xvii, f. 158.
[3] From an original in the possession of Gervase Holles, who gave a
facsimile of it in his MS. collections towards a history of Lincolnshire.
[4] Mixbury, Oxfordshire.

de me 7 de heredibus meis sicut pater suus de patre meo tenuit per
seruicium dimidii militis Bernardo Cachelen teste 7 Eustachio de
Fresceneuilla 7 Hugone de Sancto Germano 7 Radulfo clero 7
Milone sacerdote 7 Radulfo de Halerone 7 Herberto de Piri . 7 .
Willelmo de Braiosa 7 hoc iure tenendum. Valete. (*c.* 1170.)

Tag for seal.

Add. Chart. 22011

(See page 164.)

35. Gillebertus de Pinchenni omnibus hominibus suis 7 amicis tam
Francis quam Anglicis salutem . Sciatis me cognouisse 7 reddidisse
Roberto de Pinchenni 7 heredibus suis terram Sulgraue[1] 7 de
Helintonia[2] tenendum de me 7 de heredibus meis eodem seruitio
quo pater eius tenuit de meo . scilicet seruitio militis 7 dimidii .
quietum de releuatu[3] . 7 de omnibus ocasionibus (*sic*) que inter nos
antea fuerunt . pro quinque marcis quas mihi dedit . Huius rei
testes sunt . Simon filius Petri . Simon de Waldgraue . Willelmus
de Glanuilla . Willelmus de Bucheton' Willelmus filius Ricardi .
Ansculf de Pinchenni . Hugo de Pinchenni . Robertus de Estwella .
Anscher de Pichenni . Robertus Nigra Nox . Willelmus de Plum-
tonia . Henricus de Cugenho . Henricus Mala Opera . Willelmus .
Simon 7 Petrus *frater* eius . Philippus de Insula . Main de Pin-
chenni . Willelmus de Pinchenni . Alexander . Simon filius Radulfi .
Ansel . Robertus barefot . Hugo filius Ricardi . Wille[4] . Robertus
de Wedonia . Alexander . Henricus de Rollesham . Tomas sacerdos .
Rocius sacerdos . Matheus . Henricus filius Marescald . Gerardus
Cophin . Gillebertus de Hida . Ogerus . Rogerus de Bricleswurde .
Rogerus filius Gilleberti . 7 Petrus frater eius. (*c.* 1160.)

Tag only for seal. No endorsement.

Cott. Vesp. E. xviii, f. 33

(See page 172.)

36. Notum sit omnibus sancte ecclesie filiis clericis et laicis quod
ego Walterus de Aencurt . et Johannes filius meus et heres conces-
simus et dedimus deo et abbatie de Kyrkested' et monachis ibidem

[1] Sulgrave, Northamptonshire.
[2] The Domesday manor of Elentone in east Berkshire (D.B. i. 61 b).
The name does not survive, but the site is represented by the modern
Pinkneys Green between Marlow and Maidenhead.
[3] Followed by an erasure.
[4] The stop before Richard's surname is unnecessary.

deo seruientibus duas carrucatas terre et dimidiam in Cotes[1] cum omnibus suis pertinentiis . in masuris in pratis et pasturis . in bosco et plano et marisco cum tota terra illa Lindewde et cum centum acris terre in brueria Blankenie in elemosinam . libere et quiete de exercitu et warda et scutagio et equitatione et opere et omni seruitio quod ad militem pertinet . et omni seculari seruitio excepto danegeld et murdra . et adiutorio regis si communiter positum fuerit super comitatum . et iiii[or] auxiliis vicecomitis.[2] Et sciendum quod de his etiam consuetudinibus et seruitiis uolumus ut sint quieti si per cartam regis quietanciam poterint habere. Hanc donationem patris mei . et meam concessi et confirmaui ego Johannes de Aincurt in presentia Roberti episcopi Lincolniensis. Teste ipso Roberto episcopo Lincolniensi . et Gerardo . etc. (*c.* 1160.)

Ancient Deeds, B. 11642
(See pages 184–5.)

37. Notum sit presentibus 7 futuris quod ego Walterius Chroc 7 Aanor uxor mea donamus deo 7 monachis de Ferleia molendinum de Aseberia solutum 7 quietum de omnibus rebus sicut liberam helemosinam excepto scutagio'[3] militis 7 denegeldo quantum inde ad molendinum pertinet . 7 culturam de Methlest . & idem monachi dederunt mihi pro recognitione huius donationis decem[3] marchas argenti . 7 uxori mee anulum aureum . 7 disuagimoniauerunt idem molendinum á domina Aelizia uxore Rainaldi de Donastanuilla quinquaginta solidis. Ego autem promisi eis 7 fide mea pepigi quod facerem dom*i*num me⟨um 7⟩ uxorem meam 7 fiilium meum 7 fratres meos[4] concedere donum istud[5] nec artem quererem per quam molendinum pard⟨er⟩ent. Quod ut firmum 7 stabile esset anulo meo hoc breůe sigillo . 7 signum crucis huic carte *i*nprimo. Signum Croch +. Signum uxoris su*ę* . Huius rei testis est Gausfredus dapifer . Sanson presbiter . Hunfredus de Scotuilla . Osmundus 7 Hugo de Caldefelda . Willelmus Bigodus . Willelmus de Insula Robertus filius Osberti . magister Rainaldus . Alricus prepositus . Roscelinus. Stigandus. (*c.* 1130.)

Slits for two seals, one of them containing tag.
Endorsed: Walteri croc de molendino de Aseb*er*ia, &c. (twelfth century).

[1] Cotes Grange in Blankney, Lincolnshire.
[2] Referring to the quarterly payment of the sheriff's aid.
[3] Written in an erasure.
[4] Corrected from *meus*.
[5] The *d* is inserted, with a subscript sign.

Stowe MS. 935, f. 17 b

(See pages 185–6.)

38. Notum sit omnibus sancte ecclesie fidelibus quod ego Robertus de Aldelosa et Hamo filius meus damus et concedimus deo et sancto Johanne de Hortona et monachis ibidem deo seruientibus illam dimidiam virgatam terre quam Robertus de Ver de me jure hereditario tenuit et seruicium Cole filii Lanterii cum omnibus libertatibus et consuetudinibus et honoribus quibus ipse Cola et antecessores sui seruiuerunt michi et antecessoribus meis. Damus dico in perpetuam et liberam elemosinam tenendam sicut pater meus Osbertus umquam liberius tenuit . et ego post decessum eius . saluo iure regio de sulmagio de quo monachi respondebunt michi et heredibus meis . et Cola respondebit monachis . et seruicio domini mei scilicet escuagio . unde etiam ipsi monachi reddent quartum denarium quando dominus meus in terra sua accipiet escuagium . Testibus Ernaldo presbitero Asketillo filio meo. Unfrido fratre meo . Simone de Tenegate . Manassero . Wiberto filio Cole. (*c.* 1145.)

Cott. Chart. xxii. 2

(See page 189.)

39. Osbertus de Ardene Osberto filio suo Filippoque 7 Petro uniuersis hominibus . scilicet presentibus 7 futuris salutem. Sciatis me dedisse . Kierardo . 7 Nicholao . filiis Th⟨oma⟩s . eis 7 heredibus eorum . tenendum de me 7 meis heredibus . in feudo 7 hereditate . totum parchum de Brocheleie . preter Hennecroft . 7 Clippescroft . 7 la Haie . e Sichplode . 7 .l. acre . in Essebroc[1] . e le serd Serich . e le serd Grimbald . cum prato . e Longesleie . 7 terram Ricardi dapiferis . libere & quiete cum omni libertate . per uicesimam partem seruicii . millitis . 7 .x.x.iiii. acres in feudo . per tres solidos seruicii Hedrico presbitero. Valete. His testibus. Osbertus filius Alteri . Filippus . Petrus . Hedricus presbiter . Serlo . Johannes . Roger . Wlfsi. (*c.* 1130.)[2]

---

[1] Corrected from *Essebbroc*.

[2] Most of the obscurities in this strange document are cleared up by a charter of Robert son of Walter, son-in-law of Osbert the younger of Arden, confirming many of these properties to Girard and Nicholas, sons of Thomas, the Kierard and Nicholas of the text. In this document (Cott. Chart. xxv. 25) the gift described above appears as *Brocheleie et quicquid infra ambitum parci continetur . . . preter Clipsescroft et Hennecroft*, together with *totam haiam que est inter Tamam* (the river Tame) *et lacum, et Sippelac et totam terram Essebroc, . . . et totam terram R dapiferi*. There is no specific mention in this charter of the essarts of Serich and Grimbald

The shape of the charter suggests that a strip was originally cut from it to carry the seal. At present the illegible fragment of a seal is affixed to the charter by a recent tag and string.

Add. Chart. 20461
(See page 189.)

40. Sciant omnes posteri 7 futuri quod ego Rodbertus de Olleio concedo Ricardo de Brai seruitium Ricardi de Sancto Eadmundo ad tenendum de eo libere 7 quiete sicut de patre meo 7 de me tenuit 7 per eundem seruitium scilicet pro tenura sua .xvi.ᵐᵃᵐ partem militis perficiat . 7 preter hoc si dominus suus uoluerit mittet illum in suo seruitio semel in anno tantum spatium uie quantum est inter Oxineforþ' 7 Schenestan . 7 hoc ad omnem dispensam domini sui. Huius donationis 7 concessionis est testis ipsa domina Edit. 7 Fulco frater domini . 7 From*us* (*sic*)[1] capellanus. 7 Radulfus clericus 7 Robertus filius Widonis . 7 Willelmus filius Sewardi. (*c.* 1130.)[2]

Strip only for seal. No early endorsement.

Add. Chart. 20454
(See pages 163, note 4, and 192.)

41. Sciant tam presentes quam futuri quod ego Ernaldus de Powis dedi 7 concessi Willelmo filio meo terram meam de la hida in feudo 7 in hereditate . per grantum domini mei Radulfi de Toinio . 7 per grantum Walteri filii 7 heredis mei . 7 ceterorum filiorum meorum . scilicet . Rogeri 7 Ursi . quam terram dominus meus Radulfus de Toinio dedit michi pro seruitio 7 homagio meo . 7 pro seruitio unius militis quando debet fieri apud Cliffordiam. Et pro hac concessione dedit predictus Willelmus filius meus predicto Radulfo domino meo 7 suo unum palefridum . 7 homagium suum inde accepit et pro releuagio suo dedit ei centum solidos. Et predictam terram scilicet la Hida cum omnibus pertinenciis suis concessit predicto Willelmo filio meo 7 heredibus suis tenendam de eo 7 de heredibus suis libere 7 quiete per predictum seruitium. Hec concessio facta fuit in curia domini mei predicti Radulfi de Toinio

nor of 'Longesleie', and the lands are to be held, not, as above, for the twentieth of a knight's service, but 'for the twenty-sixth part of a knight for the service of the earl' (of Warwick). The date of this latter charter is approximately 1150.

[1] Probably for *Fromundus*.

[2] Printed from the fifteenth-century copy in the Great Coucher of the Duchy of Lancaster in *Transactions of the William Salt Archaeological Society*, N.S. xvii. 240.

apud Eseleam. Et ut hec concessio domini mei Radulfi de Toinio 7 mea firma sit 7 stabilis ⁀ sigillorum nostrorum[1] apositione confirmamus. His testibus .Radulfo de Toinio . Goce de Dinan . Waltero de Chandos . Rotberto de Chandos . Osberto de Haneleche. Willelmo de Clintona . Waltero filio Ernaldi de Powis . 7 Rogero 7 Urso fratres sui (*sic*) . Nicholao de Chamflur . Urrio de la haie . Valtero filio Ricardi . Stephano de Chameis . Villelmo de Estham 7 Sansone filio eius . Sansone de Weruesleches . Galfrido Talebot . Rotberto Oliphard . magistro Hugone de Clifford . 7 multis aliis. (*c.* 1145.)

Two equestrian seals on cords. No early endorsement.

Harl. MS. 3688, f. 59

(See pages 208–9.)

42. Notum sit omnibus fidelibus presentibus et futuris quod ego Gaufridus de Turuilla dedi Iohanni de Leia unam hidam terre de meo dominio in Westona cum omnibus que ad ipsam pertinent . sicut prolocutum fuit coram me et coram hominibus meis . et cum hida dedi ei molendinum quod Willelmus tenuit cum omnibus que ad ipsum pertinent in terra et in prato . quod totum concessi ei in feudum et hereditatem . et heredibus suis libere et quiete ab omni servicio et exactione . preter quod Iohannes et heredes sui facient mihi stationem in castello de Westona xl dies in tempore werre cum dextrario et runcino . et in tempore pacis iii ebdomadas. Notum sit interea quod hoc ideo feci Iohanni quia reddidit mihi hereditatem suam . uidelicet terram de Leia . quam dedi canonicis de Messend' in elemosinam. Et predictus Iohannes eam clamavit quietam predictis canonicis . fide etiam firmauit acquietare eam canonicis pro posse suo contra omnes homines de se et quietamclamauit et fidefirmauit. Testibus. abbate de Messend' et Hugone de Noers . Willelmo de Puteham . Pagano de Puteham . Osberto de Santerdon . Osberto . Gondwino de Brocton' Radulfo filio Tosti . Roberto de Santerdone . Osberto fratre eius . et toto halimot de Westuna . Galfrido sacerdote . et Willelmo sacerdote . Radulfo fabro . Roberto filio Gold' . Alurico fratre sacerdotis . Reginaldo filio Walteri . Henrico filio Goldwini . Gilberto minutore . et filio eius . Hunfrido et Hereberto et omnibus aliis eiusdem ville. Certum sit quod ego Petrus abbas de Messenden et Ern' abbas de Dodeluilla . et magistro (*sic*) Hamone (*sic*) cancellario (*sic*) de Lincolnia testes sumus quod hoc est rescriptum de uerbo in uerbum ipsius carte quam Gaufridus de Turuilla dederat Iohanni de Leia in confirmacione terre sue.

---

[1] Corrected from *sigillum meum*.

quam ei dedit apud Westonam pro mutacione terre de Leia quam
ipse Gaufridus dedit canonicis de Messenden in perpetuam elemosinam.[1]

Ancient Deeds, A. 11337

(See page 207.)

43. Hugo de Bolebec omnibus hominibus suis . 7 omnibus amicis
suis Francigenis 7 Anglis . qui sunt . 7 qui futuri . sunt . salutem .
Sciatis quia Roberto del Broc reddidi totam terram patris sui . de
Cestresham[2] . 7 del Broc[3] . 7 inde homagium ab illo accepi 7 suum
releuamen mihi dedit . rogatu patris sui . 7 aliorum amicorum eius .
qui illum mihi presentauit sicut filium 7 heredem suum . Sic ei
reddidi ad tenendum de me 7 de heredibus meis libere . per .xxx.
solidos reddendo per annum . videlicet .x. solidos ad festum sancti
Johannis . 7 .x. ad uincula sancti Petri . de terra sua de Cestresham .
7 de terra sua del Broc ꝯ x. solidos . ad festum sancti Martini . Quod
si rex Anglie ierit in Waliam cum exercitu suo . 7 ego iero corpus
meum cum eo ꝯ tunc ipse Robertus inueniet mihi unum equum
.xl. diebus . cum sella . 7 capistro . 7 unum saccum lineum . 7 alium
laneum . 7 unum hominem ad custodiam equi . 7 hoc erit ad meum .
proprium custamentum . Qui equus cum apparatu erit appreciatus .
sicut ad summam portandum . Qui si item uenerit ꝯ reddetur
Roberto . si autem non uenerit ꝯ precium equi . ipsi computabitur .
in primo seruicio suo. Uolo itaque 7 precipio . quatinus ipse Robertus
7 heredes sui teneant hanc predictam terram libere 7 quiete 7
absolute ab omnibus aliis seruiciis . per hos .xxx. solidos . ita reddendo per annum . 7 pro seruicio supradicto . de exercitu Walie .
sic tenuerunt antecessores sui . de meis antecessoribus . 7 sic uolo .
ut ipse teneant . 7 heredes sui . de me 7 de heredibus meis . hereditarie . ab omnibus quie . . . is seruiciis . Test*es* . Emma de Auber-
uill*a* . Rauening' de Messend' . 7 Robertus filius suus . Petrus
capellanus Willelmus de Wedona . Gaufredus ruffus . Rogerus de
Clincampe . Gilebertus filius Radulfi . 7 Radulfus filius eius . Hugo
de Cestresham . 7 Ricardus frater eius . Robertus camerarius . 7
Robertus de Efure. (*c.* 1170.)

Slit for seal tag. No endorsement.

[1] For the approximate date of this charter see above, 208, note 3. The
note certifying the accuracy of the transcript from which the copy in
the cartulary was derived must have been written before 1182, when
Hamo, chancellor of Lincoln, died.   [2] Chesham, Buckinghamshire.

[3] Representing the manor of 'Broch' held in 1086 by Hugh de Bolbec I.
It cannot be identified with any certainty.

Add. MS. 28024, f. 53 b

(See pages 20 and 214.)

44. H rex Anglorum omnibus baronibus et[1] vauasoribus qui
wardam debent facere ad castellum de Rochingeham salutem Precipio vobis quod sitis residentes in castello meo de Rochingeham ita
bene et plenarie per summonicionem Michaelis de Hameslap' qui
custodit castellum sicut iuste esse debueritis et nisi feceritis ipse
justificet vos per pecuniam vestram donec ita sitis Et si ipse vos non
poterit justificare vicecomites mei in quorum ministeriis terras
habetis[2] donec hoc faciatis. T' Gloec.[3] (*sic*) apud Ryllyngham[4] (*sic*).

Ancient Deeds, A. 14257

(See page 246.)

45. Venerabili domino priori totique conuentui de sancto Pancratio . Walterus de Pincheni salutes 7 seruicia . Sciatis quod
ecclesiam de Winteburna . quam materna mea Adeliza dedit deo 7
sancto Pancratio 7 uobis ⁊ do 7 concedo deo 7 sancto Pancratio 7
uobis post decessum clerici parentis mei cui dedi illam . 7 quamdiu
clericus ille uixerit ⁊ de uobis tenebit . 7 dabit unoquoque anno
decem solidos dum guerra durabit . 7 cum deus pacem dederit ⁊
dabit unam marcam argenti . Post autem eius decessum ⁊ habebitis
eam solidam 7 quietam . Testibus . Hugone de Cumbreuilla . 7
duobus fratribus eius Rogerio 7 Reinaldo de Insula . ut particeps
fiam omnium beneficiorum ecclesie uestre. (*c.* 1144.)

Slit for seal tag.

Endorsed: Walterii de Pincheni. De ecclesia de Winterburne (late
twelfth century) de Wiltesire (thirteenth century) xv (fifteenth century) E.

Harl. MS. 4714, f. 21

(See pages 247–8.)

46. Roberto dei gratia Lincolniensi episcopo et omnibus sancte
matris ecclesie filiis ⁊ Osbertus de Wanci salutem . Sciatis me dedisse
et concessisse deo et sancte Marie et monachis de Bitlesdena in
perpetuam elemosinam quandam partem terre mee de Estwella,
illam scilicet partem totam . que est inter Bicheho et Bishopespel'
(*sic*) et inter viam regiam et Gudlachesho cum omnibus pertinenciis
in pratis et pascuis et ceteris necessariis Quedam uero pars predicte

---

[1] *et* omitted in MS.   [2] *faciant* is required here.

[3] Presumably for *Milone de Gloecestria*. If so, this writ must have been
issued in the second half of Henry's reign.

[4] Apparently for 'Gyllyngham', that is, Gillingham, Dorset.

terre fuit de dote uxoris mee Aaliz .xx. scilicet et sex acre, quarum dimidiam partem, scilicet tredecim acras ipsa dedit eis pro salute anime sue in perpetuam elemosinam. Pro aliis uero tredecim acris ego dedi ei escambium ad valorem predictarum acrarum ipsa volente et concedente . et preterea, dedi monachis Gudlachesho . que est quedam pars de Bicheho ad ospitandum eos et totam communem pasturam *:* de Estwella in bosco et plano concessi eis. Hec omnia dominus meus Gilbertus de Pikini prece mea carta sua confirmauit. Hanc donacionem feci et concessi consilio uxoris mee Aaliz et Roberti filii et heredis mei et ceterorum filiorum et amicorum meorum pro salute anime mee et omnium antecessorum meorum, liberam et quietam ab omni consuetudine seculari et exaccione erga me et heredes meos defendendam et manutenendam contra omnes qui ecclesie predicte aliquam calumpniam inferre temptauerint Ipsi uero monachi in recomprehensione (*sic*) huius elemosine pro me et uxore mea post obitum nostrum sicut pro monacho illius ecclesie facient, excepto quod corpora nostra ad sepulturam non recipient Si uero vitam meam ante finem mutare voluero *:* ad religionem me suscipient Si tanta warra fuerit quod animalia nostra in pace seruare non possimus . ipsi cum suis animalibus illa seruabunt absque sumptu et saluo ordine suo scilicet quod fidem uel iuramentum pro eis non ficient (*sic*)[1] . si quis ea ui auferre voluerit Si uero furto ablata fuerint . uel aliquo alio infortunio amissa uel mortua, uel occisa, uel a bestiis capta fuerint *:* dampnum non restituent Si autem euenerit quod ego sim captus . uel uxor mea uel filius *:* aliquem fratrum suorum mittent qui nos adiuuet prece non precio.[2] Carrucam unam semel in anno mihi accomodabunt Huius concessionis mee sunt testes Suanus de Brakale . et Robertus et Simon filii eius et R' clericus de Helmeden cum aliis. (*c.* 1150.)

Lansdowne MS. 415, f. 41[3]

(See pages 104 and 251.)

47. Rannulfus comes Cestrie constab' dap' baronibus justic' vic' ministris et bailliuis et omnibus fidelibus suis Francis et Anglis salutem.[4] Sciatis me dedisse Roberto comiti Legrecestrie in feodo

[1] Other charters in the cartulary which repeat this clause read *facient*.

[2] The clauses relating to loss of animals, and the possibility of the grantor's capture, are repeated in confirmations of this charter by Gilbert de Pinkeni, Osbert's lord, and Robert de Wanci, his son.

[3] Printed, not very accurately, in Nichol's *Leicestershire*, iii. 2, 830.

[4] In the manuscript, which is somewhat illegible throughout, nothing but *Francis et A* can be read of the end of the address.

et hereditate pro homagio suo Muntsorell' . uillam et castellum desuper cum omnibus pertinenciis Et preter hoc dono ei hereditarie omnes tenuras de quibus erat meus affidatus et sicut carta mea ei testatur.[1] Eapropter uolo et firmiter precipio ut ipse comes Robertus Legrecestrie predictum castellum et uillam de Muntsorell' cum predictis tenuris bene et honorifice iure hereditario de me et de heredibus meis teneat in uilla ex extra et castro et foro et mercato . in bosco et plano . in pratis et pasturis et in aquis et molendinis in uiis et semitis et forestis et in omnibus aliis locis cum soca et saca thol et them infanganthef (*sic*) et cum omnibus aliis consuetudinibus et libertatibus. T. Gilleberto comite de Clara. (*c.* 1148.)

Cott. MS. Nero C. iii, f. 178

(See pages 250–6.)

48. Hec est conuentio inter comitem Rannulfum Cestrie . et Robertum comitem Legrecestrie . et finalis pax et concordia que fuit concessa et diuisa ab eis coram secundo Roberto episcopo Lincolnie . et hominibus ipsorum . ex parte comitis Cestrie . Ricardo de Louetot . Willelmo filio Nigelli . Rannulfo vicecomite . ex parte comitis Legrecestrie Ernaldo de Bosco . Gaufrido Abbate . Raginaldo de Bordineo . scilicet quod comes Rannulfus dedit et concessit Roberto comiti Legre*cestrie* castrum de Muntsorel sibi et heredibus suis . tenendum de eo et heredibus suis hereditarie . et sicut carta ipsius comitis Rannulfi testatur . et ita quod comes Leecestr' receptare debet ipsum comitem Rannulfum et familiam suam in burgo et baliis de Muntsorel . ad guerreandum quencunque uoluerit ut de feudo suo . et ita quod comes Leecestr' non potest inde forisfacere comiti Rannulfo pro aliquo. Et si necesse fuerit comiti Rannulfo . corpus ipsius receptabitur in dominico castro de Muntsorel . et ita quod comes Leecestrie portabit ei fidem . salua fide ligii domini sui. Et si opportuerit comitem Leecestrie ire super comitem Cestrie cum ligio domino suo non potest ducere secum plusquam uiginti milites . et si comes Leecestrie uel isti uiginti

---

[1] This is evidently the charter, printed in the Hist. MSS. Commission Report on the Manuscripts of Mr. Reginald Rawdon Hastings (i. 66–67), by which the earl of Chester granted Charley with its adjacent woods and his property in Leicester itself to the earl of Leicester. The earl of Chester's statement in the latter charter that the earl of Leicester *de hac tenura fidem mihi fecit sicut domino de quo tenet* explains the reference above to the holdings in regard to which the earl of Leicester was the earl of Chester's 'affidatus'.

milities aliquid ceperint de rebus comitis Cestrie ꞉ʾ totum reddetur. Nec ligius dominus comitis Leecestrie nec aliquis alius potest forisfacere comiti Cestrie . nec suis ꞉ʾ de castris ipsius comitis Leecestrie . nec de terra sua . et ita quod comes Leecestrie nec potest propter aliquam causam . uel propter aliquem casum impedire corpus comitis Cestrie nisi eum defidauerit . quindecim dies ante. Et comes Leecestrie debet iuuare comitem Cestrie contra omnes preter ligium dominum ipsius comitis Leecestr' et comitem Simonem; Comitem Simonem potest iuuare hoc modo . quod si comes Rannulfus forisfecerit comiti Simoni . et ipse comes Rannulfus noluerit corrigere forisfactum propter comitem Leec' ꞉ʾ tunc potest eum iuuare. Et si comes Simon forisfecerit comiti Cestrie . et noluerit corrigere se propter comitem Leecestrie ꞉ʾ non iuuabit eum comes Leecestrie. Et comes Leecestr' debet custodire terras et res comitis Cestrie que in potestate ipsius comitis Leecestrie sunt ꞉ʾ sine malo ingenio. Et comes Leecestrie pepigit comiti Rannulfo . quod castrum de Rauenestona cadet . nisi concessu comitis Rannulfi remanserit. Et ita quod si aliquis uellet illud castrum tenere contra comitem Leecestrie ꞉ʾ comes Rannulfus auxiliabitur absque malo ingenio ad diruendum castrum illud. Et si comes Rannulfus fecerit clamorem de Willelmo de Alneto ꞉ʾ comes Leecestrie in sua curia habebit eum ad rectum . quamdiu ipse Willelmus manserit homo comitis Leecestrie et terram tenebit de eo. Et ita quod si Willelmus uel sui recesserint a fidelitate comitis Leecestrie propter castrum prostratum . uel quia rectum noluerit facere in curia comitis Leec' ꞉ʾ non receptabuntur in potestate comitis Cestrie neque Willelmus nec sui ꞉ʾ ad malum faciendum comiti Leecestrie. In hac conuentione remanet comiti Leecestrie castrum de Witewic firmatum . cum ceteris castris suis.

Et e conuerso . comes Rannulfus portabit fidem comiti Leecestrie salua fide ligii domini sui . et si oportuerit com*item* Cestri*e* ire super comitem Leecestrie cum ligio domino suo ꞉ʾ non potest ducere secum plusquam uiginti milites. Et si comes Cestrie uel isti uiginti milites aliquid ceperint de rebus comitis Leecestrie ꞉ʾ totum reddetur. Nec ligius dominus comitis Cestrie . nec aliquis alius potest forisfacere comiti Leecestrie nec suis . de castris ipsius comitis Cestrie nec de terra sua. Et ita quod comes Cestrie non potest propter aliquam causam . uel aliquem casum ꞉ʾ impedire corpus comitis Leecestrie . nisi eum defidauerit . quindecim dies ante. Et comes Cestrie debet iuuare comitem Leecestrie contra omnes homines preter ligium dominum ipsius comitis Cestrie et comitem Robertum de Ferreriis. Comitem Robertum potest iuuare hoc modo. Si comes Leecestrie forisfecerit comiti de Ferreriis . et ipse comes Leecestrie noluerit corrigere forisfactum propter comitem Cestrie ? tunc potest eum iuuare comes Cestrie. Et si comes Robertus de Ferreriis forisfecerit comiti Leecestrie . et noluerit se corrigere propter comitem Cestrie . non iuuabit eum comes Cestrie. Et comes Cestrie debet custodire terras et res comitis Leecestrie que in potestate ipsius comitis Cestrie sunt ? sine malo ingenio. Et comes Cestrie pepigit comiti Leecestrie quod si aliquis uellet castrum de Rauenestona tenere contra comitem Leecestrie ? comes Ranulfus auxiliabitur absque malo ingenio ad diruendum castrum illud. Nec comes Cestrie nec comes Leecestrie debent firmare castrum aliquid nouum inter Hinchelai et Couintre . nec inter Hinchelai et Hardredeshallam . nec inter Couintre et Donintonam . nec inter Dunnintonam et Leecestriam . nec ad Gataham . nec ad Cheneldestoam . nec propius . nec inter Cheneldestoam . et Belueeir . nec inter Belueeir et Hocham . nec inter Hocham et Rochingheham . nec propius . nisi communi assensu utriusque. Et si aliquis in predictis locis uel infra predictos terminos firmaret castrum ? uterque alteri erit auxilio sine malo ingenio donec castrum diruatur.

Et hanc conuentionem sicut in hac carta continetur ? affidauit uterque comes . uidelicet Cestrie et Leecestrensis in manu Roberti secundi . Lincolniensis episcopi tenendam . et posuerunt eundem episcopum obsidem huius conuentionis super Christianitatem suam . ita quod si aliquis exiret ab hac conuentione . et nollet se corrigere infra .xv. dies postquam inde requisitus fuerit sine malo ingenio ? tunc episcopus Lincolniensis et episcopus Cestrensis facient iusticiam de eo tanquam de fide mentita. Et episcopus Lincolnie et episcopus Cestrensis tradent obsides . uterque duos . quos receperunt propter conuentiones istas tenendas ? illi uidelicet qui conuentiones istas predictas tenebit. (1148–53.)

CIROGRAPHVM

(cut through in straight line.)

Endorsed: . . ntio inter R. comitem Leg' 7 R. comitem. (twelfth century) .vii. (? fifteenth century).

INDEX OF SUBJECTS, PERSONS
AND PLACES

Individuals are indexed under their own names, not their fathers', unless they possess a surname, or are associated with a particular place, when all members of the family are indexed under the surname or place-name. Chroniclers are indexed under the word which is most familiar in their names, i.e. *Florence of Worcester* under *Florence*, *Ralf de Diceto* under *Diceto*.